The Clipper Ship Era

An Epitome of Famous American and British Clipper Ships, Their Owners, Builders, Commanders, and Crews

1843-1869

By

Arthur H. Clark

Late Commander of Ship "Verena," Barque "Agnes," Steamships "Manchu," "Suwo Nada," "Venus," and "Indiana. (1863-1877)
Author of "The History of Yachting"

With 39 Illustrations

G. P. Putnam's Sons
New York and London
The Knickerbocker Press

Made in the United States of America

To

THE MEMORY OF

A FRIEND OF MY BOYHOOD

DONALD McKAY

BUILDER OF SHIPS

PREFACE

THE Clipper Ship Era began in 1843 as a result of the growing demand for a more rapid delivery of tea from China; continued under the stimulating influence of the discovery of gold in California and Australia in 1848 and 1851, and ended with the opening of the Suez Canal in 1869. These memorable years form one of the most important and interesting periods of maritime history. They stand between the centuries during which man navigated the sea with sail and oar—a slave to unknown winds and currents, helpless alike in calm and in storm—and the successful introduction of steam navigation, by which man has obtained mastery upon the ocean.

After countless generations of evolution, this era witnessed the highest development of the wooden sailing ship in construction, speed, and beauty. Nearly all the clipper ships made records which were not equalled by the steamships of their day; and more than a quarter of a century elapsed, devoted to discovery and invention in perfecting the marine engine and boiler, before the best clipper ship records for speed were broken by steam vessels. During this era, too, important discoveries were made in regard to the laws governing the winds and currents of the ocean; and this knowledge, together with improvements in model and rig, enabled sailing ships to reduce by forty days the average time formerly required for the outward and homeward voyage from England and America to Australia.

In pursuing this narrative we shall see the stately, frigate-built Indiaman, with her batteries of guns and the hammocks stowed in nettings, disappear, and her place taken by the swift China, California, and Australian clippers, which in their turn, after a long and gallant contest, at last vanish before the advancing power of steam.

Many of the clipper ships mentioned in this book, both American and British, were well known to me; some of the most celebrated of the American clippers were built near my early home in Boston, and as a boy I saw a number of them constructed and launched; later, I sailed as an officer in one of the most famous of them, and as a young sea-captain knew many of the men who commanded them. I do not, however, depend upon memory, nearly all the facts herein stated being from the most reliable records that can be obtained. So far as I am aware, no account of these vessels has ever been written, beyond a few magazine and newspaper articles, necessarily incomplete and often far from accurate; while most of the men who knew these famous ships have now passed away. It seems proper, therefore, that some account of this remarkable era should be recorded by one who has a personal knowledge of the most exciting portion of it, and of many of the men and ships that made it what it was.

Of late years there has been a confusing mixture of the terms *knot* and *mile* as applied to the speed of vessels. As most persons are aware, there are three kinds of mile: the geographical, statute, and sea mile or knot. The geographical mile is based on a measure upon the surface of the globe, and is a mathematical calculation which should be used by experts only. The statute mile, instituted by the Romans, is a measure of 5280 feet. The sea mile or knot is one sixtieth of a degree of latitude; and while this measurement varies slightly in different latitudes, owing to the elliptical shape of the globe, for practical purposes the knot may be taken as 6080 feet.

The word knot is now frequently used to express long distances at sea. This is an error, as the term knot should be used only to denote an hourly rate of speed; for instance, to say that a vessel is making nine knots means that she is going through the water at the rate of nine knots an hour, but it would be incorrect to say that she made thirty-six knots in four hours; here the term miles should be used, meaning sea miles or knots. The term knot is simply a unit of speed, and is derived from the knots marked on the old-fashioned log line and graduated to a twenty-eight-second log glass which was usually kept in the binnacle. In this book the word mile means a sea mile and not a geographical or statute mile.

I wish to make my grateful acknowledgment to the Hydrographic Office at Washington, the British

Museum, Lloyd's Register of Shipping, the American Bureau of Shipping, the Boston Athenæum, and the Astor Library, for much of the data contained in this book.

A. H. C

NEW YORK, 1910.

CONTENTS

Contents

ILLUSTRATIONS

THE CLIPPER SHIP ERA

CHAPTER I

AMERICAN SHIPPING TO THE CLOSE OF THE WAR OF 1812

THE deeds that have made the Clipper Ship Era a glorious memory were wrought by the ship-builders and master mariners of the United States and Great Britain, for the flag of no other nation was represented in this spirited contest upon the sea. In order, therefore, to form an intelligent idea of this era, it is necessary to review the condition of the merchant marine of the two countries for a considerable period preceding it, as well as the events that led directly to its development.

From the earliest colonial days, ship-building has been a favorite industry in America. The first vessel built within the present limits of the United States was the *Virginia,* a pinnace of thirty tons, constructed in 1607 by the Popham colonists who had arrived during the summer at Stage Island, near the mouth of the Kennebec River, on board the ships *Gift of God* and *Mary and John.* When these vessels returned to England, leaving forty-five persons to establish a fishing station, and a severe winter followed, the colonists became disheartened and built the *Virginia* which carried them home in safety and which subsequently made several voyages across the Atlantic.

The *Onrust,* of sixteen tons, was built at Manhattan in 1613–14, by Adrian Block and his companions, to replace the *Tiger,* which had been damaged by fire beyond repair. After exploring the coasts of New England and Delaware Bay, she sailed for Holland with a cargo of furs. The *Blessing of the Bay,* a barque of thirty tons, was built by order of Governor John Winthrop at Medford, near Boston, and was launched amid solemn rejoicings by the Puritans on July 4, 1631. This little vessel was intended to give the New England colonists a means of communication with their neighbors at New Amsterdam less difficult than that through the wilderness. So we see that ship-building was begun in America under the pressure of necessity, and it was fostered by the conditions of life in the new country.

In the year 1668, the ship-building in New England, small as it may now seem, had become sufficiently important to attract the attention of Sir Josiah Child, sometime Chairman of the Court of Directors of the East India Company, who in his *Discourse on Trade* protests with patriotic alarm: "Of all the American plantations, His Majesty has none so apt for building of shipping as New England, nor any comparably so qualified for the breeding of seamen, not only by reason of the natural industry of that people, but principally by reason of their cod and mackerel fisheries, and, in my poor opinion, there is nothing more prejudicial, and in prospect more dangerous, to any mother kingdom, than the increase in shipping in her colonies, plantations, and provinces."

The apprehension of the worthy Sir Josiah was well founded, for at that period most of the spars and much of the timber which went into the construction of the East Indiamen and the fighting ships of his royal master, King Charles II., had grown in American soil, and of 1332 vessels registered as built in New England between 1674 and 1714, no less than 239 were built for or sold to merchants abroad. Not that they were better than foreign built vessels, but on account of the plentiful supply of timber they could be built more cheaply in America than in Great Britain and on the Continent.

The industry was in a promising and healthy condition, and so continued, until in 1720 the London shipwrights informed the Lords of Trade that the New England shipyards had drawn away so many men "that there were not enough left to carry on the work." They therefore prayed that colonial built ships be excluded from all trade except with Great Britain and her colonies, and that the colonists be forbidden to build ships above a certain size. The Lords of Trade, though fine crusty old protectionists, were unable to see their way to granting any such prayer as this, and so ship-building continued to flourish in America. In the year 1769, the colonists along the whole Atlantic coast launched 389 vessels, of which 113 were square-riggers. It should not, however, be imagined that these vessels were formidable in size. The whole 389 had an aggregate register of 20,001 tons, an average of slightly over 50 tons each. Of these vessels 137, of 8013 tons, were built in Massachusetts; 45, of 2452 tons in New Hampshire; 50, of 1542 tons, in Connecticut; 19, of 955 tons, in New York; 22, of 1469 tons, in Pennsylvania. It is probable that few of them exceeded 100 tons register, and that none was over 200 tons register.

With the advent of the Revolutionary War, the rivalry on the sea between the older and the younger country took a more serious turn. Centuries before clipper ships were ever thought of, England had claimed, through her repeated and victorious naval wars against Spain, Holland, France, and lesser nations, the proud title of Mistress of the Seas, but in the Revolutionary War with her American colonies and the War of 1812 with the United States, her battleships and fleets of merchantmen were sorely harassed by the swift, light-built, and heavily-armed American frigates and privateers. While it cannot be said that the naval power of England upon the ocean was seriously impaired, yet the speed of the American vessels and the skill and gallantry with which they were fought and handled, made it apparent that the young giant of the West might some day claim the sceptre of the sea as his own.

During the latter half of the eighteenth century, however, the leading nation in the modelling and construction of ships was France, and during this period the finest frigates owned in the British Navy were those captured from the French. The frigate was indeed invented in England, the first being the *Constant Warwick,* launched in 1647, by Peter Pett, who caused the fact of his being the inventor of the frigate to be engraved upon his tomb; but in the improvement of the type, England had long been outstripped by her neighbor across the channel. William James,[1] the well known historian of the British Navy, makes mention of the French forty-gun frigate *Hebe* which was captured by the British frigate *Rainbow* in 1782, and records that "this prize did prove a most valuable acquisition to the service, there being few British frigates even of the present day (1847) which, in size and exterior form, are not copied from the *Hebe.*" As late as 1821 the *Arrow,* for many years the fastest yacht owned in England, was modelled from the lines of a French lugger, recently wrecked upon the Dorset coast, which proved to be a well known smuggler that had for years eluded the vigilance of H. M. excise cutters, always escaping capture, although often sighted, through her superior speed.

[1] A frigate was a ship designed to be a fast, armed cruiser and mounted from twenty to fifty guns; when a naval vessel mounted less than twenty guns she became a sloop of war, and when she mounted more than fifty guns she became a line-of-battle ship. The frigate was always a favorite type of vessel with the officers and men of the navy, as she was faster and more easily handled than a line-of-battle ship, and was at the same time a more powerful fighting and cruising vessel than a sloop of war. Frigate-built means having the substantial construction, arrangement of the decks, masts, spars, rigging, and guns of a frigate.

The United States no less than Great Britain was indebted to France for improvements in the models of her ships at this period. During the Revolutionary War, when a treaty was entered into between France and the United States in 1778, a number of French frigates and luggers appeared in American waters. The luggers, rating from one hundred and fifty to two hundred tons and some even higher, belonged to the type used by the privateersmen of Brittany, a scourge upon every sea where the merchant flag of an enemy was to be found. They were the fastest craft afloat in their day. When the French frigates and luggers were dry docked in American ports for cleaning or repairs, their lines were carefully taken off by enterprising young shipwrights and were diligently studied. It was from these vessels that the first American frigates and privateers originated, and among the latter were the famous Baltimore vessels which probably during the War of 1812 first became known as "Baltimore clippers."

Congress ordered four frigates and three sloops of war to be built in 1778, and almost countless privateers suddenly sprang into existence at ports along the Atlantic seaboard, most of them copied from models of the French vessels. One of the frigates, the *Alliance,* named to commemorate the alliance between France and the United States, was built at Salisbury, Massachusetts, by William and John Hackett. Her length was 151 feet, breadth 36 feet, and depth of hold 12 feet 6 inches, and she drew when ready for sea 14 feet 8 inches aft and 9 feet forward. She was a favorite with the whole navy by reason of her speed and beauty, and on her first voyage she had the honor of conveying Lafayette to France. At the close of the war she was sold by the Government and became a merchantman famous in the China and India trade. Several of the privateers were built and fitted out at Portsmouth, New Hampshire, and Newburyport, Massachusetts. Those in which Nathaniel Tracy was interested captured no less than 120 vessels, amounting to 23,360 tons, which with their cargoes were condemned and sold for 3,950,000 specie dollars; and with these prizes were taken 2220 prisoners of war. Many other instances of this nature might, of course, be mentioned, but the important point is the fact that in the latter part of the eighteenth century and the early part of the nineteenth, as well, the fastest vessels owned or built in the United States and Great Britain were from French models.[1]

[1] When peace was declared in 1783, the Government of the United States sold or otherwise disposed of all its vessels, a fact that was quickly taken advantage of by the Barbary corsairs. They at once began to prey upon American merchant shipping in the Mediterranean and even in the Atlantic, and made slaves of the captured crews. The French and English, too, in their wars with each other, by no means respected the neutrality of American commerce, the former being the worse offenders. It was not, however, until 1794 that Congress again authorized the formation of a navy, under the Secretary of War, and in 1798 the office of Secretary of the Navy was created. Among the vessels built in 1794–98 was the frigate *Constitution*, the famous "Old Ironsides" which still survives. The separate States had meanwhile maintained vessels for the protection of their

The characteristics of the French model were a beautifully rounded bow, by no means sharp along the water-line, easy sectional lines developing into a full, powerful forebody and midship section, and great dead rise at half floor. The greatest breadth was well forward of amidships and at the water-line, with a slight, gracefully rounded tumble home to the plank-sheer. The after-body was finely moulded, clean, sharp, and long, with a powerful transom and quarters. The time-honored cod's head and mackerel's tail: the figureheads and ornamentation of the quarters and stern, were veritable works of art. By comparing the models of the British frigates of that day to be seen in the Naval Museum at Greenwich, and the lines of the American frigates and Baltimore clippers of the same period, with the models still preserved in the Louvre, it is easy to trace a family likeness among them all, the parent being of French origin. The grandparent also might easily be identified, in the Italian galleys of Genoa and Venice, though this is of no importance to our present purpose.

That the American vessels showed a marked superiority in point of speed over British men-of-war and merchant ships during these two wars is the more remarkable from the fact that frigates had been built in England for a century and a half, as we have seen, and, while it is true that two vessels for the British Government were built at Portsmouth previous to the Revolutionary War—the

---

own coasts, and, of course, there had been no cessation in the building of merchant ships during the period preceding the War of 1812.

Faulkland, fifty-four guns, in 1690, and the *America,* fifty guns, in 1740—still, at the outbreak of the Revolution, the shipwrights of America scarcely knew what a frigate was, and much less had thought of building one. It had been the policy of Great Britain to keep her American colonies as much as possible in ignorance concerning naval affairs, doubtless from fear of their growing ambition. They were therefore led to copy the models of French vessels, not only from choice, on account of their excellence, but from necessity as well. Thus it came about that the frigates of Great Britain and the United States were developed from the same source.

A sailing ship is an exceedingly complex, sensitive, and capricious creation—quite as much so as most human beings. Her coquetry and exasperating deviltry have been the delight and despair of seamen's hearts, at least since the days when the wise, though much-married, Solomon declared that among the things that were too wonderful for him and which he knew not, was "the way of a ship in the midst of the sea." While scientific research has increased since Solomon's time, it has not kept pace with the elusive character of the ship, for no man is able to tell exactly what a ship will or will not do under given conditions. Some men, of course, know more than others, yet no one has ever lived who could predict with accuracy the result of elements in design, construction, and rig. History abounds in instances of ships built for speed that have turned out dismal failures, and it has occasionally happened that ships built with no especial expectation of speed have proven fliers. It would seem, after ages of experience and evolution, that man should be able at last to build a sailing ship superior in every respect to every other sailing ship, but this is exactly what he cannot and never has been able to accomplish. A true sailor loves a fine ship and all her foibles; he revels in the hope that if he takes care of her and treats her fairly, she will not fail him in the hour of danger, and he is rarely disappointed.

While all this is true in the abstract, yet it is not difficult to account for the performance of ships in retrospect, and in this particular matter, the superior speed of American frigates during the two wars with the mother country, it is quite easy to do so.

In the first place, British men-of-war and merchantmen were at that time built with massive oak frames, knees, and planking, the timber of which had lain at dockyards seasoning in salt water for many years, and was as hard and almost as heavy as iron, while they were fastened with weighty through-and-through copper bolts; so that the ships themselves became rigid, dead structures—sluggish in moderate winds, and in gales and a seaway, wallowing brutes—whereas the American frigates and privateers were built of material barely seasoned in the sun and wind, and were put together as lightly as possible consistent with the strength needed to carry their batteries and to hold on to their canvas in heavy weather. Also, the British ships were heavy aloft—spars, rigging, and blocks—yet their masts and yards were not so long as those of the American ships, nor did they spread as much sail, although their canvas was heavier and had the picturesque "belly to hold the wind," by which, when close-hauled, the wind held the vessel.

Then the British men-of-war were commanded by naval officers who were brave, gallant gentlemen, no doubt, but whose experience at sea was limited to the routine of naval rules formulated by other gentlemen sitting around a table at Whitehall. The infraction of one of these regulations might cost the offender his epaulets and perhaps his life. In this respect the captains of the American Navy enjoyed a great advantage, for at this early period the United States authorities had their attention fully occupied in preserving the government, and had no time to devote to the manufacture of red tape with which to bind the hands and tongues of intelligent seamen. We think, and rightly, too, of Paul Jones, Murray, Barry, Stewart, Dale, Hull, Bainbridge, and others, as heroes of the navy, yet it is well for us sometimes to remember that all of these splendid seamen were brought up and most of them had commanded ships in the merchant marine. They were thus accustomed to self-reliance, and were filled with resource and expedient; they had passed through the rough school of adversity, and their brains and nerves were seasoned by salted winds, the ocean's brine mingling with their blood.

What wonder then that the American frigates, so built and so commanded, proved superior in point of speed to the British men-of-war? Less wonder still that the American privateers, whose men in the forecastle had in many instances commanded ships, should sweep the seas, until the despairing merchants and ship-owners of Great Britain, a nation whose flag had for a thousand years "braved the battle and the breeze" and which boasted proudly and justly that her home was upon the sea, compelled their government to acknowledge as political equals a people who had proved themselves superior upon the ocean.

So in the struggle for a national existence and rights as a nation, the foundations of the maritime power of the United States were laid. The shipbuilders and the seamen of the Revolution and the War of 1812 were the forefathers of the men who built and commanded the American clipper ships.

After the Revolutionary War the merchants of Salem, Boston, New York, and Philadelphia vied with each other in sending their ships upon distant and hazardous voyages. Notwithstanding the natural difficulties of navigating, what to their captains were unknown seas, and the unnatural obstacles invented by man in the form of obstructive laws, the merchant marine of the United States steadily increased not only in bulk, but what was of far more importance, in the high standard of the men and ships engaged in it.

Salem took the lead, with her great merchant, Elias Hasket Derby, who sent his barque *Light Horse* to St. Petersburg in 1784, and soon after sent the *Grand Turk* first to the Cape of Good Hope and then to China. In 1789, the *Atlantic,* commanded by his son, Elias Hasket Derby, Jr., was the first ship to hoist the Stars and Stripes at Calcutta and Bombay, and she was soon followed by the *Peggy*, another of the Derby ships, which brought the first cargo of Bombay cotton into Massachusetts Bay. Mr. Derby owned a fleet of forty vessels, and upon his death in 1799 left an estate valued at more than $1,000,000, the largest fortune at that time in America, as well as a name honored for integrity throughout the mercantile world. William Gray, another famous Salem merchant, owned in 1807 fifteen ships, seven barques, thirteen brigs, and one schooner, his fleet representing one quarter of the total tonnage of Salem at that time. Then there were Joseph Peabody, Benjamin Pickman, and Jacob Crowninshield, all ship-owners who contributed to the fame of this beautiful New England seaport.

Many of the merchants had been sea-captains in their youth, and it was the captains who really made Salem famous. These men, from the training of the New England schoolroom and meeting-house, went out into the world and gathered there the fruits of centuries of civilization, which they brought home to soften the narrow self-righteousness of their fellow-citizens. In later years these captains carried missionaries to India, China, and Africa, unconscious that they were themselves the real missionaries, whose influence had wrought so desirable a change in New England thought and character. When Nathaniel Hawthorne served in the Custom House at Salem, the friends in whom he most delighted were sea-captains, for it was through their eyes that he looked out upon the great world, and gathered the knowledge of human nature that enabled him to portray in such grim reality the hidden springs of human thought and action. These captains were the sons of gentlemen, and were as a class the best educated men of their time in the United States, for they could do more important and difficult things, and do them well, than the men of any other profession. The old East India Museum at Salem is a monument to their taste and refinement. Nowhere else, perhaps, can be found another little museum as unique and beautiful, of treasures brought home one by one from distant lands and seas by the hands that gave them.

Boston, too, had her ships and seamen. From that port were sent out in 1788 the *Columbia,* a ship of two hundred and thirteen tons, and the sloop *Washington,* of ninety tons, commanded by Captains John Kendrick and Robert Gray, who took them round Cape Horn to the northwest coast of America, and then after trading for cargoes of furs, went across to China. The *Columbia* returned to Boston by way of the Cape of Good Hope, and was the first vessel to carry the United States ensign round the globe. Subsequently she discovered the majestic river that bears her name, and so won the great Northwest for the flag under which she sailed. The *Massachusetts,* of six hundred tons, the largest merchant vessel built in America up to her time, was launched at Quincy in 1789 and was owned in Boston. She sailed for Canton and was sold there to the Danish East India Company for $65,000.

Ezra Weston was the most famous of the old time Boston ship-owners. He began business in 1764, and owned his own shipyard, sail-loft, and extensive rope-walk at Duxbury, Massachusetts, where his vessels were built and equipped. In 1798 his son Ezra became a partner, and this firm continued until the death of the father in 1822. The son Ezra then went on in his own name until 1842, when his sons Gersham, Alden, and Ezra, were taken into the firm, and they continued it until 1858, in all some ninety-three years, the last place of business being Nos. 37 and 38, Commercial Wharf. From the year 1800 to 1846 the Westons owned twenty-one ships, ranging in tonnage from the *Hope,* of 880 tons, to the *Minerva,* of 250 tons; one barque, the *Pallas,* of 209 tons; thirty brigs, from the *Two Friends,* of 240 tons, to the *Federal Eagle,* of 120 tons; thirty-five schooners, from the *St. Michael,* of 132 tons, to the *Star,* of 20 tons; and ten sloops, from the *Union,* of 63 tons, to the *Linnet,* of 50 tons. The brig *Smyrna,* one of the Weston fleet, built in 1825, of 160 tons, was the first American vessel to bear the flag of the United States into the Black Sea after it was opened to commerce. She arrived at Odessa July 17, 1830. The Westons were easily the largest ship-owners of their time in the United States, and not only built but loaded their own vessels. Their house-flag was red, white, and blue horizontal stripes.

In the year 1791, Stephen Girard, who was born near Bordeaux in 1750 and had risen from cabin-boy to be captain of his own vessel, built four beautiful ships at Philadelphia for the China and

India trade—the *Helvetia, Montesquieu, Rousseau,* and *Voltaire.* These vessels, long the pride of Philadelphia, greatly enriched their owner.

The sloop *Enterprise,* of eighty tons, built at Albany and commanded by Captain Stewart Dean, was sent from New York to China in 1785. This was the first vessel to make the direct voyage from the United States to Canton. She returned during the following year with her crew of seven men and two boys all in excellent condition. When she warped alongside the wharf at New York, Captain Dean and his crew were in full uniform, and the scene, which was witnessed by an admiring throng, was enlivened by "martial music and the boatswain's whistle."

Thomas Cheesman was one of the first shipbuilders in New York, and he was succeeded in business, before the end of the eighteenth century, by his son Forman, born in 1763. The latter built the forty-four-gun frigate *President,* launched in the year 1800 at Corlear's Hook—by far the largest vessel built in New York up to that time. Previous to this, however, he had built the *Briganza* and the *Draper,* each of three hundred tons, and the *Ontario,* of five hundred tons. Thomas Vail, William Vincent, and Samuel Ackley also built several vessels prior to the year 1800. The ships *Eugene, Severn, Manhattan, Sampson, Echo, Hercules, Resource, York,* and *Oliver Ellsworth* were launched from their yards. In 1804 the *Oliver Ellsworth,* built by Vail & Vincent and commanded by Captain Bennett, made the passage from New York to Liverpool in fourteen days, notwithstanding that she carried away her foretopmast, which was replaced at sea.

All of these shipyards were below Grand Street, on the East River. Samuel Ackley's yard was at the foot of Pelham Street, and here the *Manhattan,* of six hundred tons, was built for the China and East India trade. She was regarded as a monster of the deep, and when she sailed upon her first voyage in 1796, it took nearly all the deep water seamen in the port to man her. Henry Eckford opened a shipyard at the foot of Clinton Street in 1802. From this yard he launched, in 1803, John Jacob Astor's famous ship *Beaver,* of four hundred and twenty-seven tons. It was on board this ship that Captain Augustus De Peyster made his first voyage as a boy before the mast. Subsequently he commanded her, and upon retiring from the sea in 1845 he became the Governor of the Sailors' Snug Harbor at Staten Island. The *Beaver* once made the homeward run from Canton to Bermuda in seventy-five days. Christian Bergh began shipbuilding in 1804 with the ship *North America,* of four hundred tons, built for the Atlantic trade, and the brig *Gipsey,* of three hundred tons, a very sharp vessel for those days. She was dismasted off the Cape of Good Hope upon her first voyage to Batavia, and afterwards foundered in a heavy squall, all hands being lost. The *Trident,* of three hundred and fifty tons, was built by Adam and Noah Brown in 1805, and the *Triton,* of three hundred and fifty tons, by Charles Brown during the same year, both for the China and India trade. John Floyd began ship-building in 1807, and launched the *Carmelite,* a ship of four hundred tons, during that year, but was soon appointed naval constructor at the Brooklyn Navy Yard.

Until 1794 ships had been built from skeleton models composed of pieces that showed the frames, keel, stem, and stern post, but were of little use in giving an accurate idea of the form of a vessel, while it required much time and labor to transfer the lines of the model to the mould loft. In this year, however, Orlando Merrill, a young shipbuilder of Newburyport, at that time thirty-one years old, invented the water-line model, which was composed of lifts joined together, originally by dowels and later by screws. These could be taken apart and the sheer, body, and half-breadth plans easily transferred to paper, from which the working plans were laid down in the mould loft. This ingenious though simple invention, for which, by the way, Mr. Merrill never received any pecuniary reward, revolutionized the science of ship-building. The original model made by him in 1794 was presented to the New York Historical Society in 1853. Mr. Merrill died in 1855 at the age of ninety-two.

CHAPTER II

BRITISH SHIPPING AFTER 1815—THE EAST INDIA COMPANY

GREAT BRITAIN and the United States signed a treaty of peace and good-will at Ghent in 1814. During the following year the wars of England and France ended on the field of Waterloo. And so at last the battle flags were furled. The long-continued wars of England had, through neglect, reduced her merchant marine to a low standard of efficiency, and both men and ships were in a deplorable condition. There was no government supervision over British merchant shipping except taxation, the only check, and that but partially effective, being the Underwriters at Lloyd's. Unscrupulous ship-owners might and often did send rotten, unseaworthy vessels to sea, poorly provisioned, short of gear and stores, with captains, mates, and crews picked up from low taverns along the docks. These vessels were fully covered by insurance at high rates of premium, with the hope, frequently realized, that they would never be heard from again.

The "skippers," "maties," and "jackies" alike belonged to the lowest stratum of British social classification, which, according to the chronicles of those days, was pretty low. They were coarse, vulgar, ignorant men, full of lurid oaths; their persons emitted an unpleasant odor of cheap rum and stale tobacco; they had a jargon of their own and were so illiterate as to be unable to speak or write their own language with any degree of correctness. In a certain sense the captains were good sailors, but their knowledge and ambition were limited to dead reckoning, the tar bucket and marlinspike, a wife in every port, and plenty of rum and tobacco with no desire or ability to master the higher branches of navigation and seamanship. Mariners that a landsman delights to refer to as "real old salts," of the Captain Cuttle and Jack Bunsby species, are amusing enough, perhaps, in the hands of a skilful novelist, but not at all the class of men that one would willingly select to assist in carrying forward the commerce of a great maritime nation.

Then the stupid and obsolete Tonnage Laws encouraged and almost compelled an undesirable type of vessels, narrow, deep, flat-sided, and full-bottomed —bad vessels in a seaway, slow, and often requiring a considerable quantity of ballast, even when loaded, to keep them from rolling over.

It is, of course, always hazardous to deal in generalities, but I think that this may be accepted as a fair description of the merchant marine of Great Britain up to 1834, when the Underwriters at Lloyd's and the better class of ship-owners founded Lloyd's Register of Shipping, to provide for the proper survey and classification of the merchant ships of Great Britain. This first important step in a much needed reform was followed in 1837 by the appointment of a committee by Parliament to investigate the general condition of shipping engaged in foreign trade. The committee reported as follows:

"The American ships frequenting the ports of England are stated by several witnesses to be superior to those of a similar class amongst the ships of Great Britain, the commanders and officers being generally considered to be more competent as seamen and navigators, and more uniformly persons of education, than the commanders and officers of British ships of a similar size and class trading from England to America, while the seamen of the United States are considered to be more carefully selected, and more efficient. American ships sailing from Liverpool to New York have a preference over English vessels sailing to the same port, both as to freight and the rate of insurance; and, the higher wages being given, their whole equipment is maintained in a higher state of perfection, so that fewer losses occur; and as the American shipping having increased of late years in the proportion to 12¾% per annum, while the British shipping have increased within the same period only 1½% per annum, the constantly increasing demand for seamen by the rapidly growing maritime commerce of the whole world, the numbers cut off by shipwrecks, and the temptations offered by the superior wages of American vessels, cause a large number of British seamen every year to leave the service of their own country, and to embark in that of the United States; and these comprising chiefly the most skilful and competent of our mariners, produce the double effect of improving the efficiency of the American crews, and in the same ratio diminishing the efficiency of the British merchant service."

In 1843 a circular was issued from the Foreign Office to all British consuls requesting information on the conduct and character of British shipmasters, especially with regard to the "incompetence of British shipmasters to manage their vessels and crews, whether arising from deficiency of knowledge in practical navigation and seamanship, or of moral character, particularly want of sobriety." The consular reports revealed a startling condition of affairs, requiring immediate attention, and led to the establishment in 1847, of the Marine Department of the Board of Trade, with authority to supervise maritime affairs. From such unpromising material the formation was begun of the greatest merchant marine that has ever existed.

Meanwhile, one of the most important branches of British commerce, the East India trade, had been following an independent career, for the ships of the East India Company, although engaged in commercial pursuits, were under the direct patronage of the government, and cannot be regarded as forming part of the merchant marine of Great Britain. Yet as this Company had an important bearing upon the mercantile affairs of the nation, I propose to review as briefly as possible some of its remarkable exploits.

"The United Company of Merchant Venturers of England trading to the East Indies" was familiarly known as the "John Company," and among those endowed with a larger bump of reverence, as the "Honorable John Company"; but by whatever name it may be called, this was the most gigantic commercial monopoly the world has ever known, since the days when the merchants of Tyre claimed the exclusive right to send their ships across certain waters known by common consent as Tyrian Seas.

The East India Company was founded in the year 1600, during the reign of Queen Elizabeth. The subscribed capital of £72,000 was expended on the first voyage in five vessels with their cargoes. This fleet consisted of the *Dragon,* of 600 tons, her commander receiving the title of Admiral of the squadron; the *Hector,* 300 tons, with a Vice-Admiral in command; two vessels of 200 tons each; and the *Guest,* a store ship of 130 tons. Four hundred and eighty men were employed in the expedition, including twenty merchants as supercargoes. The vessels were all heavily armed and were provided with small arms and an abundance of ammunition. They cost, with their equipment, £45,000, and their cargoes £27,000.

Friendly relations were formed with the King of Achin, in Sumatra, and a station, known in those days and long afterward as a "factory," was established at Bantam, in Java. The fleet returned to England richly laden with silks and spices in 1603. In 1609 the *Trades Increase,* of 1209 tons, the largest ship launched in England up to that time, was built, but she was wrecked and became a total loss on her first voyage. Sir Henry Middleton, her commander, died soon after. This was an unfortunate expedition and resulted in heavy losses to the Company, but in 1611 the *Globe* cleared 218%, and in the following year the *Globe, Thomas,* and *Hector* turned over profits amounting to 340% upon the capital invested. Other successful voyages followed, so that in 1617 the stock of the Company reached a premium of 203%.

The East India Company had its troubles, to be sure, which were many and great, yet it increased in power, wealth, and strength, until at the close of the eighteenth century it had become possessed of a large portion of the continent of India, maintaining its own armies, forts, palaces, Courts of Directors, Boards of Council, Governors, and Typeans.[1] Eventually, this Company became the ruler of more than one hundred million human beings, not naked savages, but civilized men and women, many of whose ancestors had been learned scholars and merchant princes long prior to the invasion of Britain by the Roman, Dane, and Saxon.

It is not, however, with the political affairs of this Company that I wish to deal, but rather with the ships and the men who navigated them. The princely emoluments known as "indulgences" in which the captains and officers of these ships participated, naturally attracted the attention of parents and guardians, so that younger sons, otherwise destined for a life of ill-requited repose in the church, the Army, or the Navy, found lucrative service with the East India Company. These perquisites, which were handed out by the Honorable Court of Di-

[1] A typean was the head merchant of one of the Company's "factories" or mercantile houses, such as were later known in China as "hongs."

East Indiamen, 1720

rectors, were no doubt intended to be of pleasing variety and magnitude. The Company adhered strictly to promotion by seniority as vacancies occurred, from ship to ship when necessary. Captains were appointed to their ships before launching, in order that they might superintend their equipment and get them ready for sea. Midshipmen were appointed by the Court of Directors, and no youth of less than thirteen or over eighteen years was eligible. Second mates were required to be at least twenty-two, chief mates twenty-three, and commanders twenty-five years of age.

Captains were entitled to fifty-six and one half tons of space on board the ships commanded by them, which they might use at their discretion, either to collect the freight or to carry cargo on their own account, credit being furnished by the company for the latter purpose at the usual interest. The rate of freight ranged from £35 to £40 per ton, though in 1796 the *Admiral Gardner,* a ship of 813 tons, commanded by John Woolmore, Esq., was chartered for "six voyages certain" from London to India and return, at £50 for every ton of cargo carried. Even at the lowest rate of £35 per ton, the voyage out and home of about eighteen months yielded a captain some £3955, and if he carried goods on his own account, as was usually the case, he realized a much larger sum. Captains were also allowed primage, which was a percentage upon the total gross freight earned by the ship, and the passage money for passengers carried, except the Company's troops, less the cost of living. Considering that the passage money to or from India or China was for a subaltern £95, and for a general officer £234, to say nothing of directors and governors and their families, and that these ships usually carried from twenty to thirty passengers, we may conclude that this also was a considerable source of revenue.

Then captains were permitted to own the dunnage used for the protection of homeward cargoes, which they supplied in the form of stone and chinaware, canes, bamboos, rattans, sapan-wood, horns, nankins, etc. All of these goods might in those days be bought at very low prices in India and China, and under the monopoly of the East India Company, they sold at very high prices in London. Most of this "dunnage," however, came to the captains in the form of presents, known in the fragrant language of the Far East as "cumshaws," from admiring Indian and Chinese merchants.

Naturally all of the cargoes were well dunnaged, so much so, indeed, as finally to attract the attention of the benevolent Court of Directors, who deemed it expedient to restrain the zeal of their captains in this direction by issuing an order that "as dunnage has been brought home in the Company's ships far beyond what is necessary for the protection of the cargo and stores, occupying tonnage to the exclusion of goods, or cumbering the ship, the court have resolved that unless what is brought home of those articles appears absolutely and *bona fide* necessary for and used as dunnage, the exceeding of such requisite quantity shall be charged against the tonnage of the commanders and officers." This dunnage business had been progressing favorably for about two centuries when this mandate was issued, and had enriched many a deserving mariner. It was estimated that an Indiaman's captain received in one way or another from £6000 to £10,000 per annum, and there is a record of one ship that made what was known as a double voyage—that is, from London to India, China, and return—a twenty-two months' cruise—whose commander made profits amounting to the tidy sum of £30,000.

The mates and petty officers were also well provided for, having forty and one half tons of space allotted among them to do with as they pleased, and all hands were supplied with wines, spirits, and beer in quantities which if stated might seem like an attempt to impose upon the reader's credulity.

A more showy if less substantial honor was conferred by the distinctive dress of the company's servants. The captains were arrayed in a picturesque uniform consisting of a blue coat with black velvet lapels, cuffs and collar, bright gold embroidery, and yellow gilt buttons engraved with the Company's crest, waistcoat and breeches of deep buff, black stock, or neck-cloth, cocked hat and side-arms. The chief, second, third, and fourth officers wore uniforms of a similar though less gorgeous character, and all were particularly requested "not on any account to appear in boots, black breeches, and stockings" and "to appear in full dress when attending the Court of Directors."

The charter of the East India Company provided that its ships should fly the long coach-whip pennant of the Royal Navy. During the last quarter of the eighteenth and first part of the nineteenth centuries, the ships were built, rigged, equipped, armed, manned, and handled like the frigates of the Royal Navy, though they were beautifully and luxuriously fitted for passengers, many of whom were personages of high social and official rank. They differed, however, from the frigates in one important particular. Whereas, the navy constructors, as we have seen, profited by the models of the French frigates, the builders of the Indiamen kept to the full-bodied, kettle-bottomed model, in order that these ships might carry large cargoes. They were of quite as bad a type as the ships of the more humble merchant marine. I have before me the particulars of one of the East India Company's ships that carried four hundred and nineteen tons of general cargo, and required eighty tons of iron kentledge to keep her on her legs. They were nevertheless grand, stately-looking ships, and were well cared for.

The crews were divided into the usual two watches, but the officers had three watches, four hours on and eight hours off. The watches were divided into messes of eight men each, who had a space allotted to them between the guns in the between-decks. Here their hammocks were slung and their chests, mess-kids, copper pots, kettles, and tin pannikins were stowed, clean and bright, under the inspection of the commander and the surgeon, who were assisted in their duties by wearing white gloves with which to test the appearance of cleanliness. The crews slept in hammocks which were stowed in nettings at seven bells in the morning watch, to the pipe of the boatswain's whistle. The decks were washed and holystoned in the morning watch, and at eight bells all hands breakfasted. On Wednesdays and Saturdays, the between-decks were turned out, washed, and holystoned. On Sunday mornings the crew was mustered and inspected by the chief officer, and then assembled for Divine service, which was read by the commander, as the Court of Directors required the captains " to keep up the worship of Almighty God, under a penalty of two guineas for every omission not satisfactorily accounted for in the log-book."

The crews were drilled at the guns and with cutlass, musket, and boarding-pikes, and other small arms, Courts-martial were held on board and the rawhide cat-o'-nine-tails was freely used by the boatswain upon the naked backs and shoulders of triced-up seamen—one, two, three dozen, perhaps, with a bucket of salt water to rinse off the blood. This was not so brutal a form of punishment as may perhaps appear to landsmen, and was probably the best method of enforcing proper discipline among the reckless men who for the most part formed the crews of ships at that period.

These vessels carried large crews, whose work was easy and who were well looked after and provided for. They had plenty of the best food and quite as much rum as was good for them. In the dog-watches they were allowed and even encouraged to enjoy themselves in the manner known on board ship as " skylarking." Saturdays they had to themselves to wash and mend their clothes, and in the dog-watches of that day they were given an extra allowance of grog, with which to drink long life and happiness to sweethearts and wives, with music, dance, and song. Seamen who had served eight years in the Company's ships were entitled to liberal pensions, as were also the wives and children of those who had been killed in the service of the Company, or who had been so maimed or wounded as to be unable to perform further service. There can be no question that the directors of the East India Company took good care of those who served them faithfully.

The East Indiamen were always fine, strong ships, built of oak, elm, and teak, copper-fastened throughout, their cost being £40 per ton ready for sea; but they were very slow, and their passages were reckoned not by days but by months. Every evening, no matter how fine the weather, royals and all light sails were taken in and stowed, and the royal yards sent on deck. If the weather looked at all as if it might become threatening during the night, the topgallantsails and mainsail were stowed and a single reef put in the topsails. Safety and comfort were the watchwords, with no desire or effort for speed. No one ever knew how fast these vessels really could sail, as they never had any one on board who tried to get the best speed out of them, but without doubt their passages might have been considerably shortened with even a moderate amount of vigilance and energy. All we know is, how slow they were. Yet these ships were fought through many a desperate battle upon the sea, with foreign men of war, privateers, and other foes, and the skill and valor of their captains, officers, and

An East Indiaman, 1788

crews shed a new lustre upon the ensign under which they sailed. Indeed, the maritime records of the East India Company read more like a naval history than the annals of ships engaged in commercial pursuits.

In some respects these Indiamen were remarkable ships, and they should, like men, be judged by the standards of the times in which they existed. They were owned by a company which for more than two centuries held a monopoly of the British China and East India trade without the spur of competition urging them to perfect their vessels and to exact vigorous service from the officers and crews who sailed them. Under such a system there could be no marked progress in naval science. It would, of course, be an exaggeration to say that there had been no improvement in British shipping from the reign of Queen Elizabeth to the Victorian era, but it was so gradual as to be perceptible only when measured by centuries. Thus we speak of the ships of the sixteenth, seventeenth, and eighteenth centuries, and upon examination are surprised to find how few and slight were the improvements made during these three hundred years in the design and construction of hulls or in spars, rigging, and sails. The only striking improvement was a modification of the really beautiful ornamentation which embellished and at the same time lumbered up the lofty hulls of the earlier ships.

Some of the Indiamen were built in Wigram's famous yard at Blackwall on the Thames, which was in existence for more than two centuries. Indeed, some of the first ships owned by the East

India Company, the *Dragon, Susannah,* and *Merchants' Hope* were launched there. During the reigns of Elizabeth, James, Charles I., Charles II., and the Georges, this yard turned out many of the ships owned in the Royal Navy, and through all these years it had in time of need been a faithful standby of the British Government. Some of the ships of the Company were, however, built in other yards and in their own building establishment at Bombay.

During the years 1819 and 1820 the Company sent to their different stations in Bengal, Madras, Bombay, China, Ceylon, and Penang, twenty-three of their own ships aggregating 26,200 tons, besides twenty-one chartered vessels measuring 10,948 tons. Among the Company's ships were the *Canning, Duke of York, Kellie Castle, Lady Melville, Thomas Coutts,* and *Waterloo,* built by Wigram, and all from 1325 to 1350 tons, each mounting 26 guns with a crew of 130 men. The *Buckinghamshire, Earl of Balcarras, Herefordshire, Thomas Granville, Minerva,* and *Charles Grant,* all from 923 to 1417 tons, 26 guns, and 130 men with the exception of the *Minerva* and *Thomas Granville* which mounted the same number of guns but had 115 and 107 men, respectively, were built by the Company at Bombay. The *Asia, Dorsetshire, Duneira, Marquis of Wellington, Prince Regent, Princess Amelia,* and *Windsor,* which were all over 1000 tons and mounted 26 guns with crews of from 115 to 130 each, were built in the Barnard yard, also on the Thames. The *London, Lowther Castle, Marquis of Camden,* and *Perseverance,* all from 1329 to 1408 tons. 26 guns, and 130 men each, were built in the Pitcher yard at Northfleet in Kent. The *Earl of Balcarras,* of 1417 tons, built in 1815 at Bombay, was the largest ship owned by the Company. She was built of India teak, copper-fastened throughout, and mounted batteries on two decks. Her crew of 133 men was made up as follows: Commander, 6 mates, 2 surgeons, 6 midshipmen, purser, gunner, carpenter, master-at-arms, armour, butcher, baker, poulterer, caulker, cooper, 2 stewards, 2 cooks, 8 boatswains, gunner's, carpenter's, caulker's, and cooper's mates, 6 quartermasters, sailmaker, 7 servants for the commander and officers, and 78 seamen before the mast.

These facts illustrate not only the manner in which the ships of the East India Company were officered and manned, but also the extravagant scale upon which the affairs of the Company were administered. Of course, a gross monopoly like this, legalized though it was by Acts of Parliament, could not continue indefinitely among a free and intelligent people. For many years mutterings of discontent, gathering in force and volume, had been heard from all parts of Great Britain, indicating the disapproval of the people concerning the methods of the Company. At last, in 1832, these mutterings burst into a storm of indignation from the people through their representatives in Parliament, which swept the frigates of the Honorable John Company off the face of the deep; for in that year commerce to the Orient was thrown open to all British ships, and knowing their utter inability to compete successfully with free and intelligent personal energy, the East India Company condemned or sold their entire fleet. Sixteen ships were broken up for their massive copper fastenings and other valuable material, while forty-six were sold, and no finer tribute can be offered to the excellent construction of these vessels than the figures which they realized at what may justly be called a forced sale.

Naturally these ships were not all sold at the some moment, as some of them were on their way to China and India when the crash came; in fact, it required about three years to close them all out; still, it was well known that the Court of Directors had decreed that they must all be sold, and this gave bargain hunters a chance to practise their wiles. At first two or three of the ships were put up at public auction; the bids were few and meagre, indicating an assumed and perhaps preconcerted apathy. Negotiations of a less public nature ensued, which resulted as follows: The *Buckinghamshire,* of 1369 tons, then eighteen years old, was sold to Thacker & Mangels for £10,550. The *Canning,* 1326 tons, seventeen years old, sold for breaking up to Joseph Somes at £5750. The *Minerva,* 976 tons, eighteen years old, ready for sea, to Henry Templer, at £11,800; this ship, after thirty-seven years of service in the India trade was wrecked off the Cape of Good Hope in 1850. The *Earl of Balcarras,* 1417 tons, nineteen years old, to Thomas A. Shuter for £15,700; this ship after fifty-two years' service, became a receiving hulk on the west coast of Africa. The *Bombay,* 1246 tons, twenty-two years old, sold to Duncan Dunbar for £11,000, was wrecked after fifty-nine years of service. The *Lowther Castle,* 1408 tons, nineteen years old, went to Joseph Somes for £13,950. The *Waterloo,* 1325 tons, eighteen years old, was sold for breaking up at £7200. The *Thames,* 1360 tons, thirteen years old, went to James Chrystall at £10,700. The remaining ships of the fleet brought equally good prices. Thus ended the maritime exploits of the "United Company of Merchant Venturers of England trading to the East Indies"; although its influence upon the merchant marine of Great Britain continued for many years.

With the opening of the China and India trade to all British ships, there came the long-wished for competition—one of the hinges upon which commerce swings—and a number of British ship-owners, hardly known before, now came into prominence. Among them were Green, Wigram, Dunbar, and Somes, of London, and the Smiths, of Newcastle. So strongly was the example of the East India Company impressed upon their minds that they still continued to construct frigate-built ships, though with some slight effort toward economy and speed. Many of the former captains, officers, and seamen of the East India Company sailed for the private firms, and so the personnel of the British merchant marine was much benefited. The private ships, of course, were not permitted to fly the naval pennant, but in other respects the service remained pretty nearly the same. Much of the wasteful extravagance was naturally eliminated, and the "indulgences" were substantially reduced, but the time-honored practice of "making snug for the night" was too ancient and comfortable a custom to be very speedily abolished.

Joseph Somes, one of the promoters of Lloyd's Register, bought a number of the Company's old ships, as we have seen, and in addition he built the *Maria Somes, Princess Royal, Sir George Seymour,* and *Castle Eden.* Thomas and William Smith, of Newcastle, were an old ship-building firm, who had in 1808, at their yard in St. Peter's, constructed the frigate *Bucephalus,* 970 tons, 52 guns, for the Royal Navy, while in later years they built many merchant vessels. The finest of their new ships were the *Marlborough* and the *Blenheim,* of 1350 tons each, built under special government survey and granted certificates as frigates equipped for naval service. This firm also built the *Gloriana,* 1057 tons, *Hotspur,* 1142 tons, and *St. Lawrence,* 1049 tons, all of the frigate type, though employed as merchantmen.

Duncan Dunbar owned a number of fine ships and eventually became the largest ship-owner of his time in Great Britain. Many of his vessels were built in India. The *Marion,* 684 tons, built in Calcutta in 1834, was in active service until 1877, when she was wrecked on the Newfoundland coast. The *David Malcolm* was built in 1839, and the *Cressy,* 720 tons, and the *Hyderabad,* 804 tons, in 1843, at Sunderland.

Robert Wigram and Richard Green, at one time partners, built and owned their own ships, known as the "Blackwall frigates." In 1834–35, they brought out the *Malabar, Monarch,* and *Windsor Castle,* and subsequently the *Carnatic, Prince of Wales, Agamemnon, Alfred,* and others, from 1200 to 1400 tons each. As late as 1849 the *Alfred,* of

The "Marlborough" and "Blenheim"

only 1291 tons, commanded by Captain Henning, carried a crew of eighty men, which included five mates, three boatswains, two carpenters, four quartermasters, a number of stewards and cooks, with sixty men before the mast.

These were the last of the frigate-built ships; for when the Navigation Laws were repealed in 1849, and the carrying trade of Great Britain and her colonies was thrown open to all nations, the British merchants and ship-builders found it necessary to construct a very different type of vessel in order to compete in the ocean carrying trade.

Farewell, then, to the gallant old Indiaman, with her hammock nettings, bunt jiggers, rolling tackles, jeers, gammon lashings, bentinck shrouds, and cat harpings, dear to sailors' hearts; and good-bye to her sailors, too, sons of the men who fought in the victorious fleets of Nelson, fellows who drank gunpowder in their rum before stripping to battle with the enemy, who could stand triced up by the thumbs and take their four-and-twenty of rawhide on the naked back without wetting an eyelash. And farewell to the merry dance and song, the extra dram of grog in the dog-watch, and jovial toasts to sweethearts and wives, as the sun sinks beneath the blue wave and the cool evening trade wind fills the sails.

CHAPTER III

THE NORTH ATLANTIC PACKET SHIPS, 1815–1850

WHILE progress in ship-building in the United States had been constant up to the War of 1812, American ship-owners and builders had been much hampered by the interference of both Great Britain and France, but in 1815, when the smoke of battle had cleared away and the rights of American ships and seamen had been established upon the sea, ship-building was taken up with renewed energy.

The famous New York–Liverpool packets came out in 1816. The pioneer, Black Ball Line, established by Isaac Wright, Francis and Jeremiah Thompson, Benjamin Marshall, and others, led the van for years. The original ships belonging to this line were the *Amity, Courier, Pacific,* and *James Monroe,* of about 400 tons; they were followed by the *New York, Eagle, Orbit, Nestor, James Cropper, William Thompson, Albion, Canada, Britannia,* and *Columbia,* vessels of from 300 to 500 tons register. For the first ten years the passages of the fleet averaged 23 days outward and 40 days to the westward. The fastest outward passage was made by the *Canada* in 15 days, 18 hours, and her total averages —19 days outward and 36 days homeward—were the best of that period.

These ships were all flush deck, with a caboose or galley and the housed-over long-boat between the fore- and main-masts. The long-boat, which was, of course, securely lashed, carried the live stock,—pens for sheep and pigs in the bottom, ducks and geese on a deck laid across the gunwales, and on top of all, hens and chickens. The cow-house was lashed over the main hatch, and there were also other small hatch-houses and a companion aft leading to the comfortable, well-appointed cabins, which were lighted by deck skylights, candles, and whale-oil lamps. The steerage passengers lived in the between-decks amidships, and the crew's forecastle was in the fore-peak. The stores, spare sails, gear, etc., were kept in the lazarette abaft the cabins, with a small hatch leading to the main-deck. The hulls were painted black from the water-line up, with bright scraped bends, which were varnished, and the inner side of the bulwarks, rails, hatch-houses, and boats were painted green. It was said that some of the early Black Ball captains had commanded privateers during the War of 1812. At all events, these little ships, with their full-bodied, able hulls, and their stout spars, sails, and rigging, were driven outward and homeward across the Atlantic, through the fogs and ice of summer and the snow, sleet, and gales of winter, for all the speed that was in them. They were in their day the only regular means of communication between the United States and Europe. Their captains were the finest men whose services money could secure, and to their care were entrusted the lives of eminent men and women, government despatches, the mails and specie.

Rain or shine, blow high, blow low, one of the Black Ball liners sailed from New York for Liverpool on the first and sixteenth of each month, and for many years these were the European mail days throughout the United States.

In 1821, Thomas Cope of Philadelphia started his line of packets between that port and Liverpool with the ships *Lancaster,* of 290 tons, and *Tuscarora,* of 379 tons, which were soon followed by larger vessels, among them some of the finest ships on the Atlantic.

The Red Star Line of Liverpool packets from New York was also established in 1821 with the *Panther, Meteor, Hercules,* and second *Manhattan,* and soon after, the Swallow Tail Line of Grinnell, Minturn & Co., came into existence with the *Napoleon, Silas Richards, George,* and *York.* Grinnell, Minturn & Co.'s London Line was established in 1823 with the *Brighton, Columbia, Cortes,* and *Corinthian,* of less than 500 tons each, and during this year John Griswold's London Line was also started with the *Sovereign, President, Cambria, Hudson,* and the second *Ontario.*

The opening of the Erie Canal in 1825 gave a great impetus to commerce, causing New York to become the eastern gateway of the United States, and from that date to 1850 may be counted the glorious years of the Atlantic packet ships.

The Dramatic Line to Liverpool was started in 1836 with the *Siddons, Shakespeare, Garrick,* and *Roscius,* under the management of E. K. Collins. These vessels did not much exceed 700 tons, and when, in 1837, Brown & Bell built the *Sheridan,*

The "England"

of 895 tons for this line, she was regarded as too large for a Liverpool packet, and after a few voyages was placed in the China trade.

The first Havre line of packets was founded by Francis Depaw in 1822 with the *Stephania, Montana, Henry IV., Helen Mar, Louis Philippe,* and *Silvia de Grasse.* A second line was formed in 1827 with the *Baltimore, Charles Carroll, Erie, France, Oneida, Mercury, Utica, Rhone, William Tell,* and in 1832 a third line, with the *Formosa, Galia, Albany, Duchesse d'Orléans, Isaac Bell, Queen Mab,* and *Don Quixote.*

In 1831 the New Orleans Line from New York was formed with the *Nashville, Huntsville, Louisville, Creole,* and *Natchez.* These were the first packet ships built with full poop-decks, then quite a new feature in ship-building. Gradually the flush deck gave place to house- and poop-deck cabins, then to the topgallant, forecastle, and house from the foremast to the main hatch. The fashion of painting also changed, and most if not all the packets carried painted ports, while the inside green was replaced by white or light shades of other colors.

After the Black Ball Line passed into the hands of Captain Charles H. Marshall in 1836, the *Columbus, Oxford, Cambridge, New York, England, Yorkshire, Fidelia, Isaac Wright, Isaac Webb,* the third *Manhattan, Montezuma, Alexander Marshall, Great Western,* and *Harvest Queen* were gradually added to the fleet. To meet the competition of the Black Ball Line, the Swallow Tail Line built the *Washington, Independence, Pennsylvania, Roscoe, Patrick Henry, Ashburton, Hottinger, Queen of the*

West, Liverpool, New World, and *Cornelius Grinnell.*

The packet ships slowly increased in tonnage, but did not much exceed 1000 tons until 1846 when the *New World,* of 1404 tons, was built by Donald McKay, followed by the *Guy Mannering,* of 1419 tons, and the *Albert Gallatin,* of 1435 tons, built by William H. Webb in 1849, these three vessels being the largest merchant ships afloat at that period.

The Black Ball ships carried a large painted black ball below the close-reef band in their foretopsails, while the Dramatic Line, not to be outdone, carried a black X which extended diagonally, almost from clew to earring, across their foretopsails. All packet ships carried a white light at the bowsprit cap from sunset to sunrise, but side-lights did not come into use until some years later. These ships also carried a flare-up which was kept in the companion ready for immediate use.

Throughout the various changes of management the Black Ball liners carried a crimson swallowtail flag with a black ball in the centre; the Dramatic liners, blue above white with a white L in blue and a black L in white for the Liverpool ships, and a red swallowtail with white ball and black L in the centre for the New Orleans ships; the Union Line to Havre, a white field with black U in the centre; John Griswold's London Line, red swallowtail with black X in centre; the Swallowtail Line, red before white, swallowtail for the London ships, and blue before white, swallowtail for the Liverpool ships; Robert Kermit's Liverpool Line, blue swallowtail with red star in the centre; Spofford & Tileston's Liverpool Line, yellow field, blue cross with white S. T. in the centre. These flags disappeared from the sea many years ago.

The packet captain, no matter what his age might be, was usually spoken of as "the old man," a title frequently embellished by the crew with vigorous epithets, which seemed to them appropriate, but which must now, I fear, be left to the imagination of the reader. Few if any Americans sailed regularly before the mast on board of these vessels, the crews being largely composed of the most abandoned scoundrels out of British and continental jails. I shall have something further to say concerning these interesting beings in connection with their exploits on board of the California clipper ships.

Among the famous New York packet captains, and there were many of them, were Charles H. Marshall, of the *South America, James Cropper,* and *Britannia;* N. B. Palmer, of the *Siddons, Garrick, Huntsville,* and *Hibernia,* and his brother, Alexander, later of the *Garrick;* F. A. De Peyster, of the *Columbus* and *Ontario;* John Collins, an uncle of E. K. Collins, of the *Shakespeare;* John Eldridge, of the *Liverpool,* and his brother Asa, of the *Roscius,* and Oliver, another brother, who was mate with Captain John; Ezra Nye, of the *Independence* and *Henry Clay;* William Skiddy, an older brother of Francis Skiddy, of the *New World;* Benjamin Trask, of the *Virginia, Jamestown,* and *Saratoga;* Joseph Delano, of the *Columbia* and *Patrick Henry;* John Britton, of the *Constitution,* later United States consul at Southampton; Ira Bursley, of the *Hottinger;* Philip Woodhouse, of the *Queen of the West;*

James A. Wooton, of the *Havre;* William H. Allen, of the *Virginia, Waterloo, West Point,* and *Constellation;* E. E. Morgan, of the *Hudson* and *Victoria;* John Johnston, of the *Rhone* and *Isaac Bell;* and of a later period, Robert C. Cutting, of the *Adelaide;* and Samuel Samuels, of the *Dreadnought.*

It required an unusual combination of qualities to command these Western Ocean packet ships successfully. Above all things it was necessary that the captains should be thorough seamen and navigators; also that they should be men of robust health and great physical endurance, as their duties often kept them on deck for days and nights together in storm, cold, and fog. Then there were frequently desperate characters among the crew and steerage passengers, who required to be handled with moral courage and physical force, while the cabin passengers were usually gentlemen and gentlewomen of good breeding, accustomed to courtesy and politeness, which they expected to find in the captains with whom they sailed. These requirements evolved a remarkable type of men, hearty, bluff, and jovial, without coarseness, who would never be mistaken for anything but gentlemen.

The packet mates, having no social duties on shipboard to distract their attention, were able to devote their time and energies to improving the morals and manners of the crew, and it was on board the Black Ball liners that "belaying pin soup" and "handspike hash," so stimulating to honest toil, were first introduced for the benefit of mutinous or slothful mariners.

Plenty of sail was carried by the packet ships

The "Montezuma"

of this period—square lower, topmast and topgallant studding sails, skysails set on sliding gunter masts which were struck in the winter time, with three reefs in the topsails and single reefs in the topgallantsails. The racing was fast and furious. In 1837 a match was made between the Black Ball liner *Columbus,* 597 tons, Captain De Peyster, and the *Sheridan,* Captain Russell, of the Dramatic Line, then on her first voyage, for a stake of $10,000 a side, from New York to Liverpool, play or pay. The *Sheridan,* though only 895 tons, carried a crew of forty picked men before the mast, with regular pay of $25 a month, and the promise of a bonus of $50 each, provided their ship won the race. The ships sailed together from New York on Thursday, February 2, 1837, and the *Columbus* won the race in sixteen days, followed two days later by the *Sheridan.* This is the first ocean match across the Atlantic of which any record has been preserved, though, of course, there had been many informal races long before.

The *Isaac Bell,* commanded by Captain John Johnston, made three voyages from Havre to New York in less than eighteen days each, one being in the month of January, which is about the hardest month in the twelve for a ship bound to the westward. The *Independence,* 734 tons, built by Smith & Dimon in 1834, for a number of years when commanded by Captain Ezra Nye, took the President's message to England, her sailing day being fixed for the 6th of March for that purpose. She more than once made the passage from New York to Liverpool in fourteen days. In November, 1846, the

Yorkshire, Captain Bailey, made the passage from Liverpool to New York in sixteen days. This is believed to be the fastest passage ever made from Liverpool to the westward by a packet ship. The *Montezuma,* 1070 tons, and the *Patrick Henry,* 997 tons, the *Southampton,* 1273 tons, built by Westervelt & Mackay, in 1849, also the *St. Andrew,* Captain William C. Thompson, of Robert Kermit's Line, all made the passage from New York to Liverpool in fifteen days.

It should, however, be remembered that these packet ships, running regularly across the Atlantic for many years, necessarily at times encountered favorable conditions of wind and weather; whereas, a single ship making the passage occasionally, as did the clipper ships in later years, might not find so favorable a slant in a lifetime. None of the packet ships that made these remarkable passages could average more than twelve knots for twenty-four hours, and the utmost limit of their speed under the most favorable conditions was not more than fourteen knots, if as much. Most of these ships, however, made the passage from New York to Liverpool at one time or another in sixteen days, and there were few that did not at least once make the run in seventeen days. The secret of the speed of these ships was that they were commanded by men who kept them moving night and day, in all sorts of weather, and never let up on their ships or crews from the time they cast off from the wharf at New York until they ran their lines ashore on the pier-head at Liverpool. While it is true that the New York packet ships were by no means clippers, still, their models and rig were admirably adapted to the work which they had to perform. It was a splendid service and a fine prelude to the clipper ship era.

Of the earlier New York ship-builders, Henry Eckford, who came from Scotland in 1796, when twenty years of age, died in New York in 1832; Christian Bergh, who was born in Wettenburgh, Rhinebeck precinct, in 1763, died in New York in 1843; and Isaac Webb, born in Stamford, Connecticut, in 1794, the son of Wilsey Webb, died in New York in 1840. To the memories of these men, the founders of modern ship-building in the United States, the highest praise is due for their integrity, perseverance, and mechanical skill.

Of the next generation of builders, Stephen Smith, who like Isaac Webb was born in Stamford, formed with John Dimon the firm of Smith & Dimon, and prior to 1843 they had built among other vessels the packet ships *Roscoe* and *Independence,* the ship *Mary Howland,* the North River steamboats *Rochester, James Kent,* and *Oregon,* and the Greek frigate *Liberator.* Their building yard was at the foot of Fourth Street, East River. David Brown and Jacob Bell formed the firm of Brown & Bell, and had a yard at the foot of Stanton Street, a part of which had formerly been the Henry Eckford yard. Prior to 1843, this firm had built the ships *Orbit* and *William Tell* in 1821, the *Canada, Calhoun, Savannah, Pacific, Washington, Great Britain, John Jay, Britannia, George Canning, Caledonia, Hibernia,* and *Congress* from 1821 to 1831; the *Victoria, Europe, Francis Depaw, Silvia de Grasse, Vicksburg, Em-*

erald, Switzerland, Shakespeare, Garrick, Sheridan, Siddons, Roscius, and *Cornelia* from 1831 to 1841; and the *Liverpool, Queen of the West,* and *Henry Clay* in the period from 1841 to 1843, inclusive. Besides these, they built fifteen other ships, seven steamers, eight barques and brigs, thirty-nine steamboats, six ferry- and tow-boats, nineteen sloops and schooners, seven pilot boats, and four yachts.

Upon the death of Isaac Webb in 1840, his son William H. Webb, then only twenty-four years of age, continued the firm of Webb & Allen which built during the next ten years the packet ships *Montezuma, Yorkshire, Havre, Fidelia,* second *Columbia, Sir Robert Peel, Splendid, Bavaria, Isaac Wright, Ivanhoe, Yorktown, London, Guy Mannering, Albert Gallatin, Isaac Webb,* and *Vanguard.* Their yard extended from the foot of Fifth to Seventh Street, East River.

Jacob A. Westervelt, born at Hackensack, New Jersey, in 1800, was the son of a ship-builder. He went to sea before the mast and upon his return served his apprenticeship with Christian Bergh, subsequently becoming a partner in the firm and retiring with an ample fortune in 1837. Mr. Westervelt then made an extensive trip through Europe, and after returning built two ships at Williamsburg. He formed the firm of Westervelt & Mackay and built a number of London and Havre packet ships, among which were the *Ocean Queen, West Point, Toronto, Devonshire,* and *American Eagle.* The front door of Mr. Westervelt's house in East Broadway was ornamented with a beautiful carved stone cap representing the stern of a packet ship. In later

The "Yorkshire"

years, he took his sons Daniel and Aaron into partnership, the firm being known as Westervelt & Co. Jacob A. Westervelt was Mayor of New York in 1854.

George Steers, destined to become famous as the designer of the *Adriatic,* the *Niagara,* and the yacht *America,* was born in Washington, D. C., in the year 1819, and in 1843, after having built a number of fast sail- and row-boats for racing, entered into partnership with William Hathorne, the firm being known as Hathorne & Steers. Up to this time Mr. Steers, though he had shown unusual ability as a mechanic, cannot be said to have done anything predicting his future triumphs. Other firms that were building good vessels at this time were Thomas and William Collier; Perin, Patterson & Stack; Laurence & Folkes, and John Englis, some of whom we shall hear of again.

The merchants of Boston after the War of 1812, built or bought most of their vessels at Medford, Newburyport, Salem, Scituate, and Duxbury, within the State, and at Portsmouth, New Hampshire, and other ports where timber was more plentiful. It was not until 1834, when the East Boston Timber Company was incorporated by James Paige, Francis Oliver, and Gideon Barstow, that ship-building began to flourish about Boston. Stephen White was the moving spirit in this transaction, as in 1833 he had bought on behalf of himself and associates, eighty thousand feet of land in East Boston, between Border and Liverpool streets, at three cents per foot, for the establishment of a timber yard and dock. Mr. White also purchased Grand Island, in the Niagara River, which was covered with valuable timber. Sawmills were erected on the island, and a supply of the finest quality of ship timber was created, and brought by the Erie Canal to tidewater, thence by coasting vessels to East Boston. This attracted ship-builders from other towns, and eventually made Boston a famous ship-building centre. Stephen White owned the first ship built in East Boston, the *Niagara,* of 460 tons, appropriately named after the river from which the timber used in her construction had come. She was built in 1834, by Brown, Bates & Delano in their yard at the foot of Central Square, and was launched amid an uproar of guns, fire-crackers, shouts, and music, with a bottle of good Medford rum trickling down her port bow.

The first Boston ferry-boats, the *East Boston, Essex,* and *Maverick,* were built at East Boston in 1834–35, but nothing further was done in ship-building there until 1839, when Samuel Hall a well-known builder, of Marshfield and Duxbury, removed to East Boston and established a yard at the west end of Maverick Street. Mr. Hall not only contributed to the reputation and welfare of East Boston by building a large number of splendid vessels and providing employment for a great number of men, but he was also active in all municipal affairs. In appreciation of his successful efforts for the introduction of Cochituate water into East Boston in 1851, his fellow-citizens presented him with a thousand-dollar service of plate, consisting of eleven pieces, with the usual inscription, with which most of us are more or less familiar.

The Briggs Brothers, of South Boston, came from

an old and celebrated ship-building family of Scituate, their great-grandfather having been a shipbuilder of note in colonial times, while their grandfather, James Briggs, was the builder of the famous *Columbia,* in 1773. After his death the yard was continued by his sons, Henry and Cushing, who built some of the finest ships sailing out of Boston, besides many of the New Bedford and Nantucket whalers, during the first half of the last century. The brothers E. & H. O. Briggs, who established their yard at South Boston in 1848, were the sons of Cushing Briggs, and they possessed the skill in design and thorough knowledge of construction for which the family had long been famous among the merchants and underwriters of Boston.

At Medford, on the Mystic, Thatcher Magoun established his shipyard in 1802, and there built the brig *Mt. Etna,* of 187 tons, in 1803, followed by other merchant vessels as well as privateers for the War of 1812. The *Avon,* the most famous of these privateers, was launched in twenty-six days after her keel was laid. In 1822, Mr. Magoun built the *Amethyst, Emerald, Sapphire,* and *Topaz,* ships of about 350 tons, for the Boston and Liverpool Packet Company, which ran for a few years between Boston, Charleston, S. C., and Liverpool, and home direct to Boston. One of the novel features of this line was the arrangement as to agents, their office being at the end of India Wharf, but in Liverpool each ship had a separate agent, as it was imagined that four agents would attract so many times the more business. It is evident that the promoters of this line had something to learn concerning Liverpool ship-brokers and their system of working freights, for the enterprise was not successful.

Another Liverpool Line was started in Boston in 1828, and the ships *Boston, Lowell, Liverpool, Plymouth,* and *Trenton* of this line were built by Mr. Magoun. He also built between 1822 and 1829, the ships *Lucilla,* 369 tons, owned by Daniel P. Parker; *Brookline,* 376 tons, and *Courser,* 300 tons, owned by Henry Oxnard; and the *Margaret Forbes,* 398 tons, owned by Bryant & Sturgis, all sailing out of Boston. Other Medford ship-builders were Sprague & James, Isaac Taylor, Hayden & Cudworth, J. O. Curtis, Waterman & Elwell, Samuel Lapham, and Paul Curtis. Their ships were known all over the world as fine, well-built vessels. In 1845 one quarter of all the shipwrights in Massachusetts were employed in Medford, and 9660 tons of shipping were launched from its building yards.

The leading ship-builder at Newburyport was John Currier, Jr., who from 1831 to 1843 built the ships *Brenda, Republic, Oberlin, St. Clair, Leonore,* and *Columbus* for the Black Ball Line, and in 1836 the *Talbot, Flavio, Navigator, Huntress, Strabo,* and *Virginia,* ranging from 339 to 365 tons, as well as several barques, brigs, and schooners. The firms of George W. Jackman and Currier & Townsend had not been formed at this date.

Portsmouth, New Hampshire, was also noted for her ships and seamen, the principal builders in 1840 being George Raynes, Fernald & Pettigrew, and Toby & Littlefield, while the Shackfords and Salters had been sea-captains for generations. Mr.

Raynes was born at York, Maine, in 1799 and in 1835 removed to Portsmouth where he established a shipyard upon the famous Boyd estate, with its fine old trees, lawns, and gardens of vegetables, fruits, and flowers sloping to the clear blue water's edge. The family residence, erected by Colonel George Boyd in 1767, was an excellent example of colonial architecture. In later days it became known as the Raynes mansion, and for many years was one of the show places of Portsmouth. The original beauty of the grounds was preserved so far as possible, and this was perhaps the most beautiful and picturesque shipyard of modern times.

The most famous clipper-ship builder of his time, Donald McKay, was born at Shelburne, Nova Scotia, in 1810, and was a descendant of that sturdy Highland chieftain, Donald McKay, who died at Tain, County Ross, Scotland, in 1395. At about the age of sixteen, Donald went to New York, where he worked and learnt his trade in the shipyards of Isaac Webb, Brown & Bell, and perhaps others. By his energy and mechanical talents, he soon became a master shipwright, and turned his face toward the Eastern country again. In 1840 he finished the ship *Delia Walker,* of 427 tons, for John Currier at Newburyport. This vessel was owned by Dennis Condry, who, when visiting his ship from time to time, was impressed by Mr. McKay's superior mechanical ability and energetic manner of handling his men. In 1841, Mr. McKay became a partner in the firm of Currier & McKay, and the barque *Mary Broughton,* 323 tons, was built by them during this year, followed in 1842 by the ships

Courier, 380 tons, and *Ashburton,* 449 tons. The firm then dissolved, the models and moulds being equally divided—with a saw.

The little ship *Courier* was the first vessel designed by Mr. McKay. She was owned by W. Wolfe & A. Foster, Jr., of New York, who employed her in the Rio coffee trade. She proved a wonder for speed, and outsailed everything, big and little, that she fell in with at sea. No one at that time believed that such a vessel could be built outside of New York or Baltimore. She not only made a great deal of money for her owners, but at once brought her designer prominently before the maritime public.

In 1843 the firm of McKay & Pickett was formed, and the New York packet ships *St. George,* 845 tons, in 1843, and *John R. Skiddy,* 930 tons, in 1844, were built by them at Newburyport. In this year Enoch Train, a well-known ship-owner and merchant of Boston, engaged in the South American trade and who had already sent the ships *Cairo, St. Patrick,* and *Dorchester* to England, decided to put on a regular line of packets between Liverpool and Boston. While crossing the Atlantic on board one of the early Cunarders, for the purpose of establishing his European agencies, it happened that he found himself a fellow-passenger with Dennis Condry, owner of the *Delia Walker,* the gentleman who had been so much impressed during his visits to Newburyport, by the energy and skill of Donald McKay. Mr. Train and Mr. Condry soon became acquainted and naturally talked a good deal about shipping. Mr. Train was in doubt as to whom he should entrust the building of his ships; he did not like to construct them in New York, yet he felt unwilling to risk failure through employing local talent, however able, for Boston builders were inexperienced in building this class of vessel, while the construction of packet ships had been developed to a high degree of perfection in New York. His doubts were freely expressed, but Mr. Condry had a strong conviction on this subject, and so convincing were his arguments in favor of his young ship-builder friend, that Mr. Train, before landing at Liverpool, had promised that he would see Mr. McKay upon his return to the United States.

The meeting at Newburyport of these two really great men, Enoch Train and Donald McKay, should be memorable in the maritime annals of the United States. It was the swift contact of flint and steel, for within an hour a contract had been signed for building the *Joshua Bates,* the pioneer ship of Train's famous Liverpool Line, and Mr. Train was returning to his home in Boston. He visited Newburyport frequently while his ship was building, and whether Mr. McKay, during the four years that had elapsed, had further developed the qualities which Dennis Condry had so admired, as seems probable, or whether Mr. Train's perceptive faculties were keener than those of his fellow-passenger, it is a fact that on the day when the *Joshua Bates* was launched and floated safely on the Merrimac River, Mr. Train grasped Donald McKay by the hand and said to him: "You must come to Boston; we need you; if you wish financial assistance to establish a shipyard, let me know the amount and you shall have it."

So the young ship-builder had on that day launched his last ship at Newburyport. He soon closed the pleasant relations which had existed with his partner, and at the age of thirty-four opened his great shipyard at the foot of Border Street, East Boston. There he built in rapid succession, between 1845 and 1850, the packet ships *Washington Irving, Anglo-Saxon, Ocean Monarch, Anglo-American,* and *Daniel Webster* for Train's Liverpool Line. These ships carried a black T in their foretopsail below the close reef band, and flew the Enoch Train signal, a red field with white diamond. The ships *New World* and *Cornelius Grinnell* were built here for Grinnell, Minturn & Co.'s Swallowtail Line; the *A. Z., L. Z.,* and *Antarctic* for Zerega & Co., New York; the *Jenny Lind* for Fairbank & Wheeler, Boston; the *Parliament, Plymouth Rock, Reindeer,* and barque *Helicon* for George B. Upton, Boston; the *Moses Wheeler* for Wheeler & King, Boston; and the barque *Sultana* for Edward Lamb & Co., Boston. These vessels were much admired in New York, London, Liverpool, and other seaports, and established the reputation of Donald McKay as a ship-builder equal to the best.

CHAPTER IV

OPIUM CLIPPERS AND EARLY CLIPPER SHIPS, 1832–1848

THE origin of the word clipper is not quite clear, though it seems to be derived from the verb clip, which in former times meant, among other things, to run or fly swiftly. Dryden uses it to describe the flight of a falcon [1]:

"Some falcon stoops at what her eye designed,
And, with her eagerness the quarry missed,
Straight flies at check, and clips it down the wind."

The word survived in the New England slang expression "to clip it," and "going at a good clip," or "a fast clip," are familiar expressions there to this day. It therefore seems reasonable to suppose that when vessels of a new model were built, which were intended, in the language of the times, to clip over the waves rather than plough through them, the improved type of craft became known as clippers because of their speed. It is probable that the swift privateers built at Baltimore during the War of 1812 became known as "Baltimore clippers," and while the first application of the term in a

[1] *Annus Mirabilis,* stanza 89 (1667).

nautical sense is by no means certain, it seems to have had an American origin.

The first clipper constructed in Great Britain was the schooner *Scottish Maid,* one hundred and fifty tons, built in 1839 by Alexander Hall & Co., of Aberdeen, to compete with the paddle steamers between Aberdeen and London. She proved a very fast vessel, and saw half a century of service before she was wrecked on the coast of England. Three schooners of the same model and tonnage, the *Fairy, Rapid,* and *Monarch,* were built by this firm in 1842. These four were the first Aberdeen clippers. The earliest competition between American and British clippers was in the China seas. As early as 1831 three small English schooners, the *Jamesina, Lord Amherst,* and *Sylph,* were engaged in the opium trade, which proved exceedingly lucrative. In 1833 the *Jamesina* sold opium from India to the value of £330,000 at Foo Chow, Amoy, Ningpo, and other ports in China. This business increased and attracted the attention of the American merchants in China. In 1841, the *Angola,* a schooner of 90 tons, built by Brown & Bell, of New York, for Russell & Co., China, was despatched to Hongkong. She was followed in 1842 by the schooners *Zephyr,* 150 tons, built by Samuel Hall at East Boston; *Mazeppa,* 175 tons, built by Brown & Bell, and *Ariel,* 100 tons, built by Sprague & James, Medford, and in 1843 by the brig *Antelope,* 370 tons, built by Samuel Hall at East Boston. These vessels, owned by John M. Forbes and Russell & Co., soon controlled the opium-trade and became known as opium clippers. It was necessary that they should be swift in order to contend with the strong tides and currents on the China coast, and to beat against the monsoons in the China Sea. The *Antelope,* under the command of Captain Philip Dumaresq, still has the reputation of having been the only square-rigged vessel which could beat through the Formosa Channel against the northeast monsoon. Moreover, these vessels required speed to escape from the heavily manned piratical craft which infested the China seas, and which were formidable vessels, especially in light winds and calms, when they were propelled by long sweeps.

In 1846, Alexander Hall & Co. built the clipper schooner *Torrington* for Jardine, Matheson & Co., to compete with the American opium clippers in China. This schooner, the first British clipper in the China seas, was followed by the *Wanderer, Gazelle, Rose,* the brig *Lanark,* and others, until almost every British and American firm in China owned one or more of these smart vessels. The competition among them was keen, and the American clippers had decidedly the best of it. The last of these famous little vessels were the sister schooners *Minna* and *Brenda,* of 300 tons each, built in 1851 by George Raynes at Portsmouth, for John M. Forbes, of Boston, and others, and the schooner *Wild Dayrell,* 253 tons, built in 1855 by the well-known yacht builders J. White, of Cowes, Isle of Wight, for Dent & Co., China. These opium clippers, all beautifully modelled and equipped with long raking masts and plenty of canvas, like yachts rather than merchant vessels, were heavily armed and carried large crews. They all made a great deal of money for their owners until they were superseded by steamers.

From the earliest times in maritime history it had been the custom to build large vessels of a model suitable for carrying heavy cargoes—" ships of burden " they were called,—while the vessels designed for speed,—the galley of the Mediterranean, caravel of Portugal and Spain, lugger of France, cutter of England, yacht of Holland, schooner and sloop of America, had been comparatively small. To the latter class belonged the earlier British and American clippers of the nineteenth century. The Baltimore clippers, as we have said, were modelled after the French luggers which visited American ports during the Revolutionary War. They gained a world-wide reputation for speed as privateers during the War of 1812, and later also as African slavers, many of them sailing under the flags of Portugal and Spain. These vessels were brigs, brigantines, fore-and-aft or topsail schooners, and rarely exceeded two hundred tons register.

So far as history records, no one had ever attempted to reproduce the lines of a small, swift vessel in a large one, until in 1832 Isaac McKim, a wealthy merchant of Baltimore, commissioned Kennard and Williamson, of Fell's Point, Baltimore, to build a ship embodying as far as possible the lines of the famous Baltimore clipper brigs and schooners. This ship was the *Ann McKim,* named in honor of the owner's wife, of 493 tons register, a large vessel for those days. She measured: Length 143 feet, breadth 31 feet, depth 14 feet, and drew 17 feet aft and 11 feet forward. She possessed many of the striking features of the Baltimore clippers of that period; namely, great dead-rise at her mid-ship section, long, easy convex water-lines, low free-board, and raking stem, stern-post and masts, and was really an enlarged clipper schooner rigged as a ship.

The *Ann McKim* was a remarkably handsome vessel, built as the pet ship of her owner without much regard to cost. Her frames were of live oak, she was copper-fastened throughout and her bottom was sheathed with red copper imported for this purpose. The flush deck was fitted with Spanish mahogany hatch combings, rails, companions, and skylights. She mounted twelve brass guns, and was equipped with brass capstan heads, bells, etc., and carried three skysail yards and royal studding-sails. She proved to be very fast, though of small carrying capacity, and the latter quality together with her elaborate and expensive fittings caused the older merchants to regard her unfavorably; so that for some years they still adhered to their full-bodied ships. The *Ann McKim* sailed in the China trade for a number of years, and upon the death of Mr. McKim in 1837, she was purchased by Howland & Aspinwall, of New York, and was commanded by Captain Perry. Eventually she was sold at Valparaiso in 1847, and ended her days under the Chilian flag.

Although the *Ann McKim* was the first clipper ship ever constructed, it cannot be said that she founded the clipper ship era, or even that she directly influenced ship-builders, since no other ship was built like her; but she may have suggested the clipper design in vessels of ship rig, and owing to the fact that she fell into the hands of Howland & Aspinwall, she without doubt hastened the opening of that era, as the first really extreme clipper ship, the *Rainbow,* was owned by that firm.

It is difficult at this distance of time to determine exactly what influence the *Ann McKim* exercised upon the science of ship-building, though from the fact that no ship had ever been built like her, it is probable that she was an object of considerable interest in the maritime world, and it is certain that during the years following her appearance a more determined effort was made in the United States to improve the model and sailing qualities of ships. Among the most notable of these attempts were the *Courier,* already mentioned, built by Donald McKay in 1842, and the *Akbar,* a ship of six hundred and fifty tons, built by Samuel Hall at East Boston in 1839, for John M. Forbes, and others, who employed her in the China trade. On her first voyage the *Akbar* made the passage from New York to Canton in one hundred and nine days, beating up the China Sea against the northeast monsoon. On this voyage she was commanded by Captain James Watkins, in after years commodore of the Pacific Mail Steamship Co. Later she was commanded by Captain Philip Dumaresq, who made a number of rapid passages in her to and from China. Then came the *Helena,* of 650 tons, built by William H. Webb in 1841. This ship was owned by N. L. and G. Griswold, and also sailed in the China trade under the command of Captain Benjamin, who made some fine passages. The *Paul*

Jones, of 620 tons, built by Waterman & Elwell at Medford in 1842, was owned by John M. Forbes and Russell & Co., of China. She was commanded by Captain N. B. Palmer and on her first voyage in 1843 she sailed from Boston for Hong-kong, January 15th, crossed the equator 26 days out, was 54 days to the Cape of Good Hope, 88 days to Java Head, and arrived at Hong-kong 111 days from Boston. In 1848, this ship made the run from Java Head to New York in 76 days.

In 1844, A. A. Low & Brother, of New York, contracted with Brown & Bell to build the *Houqua,* of 706 tons, constructed for Captain N. B. Palmer. She made a number of very fast passages. On her first voyage she made the passage from New York to Java Head in 72 days, thence to Hong-kong in 12 days, total 84 days. Her best records from China were as follows: From Hong-kong, December 9, 1844, passed Java Head 15 days out, was 70 days to the Equator in the Atlantic, thence 20 days to New York, total 90 days—distance by log, 14,272 miles. December 9, 1845, sailed from Hong-kong, passed Java Head 16 days out, arrived at New York, March 10, 1846, 91 days' passage. Under the command of Captain McKanzie, in 1850, she made the passage from Shanghai to New York in 88 days, the shortest passage up to that time. This ship was named in honor of Houqua, the well-known Canton merchant who was beloved and respected by American and English residents in China, no less for his integrity than for his great kindness and his business ability.

In 1844 also William H. Webb built the *Montauk,*

540 tons, for A. A. Low & Brother, and the *Panama,* 670 tons, for N. L. & G. Griswold, both vessels for the China trade, and Samuel Hall, of East Boston, built the barque *Coquette,* 420 tons, commanded by Captain Oliver Eldridge. The *Coquette* sailed from Boston, June 29, 1844, was 76 days to Java Head, and 99 days to Canton. She was owned by Russell & Co., of China, and made several fast passages between Calcutta and ports in China. Young James H. Perkins made a voyage to China as a passenger on board this vessel, and his famous schooner yacht *Coquette,* which defeated the sloop *Maria* in a match off Sandy Hook in 1846, was named for the clipper barque.

These were among the first clipper ships built in the United States, and while by no means extreme clippers, they were sharper and finer models than any vessels which had been constructed up to that time, and clearly indicated the dawn of a new epoch in naval architecture.

I have now brought this narrative to the opening of the clipper ship era, and have endeavored to sketch the development of the merchant marine of Great Britain and the United States from the common starting point—where the ship-builders of both countries derived their best knowledge of ship models and construction from the French—as they advanced along diverging lines under different climatic, social, and political conditions, until we now find them at points widely distant from each other—Great Britain with her stately, frigate-built Indiaman, embodying the glories of the past; the United States with her wild packet ship scending into a long, sweeping head sea, and flinging a rainbow of flying spray across her weather-bow, in which was imaged the promise of a glorious future.

In 1841, John W. Griffeths, of New York, proposed several improvements in marine architecture, which were embodied in the model of a clipper ship exhibited at the American Institute, in February of that year. Later he delivered a series of lectures on the science of ship-building, which were the first discourses upon this subject in the United States. Mr. Griffeths advocated carrying the stem forward in a curved line, thereby lengthening the bow above water; he also introduced long, hollow water-lines and a general drawing out and sharpening of the forward body, bringing the greatest breadth further aft. Another improvement which he proposed was to fine out the after body by rounding up the ends of the main transom, thus relieving the quarters and making the stern much lighter and handsomer above the water-line.

This proposed departure from old methods naturally met with much opposition, but in 1843 the firm of Howland & Aspinwall commissioned Smith & Dimon, of New York, in whose employ Mr. Griffeths had spent several years as draughtsman, to embody these experimental ideas in a ship of 750 tons named the *Rainbow.* This vessel, the first extreme clipper ship ever built, was therefore, the direct result of Mr. Griffeths's efforts for improvement. Her bow with its concave waterlines and the greatest breadth at a point considerably further aft than had hitherto been regarded as practicable, was a radical departure, differing not merely in degree but in kind from any ship that preceded her. One critical observer declared that her bow had been turned "outside in," and that her whole form was contrary to the laws of nature. The *Rainbow* was designed and built with great care and was not launched until January, 1845.

Mr. Griffeths relates a good story about the masting of this vessel. It appears that Mr. Aspinwall, who had an excellent idea of what a ship ought to be, had come to the conclusion that the masting of vessels was a question of no small moment in shipbuilding, and determined that his new ship should have the benefit of foreign aid in placing the masts. Accordingly, he informed the builders that he would obtain assistance from abroad, for their benefit as well as his own. The builders naturally paid little attention to this information. The port-captain, who was appointed to superintend the construction, was directed by Mr. Aspinwall to select the best authorities in Europe on masting ships. The European experts were written to in reference to this important matter, and after they had duly considered the principal dimensions of the vessel, the trade in which she was to be employed, etc., a spar draft and elaborate calculations were prepared and forwarded to New York.

In the meantime, the construction of the *Rainbow* had progressed steadily. The clamps being ready, the deck beams were placed according to the original drawings, the framing of the decks completed, hatches and mast partners framed, channels and mast-steps secured; the masts and yards were also made and the ship planked and caulked by the time the important despatches arrived. They were examined by the port-captain, Mr. Aspinwall was informed that they were all right, and the port-captain was requested to give the information to the builders, which, of course, was done. The ship, however, was finished without the slightest alteration from the original plans. Mr. Aspinwall, who never doubted that his pet project had been carefully carried out, attributed much of the success of this vessel to the placing of her masts by foreign rules.

The sharp model of the *Rainbow* gave rise to a great deal of discussion while she was on the stocks in course of construction. It was generally admitted by the recognized shipping authorities of South Street, that she was a handsome vessel, but whether she could be made to sail was a question on which there were varieties of opinion. She proved an excellent ship in every way and exceedingly fast. Her second voyage to China out and home, was made in six months and fourteen days, including two weeks in port discharging and loading cargo. She went out to China against the northeast monsoon in ninety-two and home in eighty-eight days, bringing the news of her own arrival at Canton. Captain John Land, her able and enthusiastic commander, declared that she was the fastest ship in the world, and this was undeniably true; finding no one to differ from him, he further gave it as his opinion that no ship could be built to outsail the *Rainbow,* and it is also true that very few vessels have ever broken her record. She was lost on her fifth voyage while bound from New York for Valparaiso in 1848 under command of Captain Hayes, and it was supposed that she foundered off Cape Horn.

The *Ariel,* 572 tons, was built by John Currier at Newburyport in 1846, for Minot & Hooper, of Boston. This ship became celebrated in the China trade and was bought by N. L. & G. Griswold, and has a record of 90 days from Canton to New York.

In 1846, Howland & Aspinwall, for whom Captain Robert H. Waterman had been making some remarkably fast voyages in the old packet ship *Natchez,* had a clipper ship built especially for him, entrusting the design and construction to Smith & Dimon, the builders of the *Rainbow,* though all the details of spars, sails, and rigging were carried out under the supervision of Captain Waterman. This ship was the famous *Sea Witch,* of 890 tons, length 170 feet, breadth 33 feet 11 inches, and depth 19 feet. She carried a cloud of canvas; three standing skysail yards, royal studding sails, large square lower studding sails with swinging booms, ringtail, and water sails.

When loaded the *Sea Witch* lay low on the water; her hull was painted black and her masts had a considerable rake; her figurehead was an aggressive-looking dragon, beautifully carved and gilded. She had the reputation at that time of being the handsomest ship sailing out of New York, and her officers and crew were picked men, several of whom had sailed with Captain Waterman on his voyages in the *Natchez.* She sailed on her first voyage, bound for China, December 23, 1846, went to sea in a strong northwest gale, and made a remarkable fine run southward, arriving off the harbor of Rio

Janeiro in twenty-five days, where she exchanged signals with the shore and sent letters and New York newspapers by a vessel inward bound. She made the passage from New York to Hong-kong in 104 days, and arrived at New York from Canton July 25, 1847, in 81 days, making the run from Anjer Point to Sandy Hook in 62 days. On her second voyage she arrived at Hong-kong from New York, November 7, 1847, in 105 days, and arrived from Canton at New York, March 16, 1848, in 77 days. On this passage she made the run from St. Helena to Sandy Hook in 32 days. Her next voyage was from New York to Valparaiso, where she arrived July 5, 1848, in 69 days, thence to Hong-kong, where she arrived December 7, 1848, in 52 days. She arrived at New York March 25, 1849, 79 days from Canton. She next sailed from New York for Canton via Valparaiso and arrived at Canton July 23, 1849, 118 sailing days from New York. She arrived at New York March 7, 1850, from Canton in 85 days, making the run from Java Head in 73 days.

This is a most remarkable series of passages, especially considering the seasons of the year during which most of her China voyages were made. Her best twenty-four hours' run was 358 miles, a speed far in excess of any ocean steamship of that period. The *Sea Witch* during the first three years of her career, was without doubt the swiftest ship that sailed the seas, and she continued to distinguish herself later on, in her passages from New York to San Francisco under the command of Captain George Fraser.

In 1847, A. A. Low & Bro. brought out the *Samuel Russell,* of 940 tons, built by Brown & Bell and commanded by Captain N. B. Palmer, formerly of the *Houqua.* Her first voyage from New York to Hong-kong was made by the eastern passages in 114 days. On a voyage from Canton in 1851 she sailed 6780 miles in 30 days, an average of 226 miles per day, her greatest twenty-four hours' run being 328 miles. This ship was named for the eminent New York merchant, founder of the house of Russell & Co., of China, with whom the brothers Low began their career as merchants and ship-owners. She was a beautiful vessel, heavily sparred, with plenty of light canvas for moderate weather, and every inch a clipper.

The *Architect,* 520 tons, was also built in 1847, at Baltimore, for Nye, Parkin & Co., American merchants in China, and was commanded by Captain George Potter.

The *Memnon,* 1068 tons, owned by Warren Delano, was built by Smith & Dimon in 1848, and on her first voyage to China was commanded by Captain Oliver Eldridge.

These were the most celebrated of the clipper ships built in the United States prior to the discovery of gold in California in 1848, though there were, of course, many other fine vessels engaged in the China trade, which had for years brought home cargoes of tea, silk, and spices. During the twelve months from June 30, 1845 to July 1, 1846, forty-one vessels arrived at New York from China, and probably as many more at other Atlantic ports, chiefly Boston and Salem. Besides these vessels there were the

South American, African, and East India fleets, as well as the lines of splendid packet ships sailing from New York, Boston, and Philadelphia to European ports. In 1847, the ships owned in the United States and engaged in foreign commerce registered 1,241,313 tons.

The American clippers were decidedly the fastest ships built up to that time, yet much of their speed was due to the skill and energy of their commanders. The manner in which American vessels were handled at this period will be seen by extracts from the log-book of the ship *Great Britain,* 524 tons, Captain Philip Dumaresq, on her homeward voyage from China in 1849–50. She left Java Head December 22, 1849, and by January 14, 1850, had passed seven vessels bound the same way. The log from this date reads in part as follows:

" Squally, under double reefed topsails, passed a ship laying-to under a close reefed maintopsail. . . . January 24th, a southwest gale, close reefed topsails, split courses; before doing this we were going seven and one half knots close-hauled, within six points of the wind under double-reefed topsails and courses; January 25th, split all three topsails and had to heave-to; five vessels in sight, one a Dutch frigate, all hove-to; January 27th, seven vessels in sight and we outsail all of them; January 29th passed the Cape of Good Hope and anchored in Table Bay, parted both chains and split nearly all the sails; hove-to outside, blowing a gale offshore; January 30th, at 6 A.M. bore up for St. Helena; February 1st, fresh trades, passed a ship under double reefs, we with our royals and studdingsails set; February 8th, anchored at St. Helena with a stream anchor backed by remainder of one of the chains; February 10th, having procured anchors and water, left St. Helena; February 21st, crossed the line in longitude 31; March 12th, under double-reefed topsails, passed several vessels laying-to; March 17th, took pilot off Sandy Hook, 84 days from Java Head, including detentions."

Probably few if any of the vessels which Captain Dumaresq passed hove-to or under short canvas were sailing under the American flag. It is worthy of note that the *Great Britain* was at that time twenty-six years old, having been built by Brown & Bell for the New York and Liverpool packet service in 1824, and of course, was by no means a clipper.

CHAPTER V

TWO EARLY CLIPPER SHIP COMMANDERS

CAPTAIN ROBERT H. WATERMAN, the first commander of the *Sea Witch,* had been known for some years among the shipping community of New York as an exceptionally skilful seaman and navigator, but he first began to attract public attention about 1844 by some remarkably fast voyages in the ship *Natchez.* Captain Waterman was born in the city of New York, March 4, 1808, and at the age of twelve shipped on board of a vessel bound for China. After working through the grades of ordinary and able seaman, and third, second, and chief mate on board of various vessels, he sailed for a number of voyages as mate with Captain Charles H. Marshall in the Black Ball packet ship *Britannia* between New York and Liverpool. At that time he was counted one of the smartest mates sailing out of New York, and was noted for keeping the *Britannia* in fine shape, as well as for his ability in maintaining proper order and discipline among the steerage passengers and crew, who were always a source of anxiety and trouble to packet-ship captains. When his vessel was bound to the westward in 1831, one of the sailors fell overboard from aloft during a heavy gale, and Mr. Waterman saved the man's life at the risk of his own. The cabin passengers of the *Britannia* presented him with a substantial testimonial in appreciation of his humane and gallant conduct. At this time he was twenty-three years old. Two years later he was promoted to captain, and in this capacity he made five voyages round the globe.

In 1843 he took command of the *Natchez*. This ship, as we have seen in Chapter III., was one of the full-pooped New Orleans packets, and was built by Isaac Webb in 1831. Captain Waterman took her around Cape Horn to the west coast of South America, thence across the Pacific to Canton, where he loaded a cargo of tea for New York, and made the passage home in 94 days and the voyage round the globe in 9 months and 26 days. In 1844 Captain Waterman sailed again in the *Natchez* from New York for Valparaiso and made the passage in 71 days, thence to Callao in 8 days, and to Hongkong in 54 days. She again loaded tea for New York and sailed from Canton January 15, 1845, passed Java Head on the 26th, and 39 days out was off the Cape of Good Hope, crossed the equator 61 days out, arriving in New York April 3d, 78 days from Canton, a total distance of 13,955 miles. Her run from the equator to New York in 17 days, and indeed, this whole passage, was most remarkable, as the *Natchez* during her packet days had established the reputation of being an uncommonly slow ship. Captain Waterman received a grand ovation in New York upon this record passage from China, and it was suggested that he had brought the old hooker home by some route unknown to other navigators. In 1845–46 Captain Waterman made one more voyage to China in the *Natchez,* from New York direct to Hong-kong in 104 days, and returned to New York in 83 days.

A seires of voyages such as these, by a ship of the type and character of the *Natchez,* would probably have established the reputation of any one commanding her, and when we consider that "Bob" Waterman, for so he was known, was at this time a young captain of an unusually attractive personality, it is not difficult to understand the pride and admiration with which he was regarded by his friends, of whom he had many, both in New York and in the various foreign ports to which he had sailed. The owners of the *Natchez,* Howland & Aspinwall, were so favorably impressed not only by his ability as a seaman and navigator, but by his loyalty to their interests, that, as we have seen, they built the clipper ship *Sea Witch* for him in 1846. While she was building, Captain Waterman married Cordelia, a daughter of David Sterling, of Bridgeport, and Mrs. Waterman was present as a bride when the ship was launched.

In 1849, Captain Waterman resigned from the *Sea Witch* to take the Pacific Mail steamship *Northerner* from New York to San Francisco. During the three years that he had commanded the *Sea Witch,* she had made a large amount of money for her owners, and Captain Waterman had added to his reputation,—so much so, indeed, that certain good people began to say unpleasant things of him. It was alleged that Captain Waterman carried sail too hard, that he exceeded the bounds of prudence in this respect, and kept padlocks on the topsail sheets and rackings on the topsail halliards fore and aft; also that he maintained a standard of discipline far more severe than was necessary.

It is probable that Captain Waterman did carry sail rather hard—most American captains who wanted to get anywhere in those days usually did—and as to the padlocks and rackings, more than one captain used these precautions to prevent villainous or cowardly sailors from letting go sheets and halliards by the run, when according to their ideas the ship had too much canvas on her. The fact, however, remains that in the eighteen years during which Captain Waterman commanded various ships, he never lost a spar or carried away rigging of any importance, and never called on underwriters for one dollar of loss or damage. The record shows that six of the men before the mast sailed with him upon all his voyages in the *Natchez* and the *Sea Witch,* a rare occurrence at that period, or at any other time of which we have knowledge, and creditable alike to the sailors, the ships, and their commander.

The truth is that Captain Waterman was a humane, conscientious, high-minded man, who never spared himself nor any one else when a duty was to be performed. There are, and always have been, lazy, incompetent, mutinous sailors, a type of men that Captain Waterman detested. They found no comfort in sailing with him, and were glad when the voyage was ended, so that they might scramble ashore and relate their woes to the sympathetic legal "gents" who were usually to be found hanging about Pier 9, East River, when the *Sea Witch* was reported coming up the bay. We shall hear more of Captain Waterman and his crew on board of the *Challenge* in a later chapter.

The celebrated clipper-ship captain, Nathaniel Brown Palmer, the first commander of the *Paul Jones, Houqua, Samuel Russell,* and *Oriental,* was born in the pretty town of Stonington, on Long Island Sound in 1799, and came from distinguished colonial ancestry. His grandfather's only brother fell mortally wounded at the battle of Groton Heights in 1771, while his father was an eminent lawyer and a man of marked ability.

At the age of fourteen or just as the War of 1812 was fairly under way, Nathaniel shipped on board of a coasting vessel which ran to ports between Maine and New York, and continued in this service until he was eighteen, when he was appointed second mate of the brig *Hersilia,* bound down somewhere about Cape Horn on a sealing voyage.

These sealing expeditions were also at that period more or less voyages of discovery. For years there had been rumors of a mythical island called Auroras, embellished with romance and mystery by the whalers of Nantucket, New Bedford, and New London, and described as lying away to the eastward of the Horn, concerning which no forecastle yarn was too extravagant for belief. Whaling captains by the score had spent days and weeks in unprofitable search for it. On this voyage Captain J. P. Sheffield, of the *Hersilia,* landed at one of the Falkland Islands, where he left his second mate and one sailor to kill bullocks for provisions, and then sailed away in search of the fabled island.

Young Nat Palmer proceeded to capture and slay bullocks, and when, after a few days, a ship hove in sight, he piloted her into a safe anchorage, and supplied her with fresh meat. This vessel proved to be the *Espirito Santo,* from Buenos Ayres, and the captain informed Nat that he was bound to a place where there were thousands of seals, and where a cargo could be secured with little effort, but he declined to disclose its position. The mind of the young sailor naturally turned to the magio isle of Auroras, where, according to the saga preserved beside the camp-fires of corner grocery stores in New England whaling towns, silver, gold, and precious gems lay scattered along the beach in glittering profusion, the treasure of some huge galleon, wrecked and broken up centuries ago, when Spain was powerful upon the sea.

There must have been something about the whale fishery highly inspiring to the imagination, though to see one of the greasy old Nantucket or New Bedford blubber hunters wallowing about in the South Pacific, one would hardly have suspected it, yet among the spinners of good, tough tarry sea yarns, some of the authors of narratives relating to the pursuit and capture of the whale are easily entitled to wear champion belts as masters of pure fiction. Whaling is one of the least hazardous, the most commonplace, and, taken altogether about the laziest occupation that human beings have ever been engaged in upon the sea. Sailors aboard the clippers fifty years ago used to refer to whale ships as "butcher shops adrift," and on account of the slovenly condition of their hulls, spars, sails, and rigging, a "spouter" was generally regarded among seamen as one of the biggest jokes afloat. As a matter of fact the whale is about as stupid and inoffensive a creature as exists, and when occasionally he does some harm—smashing up a boat, for instance—it is usually in a flurry of fright, with no malice or intent to kill. If a whale possessed the instinct of self-defence he could never be captured with a harpoon, but he has evidently been created as he is for the benefit of mankind, and incidentally as a temptation to scribes, from the days of the indigestible Jonah even to the piscatory romancers of our own times.

Well, the captain of the *Espirito Santo,* after filling his water-casks, laying in a stock of provisions, and giving his crew a run ashore sheeted home his topsails, hove up anchor, and departed. Young Nat took such a lively interest in the welfare of this craft that he carefully watched her progress until the last shred of her canvas faded upon the horizon. He judged by the sun, for he had no compass, that her course was about south.

Three days after the departure of the *Espirito Santo,* the *Hersilia* appeared. Captain Sheffield had found nothing and seen nothing, except the cold, gray sky, and the long, ceaseless heaving of the Southern Ocean's mighty breast, a few stray, hungry, screeching albatross, and once in a while, for a moment, a whale, with smooth, glistening back, spouting jets of feathery spray high in the keen, misty air, then sounding among the caverns of the deep. He had returned, like so many other credulous mariners, empty-handed, but he found his young second mate in a white heat of enthusiasm as he reported to his commander what he had learned, and finally, with the hopefulness of youth, declared his belief that "we can follow that *Espirito Santo,* and find her, too." And they did, for in a few days she was discovered lying at anchor in a bay off the South Shetlands, islands at that time unknown in North America, though soon to become famous as the home of seals. The officers and crew of the *Espirito Santo* greeted them with surprise, while their admiration took the substantial form of assisting to load the *Hersilia* with ten thousand of the finest sealskins, with which she returned to Stonington.

This exploit spread like wildfire through New England whaling ports, and secured Captain Palmer at the age of twenty, command of the Stonington sloop *Hero,* "but little rising forty tons," on board of which he sailed again for the Antarctic seas, as tender to the *Hersilia,* in 1819. Upon this voyage, after calling at the Falkland Islands for water and provisions, they again steered for the South Shetlands, and the *Hersilia* and *Hero* returned to Stonington with full cargoes of sealskins.

In 1821, Captain Palmer again sailed in the *Hero* upon an expedition to the South Shetlands, composed of six vessels commanded by Captain William Fenning of the brig *Alabama Packet.* By this time, however, the seals had been nearly exterminated, and Captain Palmer sailed farther south in search of new sealing-grounds, until he sighted land not laid down on any chart. He cruised along the coast for some days and satisfied himself that it was not an island, and after anchoring in several bays without finding any seals, although the high cliffs and rocks were covered by multitudes of penguin, he steered away to the northward with light winds and fog.

One night the *Hero* lay becalmed in a dense fog, the cold, penetrating mist drenching her sails and dripping from the main boom along her narrow deck. At midnight Captain Palmer relieved his mate and took the deck for the middle watch. When the man at the helm struck one bell, the captain was somewhat startled to hear the sound repeated twice at short intervals, for he knew, or thought he knew, that the only living things within many leagues were whales, albatross, penguin, and the like, nor did he recall ever hearing that these harmless creatures carried bells with them. The men of the watch on deck were really alarmed, for in those days superstition had not by any means departed from the ocean. The crew had heard of the fierce Kraken of northern seas, and suddenly remembered all about the doomed and unforgiven Vanderdecken, to say nothing of mythical local celebrities, renowned in all the barrooms of coast towns between Cornfield Point and Siasconset Head, nor were their fears assuaged when at two bells the same thing happened again, and so on through the watch.

Captain Palmer, however, concluded that, strange as it seemed, he must be in company with other vessels, and so at four o'clock he left the mate in charge of the deck with orders to call him if the fog lifted, and turned in for his morning watch below. At seven bells the mate reported that the fog had cleared a little and a light breeze was springing up, and by the time Captain Palmer got on deck two large men-of-war were in sight not more than a mile distant—a frigate on the port bow and a sloop of war on the starboard quarter, both showing Russian colors. Soon the United States ensign was run up at the main peak of the *Hero* and floated gaily in the morning breeze. The three vessels were now hove to, and a twelve-oared launch was seen approaching from the frigate, her crew and officer in the stern sheets in uniform. As she swept round the stern of the *Hero* the crew tossed oars and the coxswain shot her alongside. She really looked almost as large as the little sloop; at all events the Russian officer stepped from her gunwale to the deck of the *Hero*. The officer spoke English fluently, and presented the compliments of Commander Bellingshausen, who invited the captain of the American sloop to come on board his ship.

Captain Palmer was all his life a man of purpose rather than of ceremony, though by no means deficient in dignity and self-respect. He accepted the invitation, and giving an order or two to his mate, stepped into the launch just as he stood, in sea boots, sealskin-coat, and sou'wester. They were soon alongside the frigate, and Captain Palmer was ushered into the commander's spacious and luxurious cabin. The scene was impressive; the venerable, white-haired commander surrounded by his officers in uniform, and the stalwart young American captain standing with respectful dignity, his rough weather-worn sea-dress contrasting with his fresh, intelligent, handsome face. Commander Bellingshausen smiled pleasantly, and taking his guest by the hand, said kindly, "You are welcome, young man; be seated."

After questioning Captain Palmer about himself, his vessel, and the land he had discovered, and incidentally remarking that he himself had been two years upon a voyage of discovery, the commander asked to see Captain Palmer's chart and log-book. These were sent for on board the *Hero* while an elaborate luncheon was being served, and were afterwards carefully examined. The commander then rose from his seat and placing his hand in a parental manner upon the young captain's head, delivered quite an oration: "I name the land you have discovered 'Palmer Land' in your honor; but what will my august master say, and what will he think of my cruising for two years in search of land that has been discovered by a boy, in a sloop but little larger than the launch of my frigate?" Captain Palmer was unable to offer any information on this point, but he thanked his host for the honor conferred upon him, and for his kindness and hospitality, remaining somewhat non-committal in his opinion as to the old gentleman's qualifications as an explorer.

It may be mentioned that upon all charts this portion of the Antarctic Continent is laid down as "Palmer Land," also that some twenty years elapsed before it was rediscovered by the British explorer, Sir James Ross, in command of the famous *Erebus* and *Terror* expedition.

Captain Palmer next took command of the schooner *Cadet,* owned by Borrows & Spooner, of New York, on board of which he made a number of voyages to the Spanish Main. In 1826 he took the brig *Tampico* to Carthagena, and upon his return he married a daughter of Major Paul Babcock and sister of Captain David S. Babcock, afterwards famous as commander of the clipper ships *Sword-Fish* and *Young America,* and subsequently President of the Pacific Mail Steamship Co. Captain Palmer then took the brig *Francis* on several voyages to Europe, and in 1829 was in command of the brig *Anawan,* exploring new sealing-grounds among the islands about Cape Horn. In 1833 he took command of the New Orleans packet ship *Huntsville,* and then of the *Hibernia, Garrick,* and *Siddons.* In 1842 and the years following, as we have seen, he commanded the clippers *Paul Jones, Houqua, Samuel Russell,* and *Oriental,* and in 1850 retired from the sea.

At this time he was well known, not only among his neighbors and friends at Stonington, but in the great seaports of Europe and China as "Captain Nat," and many of those who talked about what he had said and what he had done were apparently unaware that he possessed any other name. It is pleasant to reflect that the neighboring seaport of Bristol has perpetuated the title in one who is respected and beloved, not more for his genius than for his modesty and reserve.

It was, of course, impossible for a man of Captain Palmer's earnest temperament and varied activities to lead a life of pleasure and idleness, so one of the first things that he did upon his retirement was to take the auxiliary steamship *United States* from New York to Bremen where she was sold. When some of his friends rallied him, asking whether he considered this giving up the sea, Captain Palmer replied, "Well, I really don't know how you can call a trip like this going to sea."

For many years Captain Palmer was the confidential adviser of A. A. Low & Brother in all matters relating to their ships, which occupied a considerable portion of his time, and while he was a seaman *par excellence,* he also possessed other accomplishments. He had much knowledge of the design and construction of ships, and many of his suggestions were embodied in the *Houqua, Samuel Russell, Oriental,* and other ships subsequently owned by the Lows. He was also a fine all-round sportsman, being a skilful yachtsman, excellent shot, and truthful fisherman. Altogether, he owned some fifteen yachts, and he was one of the earliest members of the New York Yacht Club, joining on June 7, 1845. The beautiful schooner *Juliet,* of seventy tons, designed by himself, was the last yacht owned by him. On board of her he sailed, summer after summer, upon the pleasant waters of the New England coast that he had known from boyhood and loved so well.

Captain Palmer stood fully six feet, and was a man of great physical strength and endurance. He was an active member of the Currituck Club, and at the age of seventy-six, on his annual cruise to the Thimble Islands for duck shooting, few of the party of much younger men held so steady a gun, or could endure the fatigue and exposure for which he seemed to care nothing. Though rugged in appearance, his roughness was all on the outside; his heart was filled with kindness and sympathy for the joys and sorrows of others. His brother, Captain Alexander Palmer, a seaman only less famous than himself, once said: "My home is here in Stonington, but Nat's home is the world." Captain Palmer was deeply though not vainly religious, and was long a warden of Calvary Episcopal Church at Stonington.

In 1876 he accompanied his nephew, Nathaniel B. Palmer, his brother Alexander's eldest son, who was in feeble health, to Santa Barbara, but as the invalid derived no benefit there, they went for the sea voyage to China on board the clipper ship *Mary Whitridge.* At Hong-kong, Captain Palmer received an ovation, for, while few of his old friends there were still alive, those who were left had good memories. On the return voyage to San Francisco on the steamship *City of Pekin,* Captain Palmer's nephew died when the vessel was but one day out. This was a terrible blow to Captain Palmer, from which he never recovered. On arriving at San Francisco he was confined to his bed, and although he received every care, he died there on June 21, 1877, in his seventy-eighth year. At the close of a glorious summer day, the remains of the devoted uncle and nephew were laid at rest in the churchyard at Stonington, by the hands of those who had known and loved them well.

Captain Palmer was a fine type of the American merchant seaman of that period, and I have thought it worth while to trace the leading events of his life, because he always seemed to me to be the father of American clipper-ship captains. Probably no one ever brought up so many young men who afterward became successful shipmasters, while his character and example were an inspiration to many who never sailed with him. It is indicative of the broad and far-reaching sympathies of Captain Palmer's life, that not only a part of the Antarctic Continent bears his name—an enduring monument to his memory—but that A. A. Low & Brother named one of their finest clipper ships, the *N. B. Palmer,* and the famous schooner-yacht *Palmer,* owned for many years by Rutherfurd Stuyvesant, was also named for him. Few men in private life have had part of a continent, a clipper ship, and yacht named for them.

CHAPTER VI

THE REPEAL OF THE BRITISH NAVIGATION LAWS—THE "ORIENTAL"

THE repeal of the British Navigation Laws in 1849, after violent opposition in Parliament and the House of Lords, and from almost every British ship-builder and ship-owner, gave a new impetus to the building of clipper ships, as the British merchant marine was then for the first time brought into direct competition with the vessels of other nationalities, especially those of the United States.

During the years that had elapsed since the closing up of the East India Company in 1832, some effort had been made to improve the model and construction of British merchant ships, and as we have seen, clipper schooners had been built for the Aberdeen service and for the opium trade in China, but no attempt had been made in Great Britain to build clipper ships. British ship-owners still felt secure under the Navigation Laws, in the possession of their carrying trade with the Far East, and paid little attention to the improvements in naval architecture which had been effected in the United States.

This was not from ignorance of what had been accomplished there, for the fast American packet ships had long been seen lying in the London and Liverpool docks. In 1848, Lord William Lennox, in an article entitled *A Fortnight in Cheshire,* mentions seeing them. He says: "Here (Liverpool) are some splendid American liners. I went on board the *Henry Clay* of New York, and received the greatest attention from her commander, Captain Ezra Nye. Nothing can exceed the beauty of this ship; she is quite a model for a frigate. Her accommodations are superior to any sailing vessel I ever saw." There were also the *Independence, Yorkshire, Montezuma, Margaret Evans, New World,* and scores of other fast American packet ships which had been sailing in and out of Liverpool and London for years. The arrivals and departures of these vessels created no deep impression upon the minds of British ship-owners, because they were not at that time competing with sailing vessels for the North Atlantic trade to the United States.

The same lack of enterprise was apparent in the men who handled their vessels, as we may see from the following amusing description in De Tocqueville's *Democracy in America,* published in 1835[1]:

"The European sailor navigates with prudence; he only sets sail when the weather is favorable; if an unfortunate accident befalls him, he puts into port; at night he furls a portion of his canvas; and when the whitening billows intimate the vicinity of land, he checks his way and takes an observation of the sun. But the American neglects these precautions

[1] Second American edition, translated by H. Reeve, pp. 403–4.

and braves these dangers. He weighs anchor in the midst of tempestuous gales; by night and day he spreads his sheets to the winds; he repairs as he goes along such damage as his vessel may have sustained from the storm; and when he at last approaches the term of his voyage, he darts onward to the shore as if he already descried a port. The Americans are often shipwrecked, but no trader crosses the seas so rapidly. And as they perform the same distance in shorter time, they can perform it at a cheaper rate.

"The European touches several times at different ports in the course of a long voyage; he loses a good deal of precious time in making harbor, or in waiting for a favorable wind to leave it; and pays daily dues to be allowed to remain there. The American starts from Boston to purchase tea in China; he arrives at Canton, stays there a few days, and then returns. In less than two years he has sailed as far as the entire circumference of the globe, and he has seen land but once. It is true that during a voyage of eight or ten months he has drunk brackish water, and lived upon salt meat; that he has been in a continual contest with the sea, with disease, and with a tedious existence; but, upon his return, he can sell a pound of tea for a half-penny less than the English merchant, and his purpose is accomplished.

"I cannot better explain my meaning than by saying that the Americans affect a sort of heroism in their manner of trading. But the European merchant will always find it very difficult to imitate his American competitor, who, in adopting the system I have just described, follows not only a calculation of his gain, but an impulse of his nature."

At that time there were several American ships that could have transported De Tocqueville from Boston to Canton and back in considerably less than two years, and doubtless their captains would have supplied him with something much better than brackish water to drink, besides convincing him that what he regarded as recklessness was in reality fine seamanship, and that he had been in no greater danger of shipwreck than on board a vessel of any other nationality, besides being a great deal more comfortable.

Some time before 1849, British sea-captains must have seen the American clipper ships in the ports of China; or perhaps an Indiaman in the lone southern ocean may have been lying almost becalmed on the long heaving swell, lurching and slatting the wind out of her baggy hemp sails, while her officers and crew watched an American clipper as she swept past, under a cloud of canvas, curling the foam along her keen, slender bow. But when these mariners returned home and related what they had seen, their yarns were doubtless greeted with a jolly, good-humored smile of British incredulity. With the Navigation Laws to protect them, British ship-owners cared little about American ships and their exploits.

These Navigation Laws, first enacted in 1651 by the Parliament of Cromwell, and affirmed by Charles II. soon after his restoration to the throne, were intended to check the increasing power of

Holland upon the sea, but they had quite the contrary effect. With a few slight changes, however, they were passed along from generation to generation, until Adam Smith exposed the fallacy of Protection in his *Wealth of Nations,* which appeared in 1776. From that time on, British statesmen, few in number at first, adopted his teachings, and under the pressure of popular clamor some concessions were made, especially in the way of reciprocity treaties, but it was nearly three quarters of a century before these barbaric old laws, a legacy from the thieving barons, were finally swept away.

It may be well briefly to enumerate these laws as they stood previous to their repeal, for it is seldom that one comes across so much ingenious stupidity in so compact a form; also mainly because through their repeal the ships of Great Britain eventually became the greatest ocean carriers of the world.

(I.) Certain enumerated articles of European produce could only be imported to the United Kingdom for consumption, in British ships or in ships of the country of which the goods were the produce, or in ships of that country from which they were usually imported.

(II.) No produce of Asia, Africa, or America could be imported for consumption in the United Kingdom from Europe in any ships; and such produce could only be imported from any other place in British ships or in ships of the country of which they were the produce.

(III.) No goods could be carried coastwise from

one part of the United Kingdom to another in any but British ships.

(IV.) No goods could be exported from the United Kingdom to any of the British possessions in Asia, Africa, or America (with some exceptions in regard to India) in any but British ships.

(V.) No goods could be carried from one British possession in Asia, Africa, or America to another, nor from one part of such possession to another part of the same, in any but British ships.

(VI.) No goods could be imported into any British possessions in Asia, Africa, or America, in any but British ships, or ships of the country of which the goods were the produce; provided also, in such case, that such ships brought the goods from that country.

(VII.) No foreign ships were allowed to trade with any of the British possessions unless they had been specially authorized to do so by orders in Council.

(VIII.) Powers were given to the sovereign in Council to impose differential duties on the ships of any country which did the same with reference to British ships; and also to place restrictions on importations from any foreign countries which placed restrictions on British importations into such countries.

Furthermore, by an act passed in 1786, British subjects were prohibited from owning foreign-built vessels. This act was regarded as one of the Navigation Laws, and was repealed with them.

One of the objects of the repeal of the Navigation Laws was to enable British ship-owners to become the ocean carriers of the world, and to remove every restraint as to where they should build or buy their ships. This step was a natural sequence to the repeal of the Corn Laws in 1846, and the glorious dawn of Free Trade, by which every British subject was permitted to purchase whatever he required in the best and cheapest market, and so was able to work at a moderate wage, and to have continuous employment. Thus Great Britain, with few natural advantages, became the great workshop of the world and controlled every market upon the globe in which her manufactures were not excluded by the barrier of Protection. Even from these countries she reaped a decided benefit, for they were so hampered by Protection, which increased the expense of living, created high rates of wages for labor but with uncertain employment, and brought about increased cost of production, whether of ships or merchandise, that it became impossible for them to compete in the open markets of the world, and these avenues of trade were left open for Great Britain to exploit at her pleasure.

Such was the belief of the great leader, Richard Cobden, and his brilliant colleagues. They were convinced that if British merchants were to carry on the commerce of Great Britain they must do so untrammelled as to where they bought or built their ships; they realized the fact that cheaper and better wooden sailing vessels—then the ocean cargo carriers of the world—were being built in the United States than could be constructed in Great Britain. (Indeed, as we shall presently see, the finest, largest, and fastest ships owned or chartered in Great

Britain between the years 1850 and 1857, came from the shipyards of the United States.) They fully recognized the importance of the home ship-building industry, and did everything possible to encourage it, but they also perceived that ship-owning is of vastly more importance to a nation than ship-building, and that fleets of ships are not commerce but only the instruments with which commerce performs its work; likewise, that the nation owning the best and cheapest ships, no matter where or by whom built, must and will, other things being equal, do not only most of its own carrying trade, but also a considerable portion of that of other nations. These men were not willing any longer to sacrifice the carrying trade of their country in order that a few comparatively unimportant ship-builders, grown incompetent through long years of monopoly, might continue to thrive at the expense of the nation.

No people excel the English in courage and resource in times of national trouble, and they had long before this fought battles for freedom—freedom of thought, freedom of speech, freedom of the press, freedom of the slave, freedom to worship God, —and now the final contest for freedom, the freedom of trade, had been bravely fought and won. The result, of course, was not immediate, as it required several years to recover from the evil effects of two centuries of Protection. The fruits of victories for freedom rarely ripen quickly, and in this instance the records show that the increase of British shipping for the year before the repeal of the Navigation Laws had been 393,955 tons, while during the year following there had been a decrease of 180,576 tons; also that foreign vessels arriving from foreign ports increased from 75,278 tons to 364,587 tons in these years. It was therefore natural that there should be a feeling of despondency throughout Great Britain among those who had opposed the repeal, for they thought that their fears were being realized, and that the over-sea carrying trade, which they had regarded as their own, was being taken from them. In this hour of gloom the stout-hearted ship-owners of London and Liverpool resolved that England should again become Mistress of the Sea, and so competition, the stimulus needed to rouse their latent abilities, was the instrument of their salvation.

The first American ship to carry a cargo of tea from China to England after the repeal of the Navigation Laws was the clipper *Oriental,* of 1003 tons, built for A. A. Low & Brother in 1849, by Jacob Bell, who continued in the ship-building business after the firm of Brown & Bell was dissolved in 1848. This ship's length was 185 feet, breadth 36 feet, depth 21 feet. She sailed from New York on her first voyage, commanded by Captain N. B. Palmer, September 14, 1849, and arrived at Hong-kong by the Eastern passages in 109 days. She discharged, took on board a full cargo of tea for New York, sailed January 30, 1850, and arrived April 21st, 81 days' passage. This was Captain Palmer's last command, though he lived many years, as we have seen, to enjoy the fruits of his toil upon the sea.

The *Oriental* sailed on her second voyage from New York for China, May 19, 1850, under the command of Captain Theodore Palmer, a younger brother of Captain Nat, and was 25 days to the equator; she passed the meridian of the Cape of Good Hope 45 days out, Java Head 71 days out, and arrived at Hong-kong, August 8th, 81 days from New York. She was at once chartered through Russell & Co. to load a cargo of tea for London at £6 per ton of 40 cubic feet, while British ships were waiting for cargoes for London at £3:10 per ton of 50 cubic feet. She sailed August 28th, and beat down the China Sea against a strong southwest monsoon in 21 days to Anjer, arrived off the Lizard in 91 days, and was moored in the West India Docks, London, 97 days from Hong-kong—a passage from China never before equalled in point of speed, especially against the southwest monsoon, and rarely surpassed since. She delivered 1600 tons of tea, and her freight from Hong-kong amounted to £9600, or some $48,000. Her first cost ready for sea was $70,000. From the date of her first sailing from New York, September 14, 1849, to arrival at London, December 3, 1850, the *Oriental* had sailed a distance of 67,000 miles, and had during that time been at sea 367 days, an average in all weathers of 183 miles per day.

Throngs of people visited the West India Docks to look at the *Oriental.* They certainly saw a beautiful ship; every line of her long, black hull indicated power and speed; her tall raking masts and skysail-yards towered above the spars of the shipping in the docks; her white cotton sails were neatly furled under bunt, quarter, and yardarm gaskets; while her topmast, topgallant, and royal studdingsail booms and long, heavy, lower studdingsail booms swung in along her rails, gave an idea of the enormous spread of canvas held in reserve for light and moderate leading winds; her blocks, standing and running rigging were neatly fitted to stand great stress and strain, but with no unnecessary top-hamper, or weight aloft. On deck everything was for use; the spare spars, scraped bright and varnished, were neatly lashed along the waterways; the inner side of the bulwarks, the rails and the deck-houses were painted pure white; the hatch combings, skylights, pin-rails, and companions were of Spanish mahogany; the narrow planks of her clear pine deck, with the gratings and ladders, were scrubbed and holystoned to the whiteness of cream; the brass capstan heads, bells, belaying pins, gangway stanchions, and brasswork about the wheel, binnacle, and skylights were of glittering brightness. Throughout she was a triumph of the shipwright's and seaman's toil and skill.

No ship like the *Oriental* had even been seen in England, and the ship-owners of London were constrained to admit that they had nothing to compare with her in speed, beauty of model, rig, or construction. It is not too much to say that the arrival of this vessel in London with her cargo of tea in this crisis in 1850, aroused almost as much apprehension and excitement in Great Britain as was created by the memorable Tea Party held in Boston harbor in 1773. The Admiralty obtained permission to take off her lines in dry dock; the *Illustrated London News* published her portrait, not a very good one by the way; and the *Times* honored her arrival by a leader, which ended with these brave, wise words:

"The rapid increase of population in the United States, augmented by an annual immigration of nearly three hundred thousand from these isles, is a fact that forces itself on the notice and interest of the most unobservant and uncurious. All these promise to develop the resources of the United States to such an extent as to compel us to a competition as difficult as it is unavoidable. We must run a race with our gigantic and unshackled rival. We must set our long-practised skill, our steady industry, and our dogged determination, against his youth, ingenuity, and ardor. It is a father who runs a race with his son. A fell necessity constrains us and we must not be beat. Let our ship-builders and employers take warning in time. There will always be an abundant supply of vessels, good enough and fast enough for short voyages. The coal-trade can take care of itself, for it will always be a refuge for the destitute. But we want fast vessels for the long voyages, which otherwise will fall into American hands. It is fortunate that the Navigation Laws have been repealed in time to destroy these false and unreasonable expectations, which might have lulled the ardor of British competition. We now all start together with a fair field and no favor. The American captain can call at London, and the British captain can pursue his voyage to New York. Who can complain? Not we. We trust that our countrymen will not be beaten; but if they should be, we shall know that they deserve it."

CHAPTER VII

THE RUSH FOR CALIFORNIA—A SAILING DAY

THE world has seldom witnessed so gigantic a migration of human beings, by land and sea, from every quarter of the globe, as that which poured into California in 1848 and the years following. San Francisco, from a drowsy, Mexican trading station, composed of a cluster of some fifty mud huts, adobe dwellings, and hide houses, situated upon a magnificent bay with lofty mountains in the distance, occasionally enlivened by the visit of a New Bedford or Nantucket whale ship in need of wood and water, or a Boston hide droger which took away tallow, hides, and horns, suddenly became one of the great seaports of the world.

From April 1, 1847, to the same date in 1848, two ships, one barque and one brig arrived at San Francisco from Atlantic ports, and in the course of this year nine American whalers called in there. In 1849, 775 vessels cleared from Atlantic ports for San Francisco; 242 ships, 218 barques, 170 brigs, 132 schooners, and 12 steamers. New York sent 214 vessels, Boston 151, New Bedford 42, Baltimore 38, New Orleans 32, Philadelphia 31, Salem 23, Bath 19, Bangor 13, New London 17, Providence 11, Eastport 10, and Nantucket 8. Almost every seaport along the Atlantic coast, sent one or more vessels, and they all carried passengers. The schooner *Eureka* sailed from Cleveland, Ohio, for San Francisco via the River St. Lawrence, September 28, 1849, and carried fifty-three passengers, among whom were two families from Cleveland. Many of these vessels never reached California; some of them put into ports of refuge disabled and in distress; while others were never heard from. Most of the ships that did arrive at San Francisco made long, weary voyages, their passengers and crews suffering sore hardships and privations.

In the year 1849, 91,405 passengers landed at San Francisco from various ports of the world, of almost every nationality under the sun and representing some of the best and some of the worst types of men and women. The officers and crews, with hardly an exception, hurried to the mines, leaving their ships to take care of themselves; in some instances the crews did not even wait long enough to stow the sails and be paid off, so keen were they to join the wild race for gold. Many of these vessels never left the harbor; over one hundred were turned into store ships, while others were converted into hotels, hospitals, and prisons, or gradually perished by decay.

The first vessel, and one of the few of the California fleet of 1849, which escaped from San Francisco, was the ship *South Carolina.* This vessel sailed from New York, January 24, 1849, and returned via Valparaiso with a cargo of copper to Boston, where she arrived February 20, 1850, after a voyage out and home of some thirteen months.

A letter from San Francisco to the New York *Herald,* dated February 28, 1850, states that wages for seamen were then from $125 to $200 per month. There used to be a humorous yarn spun among seamen to the effect that during the "flush times," as those glorious days of the gold fever were called, sailors required a captain to produce a recommendation from his last crew before they would ship with him or sign articles. However this may be, it is a fact that as late as 1854, it was so difficult to induce crews to leave San Francisco that captains were frequently obliged to ship men out of jail, whether they were sailors or not, in order to get their ships to sea.

The gold mines exerted an irresistible attraction, and for a time the town was almost deserted, except for those passing through on their way to and from the mines. By degrees, however, it became apparent to some that more gold-dust was to be collected at San Francisco in business than by digging among the mountains, and with admirable energy they set about transforming this lawless camp into a prosperous trading city.

Prior to 1848, California had been for all practical purposes almost uninhabited, and now was utterly unable to provide for the needs of her vastly increased population. The newcomers produced plenty of gold, but nothing else, and they frequently found themselves on the brink of starvation. They were too busy with pick and shovel to contribute anything in the form of manufactures or supplies, so that the most ordinary articles of every-day use, to say nothing of comforts and luxuries, had to be brought from places thousands of miles distant. This precarious means of supply, together with the enormous and reckless purchasing power developed by the rapid production of gold from the mines, naturally created a speculative and artificial standard of values, and goods of every description sold for fabulous amounts: Beef, pork, and flour brought from $40 to $60 per barrel; tea, coffee, and sugar, $4 a pound; spirits, $10 to $40 a quart; playing-cards, $5 a pack; cowhide boots, $45 a pair; picks and shovels from $5 to $15 each; wooden and tin bowls from $2.50 to $7.50 each; laudanum, $1 a drop, and so on. These were by no means high prices for stevedores and laborers receiving from $20 to $30 a day, and miners who were making anywhere from $100 to $1000 a day washing dirt at the mines.

An idea of the amount of gold produced may be gained from the fact that the Pacific Mail Company, whose first steamship, the *California,* arrived at San Francisco via the Straits of Magellan, February 28, 1849, had by the end of 1852 shipped gold from that city to the value of $121,766,425.

The speculators and shippers of merchandise in the Eastern States were as deeply interested in the output of the mines of California as the gold diggers themselves. No one could predict how long this state of affairs would continue; with them speed meant everything; a week or even a day's delay might result in heavy losses, or what was to them the same thing, failure to reap large profits. They could not send their goods across the continent, and the Pacific Mail Company had all that it could attend to in conveying passengers and the mails across the Isthmus; so that the only means of transportation from the Atlantic States to San Francisco was round Cape Horn. Under these circumstances one can easily understand how the rates of freight advanced to extravagant figures, and created a demand under which the California clippers came into existence.

In these days of thrifty transportation by sea, when coal shovels have superseded watch-tackles, and ship-owners are expected to look cheerful with steamship rates at $14.00 a ton from New York to San Francisco, and $12.00 a ton from New York to Melbourne or Hong-kong, the rates of freight that the clipper ships earned from New York to San Francisco seem almost incredible. In 1850 the *Samuel Russell* received $1.50 per cubic foot, or $60 per ton of 40 cubic feet. She registered 940 tons, and being a very sharp ship would probably carry not more than 1200 tons of California cargo. But even so, her freight would amount to $72,000, or a little more than her first cost ready for sea. The other clippers at first received the same rate, but by degrees, as they increased in tonnage and in number, the rates of freight declined to $50 per ton, and then to $40 where they remained for a considerable time.

The California clipper period covers the years 1850–1860, during the first four of which nearly all of these famous ships, numbering one hundred and sixty, were built. (See Appendix I.) Most of them were launched at or near New York and Boston, though some were built elsewhere, Richmond,

Jacob A. Westervelt

Jacob Bell

Clipper-Ship Builders

Baltimore, Mystic, Medford, Newburyport, Portsmouth, Portland, Rockland, Bath, and other ports contributing to the fleet. These splendid ships—the swiftest sailing vessels that the world has even seen or is likely ever to see—sailed their great ocean matches for the stake of commercial supremacy and the championship of the seas, over courses encircling the globe, and their records, made more than half a century ago, still stand unsurpassed.

After carrying their cargoes to California at the enormous rates we have given, these ships would return round Cape Horn in ballast for another cargo at the same rate, as they could well afford to do, or would cross the Pacific in ballast and load tea for London or New York. Many of them more than cleared their original cost in less than one year, during a voyage round the globe, after deducting all expenses.

The central points about which the great ship-owning interests collected were New York and Boston. Here, too, were the most famous shipyards. All along the harbor front at East Boston and the water-front of the East River from Pike Street to the foot of Tenth Street, New York, were to be seen splendid clipper ships in every stage of construction; and beside the ship-building yards, there were rigging-lofts, sail-lofts, the shops of boat-builders, block- and pump-makers, painters, carvers, and gilders, iron, brass, and copper workers, mast- and spar-makers, and ship stores of all kinds, where everything required on shipboard, from a palm and needle, a marlinspike or a ball of spun yarn, to anchors and chains, was to be found. The shipyards were great thriving hives of industry, where hundreds of sledge-hammers, top mauls, and caulking mallets, swung by the arms of skilful American mechanics, rung out a mighty chorus, and the fresh odor of rough-hewn timber, seething Carolina pitch, and Stockholm tar filled the air with healthful fragrance. They were unique and interesting localities, the like of which have never existed elsewhere—now long passed away and all but forgotten.

The principal shipping merchants in New York were William T. Coleman & Co., Wells & Emanuel, Sutton & Co., John I. Earl, and James Smith & Son, all of whom managed San Francisco lines and usually had one or more clippers on the berth, loading night and day for California. The old Piers 8, 9, and 10, along the East River, were scenes of great activity, and throngs of people visited them to see these ships. At all the seaports along the Atlantic coast, almost every one knew something and most persons knew a good deal about ships. They were a matter of great importance to the community, for as late as 1860, nearly all the large fortunes in the United States had been made in shipping.

The captains and officers of the California clippers were as a class men of integrity, energy, and skill, nearly all of them being of the best Pilgrim and Puritan stock of New England, and trained to the sea from boyhood. Many of them were the sons of merchants and professional men, well known and respected in the communities in which they lived. Their ships carried large crews, besides being fitted with every appliance for saving labor: fly-wheel

William H. Webb

Samuel Hall

Clipper-Ship Builders

pumps, gypsy winches, gun-metal roller bushes in the sheaves of the brace, reef tackle and halliard blocks, geared capstans, and plenty of the best stores and provisions, with spare spars, sails, blocks, and rigging in abundance. The owners fitted out their vessels with rational economy and looked to their captains, whom they rewarded liberally, to see that nothing was wasted and that the ships performed their voyages quickly and well.

There was no allowance of food, as on British ships, on board the American clippers; a barrel of beef, pork, bread, or flour was supposed to last about so many days, according to the ship's company; a little more or less did not matter. The water was in charge of the carpenter, and was usually carried in an iron tank which rested on the keelson abaft the mainmast and came up to the main deck. This tank was in the form of a cylinder, and held from three to four thousand gallons; some of the larger ships carried their water in two of these tanks. Each morning at sea, water equal to one gallon for every person on board was pumped out of the tank and placed in a scuttle-butt on deck; the carpenter then made a report of the number of gallons remaining in the tank to the chief officer, who entered it in the log-book. During the day the crew took the water they needed from the scuttle-butt, the cook and steward what they required for the galley and aft; and while there was no stint, woe to the man who wasted fresh water at sea in those days, for if he managed to escape the just wrath of the officers, his shipmates were pretty sure to take care of him. The salt beef and pork were kept in a harness cask abaft the mainmast, and when a fresh barrel of provisions was to be opened, the harness cask was scrubbed and scalded out with boiling water, and so was always sweet and clean. The cooks and stewards were almost invariably negroes, and it is to be regretted that there are not more like them at the present time—especially the cooks. "Plenty of work, plenty to eat, and good pay," is what sailormen used to say of American clippers, the sort of ships on board of which good seamen liked to sail.

The forecastle on board the old type of vessels was in the forepeak, below the main deck, a damp, ill-ventilated hole, but in the California clippers it was in a large house on deck between the fore- and main-masts, divided fore and aft amidships by a bulkhead, so that each watch had a separate forecastle, well ventilated and with plenty of light. There was nothing to prevent a crew from being comfortable enough; it depended entirely upon themselves. Indeed, there were no ships afloat at that period where the crews were so well paid and cared for as on board the American clippers. Seamen who knew their duties and were willing to perform them fared far better than on board the ships of any other nationality.

Perhaps, the most marked difference between American merchant ships and those of other nations was in regard to the use of wine and spirits. On board British ships grog was served out regularly to the men before the mast, and the captain and officers were allowed wine money. Nothing of this sort was permitted on American vessels. Robert

Minturn, of the firm of Grinnell, Minturn & Co., in his evidence before a parliamentary committee in 1848, stated that teetotalism not only was encouraged by American ship-owners, but actually earned a bonus from underwriters, who offered a return of ten per cent of the insurance premium upon voyages performed without the consumption of spirits. On board the packet ships and other vessels which carried passengers, there was always wine on the captain's table, but the captain and officers rarely made use of it. The sailors were allowed plenty of hot coffee, night or day, in heavy weather, but grog was unknown on board American merchant ships.

In those days, after a New York clipper had finished loading, it was the custom for her to drop down the East River and anchor off Battery Park, then a fashionable resort, where she would remain for a few hours to take her crew on board and usually to ship from five to ten tons of gunpowder, a part of her cargo that was stowed in the main hatch, to be easily handled in case of fire. Towboats were not as plentiful in New York harbor as at present, and unless the wind was ahead or calm, the clippers seldom made use of them, for with a leading breeze these ships would sail to and from Sandy Hook much faster than they could be towed. One of the clippers getting under way off Battery Park was a beautiful sight, and an event in which a large part of the community was interested.

The people who gathered at Battery Park to see a clipper ship get under way, came partly to hear the sailors sing their sea songs, or chanties, which were an important part of sea life in those days, giving a zest and cheeriness on shipboard, which nothing else could supply. It used to be said that a good chanty man was worth four men in a watch, and this was true, for when a crew knocked off chantying, there was something wrong—the ship seemed lifeless. These songs originated early in the nineteenth century, with the negro stevedores at Mobile and New Orleans, who sung them while screwing cotton bales into the holds of the American packet ships; this was where the packet sailors learned them. The words had a certain uncouth, fantastic meaning, evidently the product of undeveloped intelligence, but there was a wild, inspiring ring in the melodies, and, after a number of years, they became unconsciously influenced by the pungent, briny odor and surging roar and rhythm of the ocean, and howling gales at sea. Landsmen have tried in vain to imitate them; the result being no more like genuine sea songs than skimmed milk is like Jamaica rum.

There were a great many Whitehall boats kept at the lower end of the Park, and the Battery boatmen were fine oarsmen, Bill Decker, Tom Daw, Steve Roberts, and Andy Fay being famous scullers. There were some smart four- and six-oared crews among them which used to swoop down and pick up the valuable prizes offered by the Boston city fathers for competition each Fourth of July on the Charles River, but the convivial life which the gay Battery boatmen led did not improve their rowing, and in 1856 they were defeated by the famous *Neptune* crew, of St. John, N. B., in a match rowed on the Charles River for the stake of $5000, and later were quite eclipsed by the even more famous Ward crew of Newburgh.

The time when these men really had to work, was on the sailing day of a California clipper. A busy scene it was, as they put the crew and their dunnage on board, one or two lots at a time, accompanied by a boarding-house runner, the sailormen being in various stages of exalted inebriation. The helpless in body and mind are hauled over the side in bowlines and stowed away in their berths to regain the use of their limbs and senses. These men have been drugged and robbed of their three months' advance wages and most of their clothing. In a few hours they will come to, and find themselves at sea on board of a ship whose name they never heard, with no idea to what part of the globe they are bound. A receipt is given for each man by the mate, who considers himself fortunate if he can muster two thirds of his crew able to stand up and heave on a capstan bar or pull on a rope. The probable condition of the crew is so well known and expected that a gang of longshoremen is on board to lend a hand in getting the ship under way. The more provident of the seamen bring well-stocked sea chests; the less thoughtful find moderate-sized canvas bags quite large enough to hold their possessions; one mariner carries his outfit for the Cape Horn voyage tied up in a nice bandanna handkerchief, the parting gift of a Cherry Street damsel —who keeps the change. Jack is in a jovial, tipsy humor, and appears to be well satisfied with his investment.

This is an anxious day for the mate, for, while he receives his instructions from the captain in a general way, yet every detail of getting the ship to sea is in his hands; and though he seems careless and unconcerned, his nerves are on edge and every sense alert; his eyes are all over the ship. He is sizing up each man in his crew and getting his gauge; when he strikes a chord of sympathy, he strikes hard, and when his keen instinct detects a note of discord, he strikes still harder, lifting his men along with a curse here, a joke there, and ever tightening his firm but not unkindly grasp of authority. The mate is not hunting for trouble—all that he wants is for his men to do their work and show him enough respect so that it will not become his unpleasant duty to hammer them into shape. He knows that this is his day, and that it is the decisive day of the voyage, for before the ship passes out by Sandy Hook his moral victory will be lost or won, with no appeal to Admiralty Boards or Courts of Justice. He knows, too, that a score of other mates and their captains are looking on with keen interest to see how he handles his crew, and their opinion is of far greater value to him than the decrees of Senates; so he intends to lay himself out and give them something worth looking at.

There is a crisp northeasterly breeze, and the blue waters of the bay dance and frolic in the sweet June sunshine. The crew are all on board, with the captain and pilot in consultation on the quarterdeck; it is nearly high water, and the tide will soon run ebb. The mate takes charge of the topgallant forecastle, with the third mate and the boatswain

Clipper-Ship Captains

Robert H. Waterman　　　　N. B. Palmer

to assist him, while the second mate, with the fourth mate and boatswain's mate work the main deck and stand by to look after the chain as it comes in over the windlass.

As the crew muster on the forecastle they appear to be a motley gang, mostly British and Scandinavian, with a sprinkling of Spaniards, Portuguese, and Italians, and one or two Americans. Some wear thick, coarse, red, blue, or gray flannel shirts, others blue dungaree jumpers, or cotton shirts of various colors; their trousers are in a variety of drabs, blues, grays, and browns, supported by leather belts or braces; they wear stiff or soft felt hats or woollen caps of many colors. But no clothes that were ever invented could disguise these men; their bronzed, weather-beaten faces and sun-baked, tattooed arms, with every swing of their bodies, betray them as sailormen, and good ones too, above the average even in those days. They would no more submit to being put into uniforms or to the cut-and-dried discipline of a man-of-war, than they would think of eating their food at a table with knives and forks.

They are all pretty full of alcohol, but the sailor instinct is so strong in them that they do their work as well, some of them perhaps better, than if they were sober. There is no romance about them or about any part of their lives; they are simply common, every-day sailors, and will never be anything else, unless they happen to encounter some inspired writer of fiction; then it is difficult to say what may become of them. Some of them have much good in their natures, others are saturated with evil, and all need to be handled with tact and judgment, for too much severity, or on the other hand any want of firmness, may lead to trouble, which means the free use of knives, belaying pins, and knuckle-dusters.

Now the flood-tide begins to slacken, and as the ship swings to the wind, the order is passed along from aft to man the windlass and heave short. We hear the mate sing out in a pleasant, cheery voice: "Now, then, boys, heave away on the windlass breaks; strike a light, it 's duller than an old graveyard." And the chantyman, in an advanced stage of hilarious intoxication, gay as a skylark, sails into song:

"In eighteen hundred and forty-six,
I found myself in the hell of a fix,
A-working on the railway, the railway, the railway.
Oh, poor Paddy works on the railway.

"In eighteen hundred and forty-seven,
When Dan O'Connolly went to heaven,
He worked upon the railway, the railway, the railway.
Poor Paddy works on the railway, the railway.

"In eighteen hundred and forty-eight,
I found myself bound for the Golden Gate,
A-working on the railway, the railway.
Oh, poor Paddy works on the railway, the railway.

"In eighteen hundred and forty-nine,
I passed my time in the Black Ball Line,
A-working on the railway, the railway,
I weary on the railway,
Poor Paddy works on the railway, the railway."

And so on to the end of the century, or till the mate sings out, "Vast heaving," lifts his hand, and reports to the captain: "The anchor 's apeak, sir." "Very good, sir, loose sails fore and aft." "Aye, aye, sir." "Aloft there some of you and loose sails. One hand stop in the tops and crosstrees to overhaul the gear." "Aye, aye, sir. Royals and sky-sails?" "Yes, royals and skysails; leave the stay-sails fast." "Lay out there, four or five of you, and loose the head sails." "Here, you fellow in the green-spotted shirt, lay down out of that; there 's men enough up there now to eat those sails." "Mr. Sampson, take some of your men aft and look after the main and mizzen; put a hand at the wheel; as he goes along let him clear the ensign halliards; while you 're waiting lay that accommodation ladder in on deck; leave the spanker fast." "On the foretopsail yard, there, if you cut that gasket, I 'll split your damned skull; cast it adrift, you lubber." "Boatswain, get your watch tackles along to the topsail sheets." "Aye, aye, sir." "Here, some of you gentlemen's sons in disguise, get that fish-davit out; hook on the pendant; overhaul the tackle down ready for hooking on." "Mainskysail yard there, don't make those gaskets up, my boy; fetch them in along the yard, and make fast to the tye."

By this time the sails are loose and the gaskets made up; courses, topsails, topgallantsails, royals, and skysails flutter in their gear, and the clipper feels the breath of life. "Sheet home the topsails." "Aye, aye, sir." "Boatswain, look out for those clew-lines at the main; ease down handsomely as the sheets come home." "Foretop there, overhaul your buntlines, look alive!" "Belay your port maintopsail sheet; clap a watch tackle on the starboard sheet and rouse her home." "Maintop there, lay down on the main-yard and light the foot of that sail over the stay." "That's well, belay starboard." "Well the mizzentopsail sheets, belay." "Now then, my bullies, lead out your topsail halliards fore and aft and masthead her." "Aye, aye, sir." By this time the mate has put some ginger into the crew and longshoremen, and they walk away with the three topsail halliards:

"Away, way, way, yar,
We'll kill Paddy Doyle for his boots."

"Now then, long pulls, my sons." "Here, you chantyman, haul off your boots, jump on that main-deck capstan and strike a light; the best in your locker." "Aye, aye, sir." And the three topsail-yards go aloft with a ringing chanty that can be heard up in Beaver Street:

"Then up aloft that yard must go,
Whiskey for my Johnny.
Oh, whiskey is the life of man,
Whiskey, Johnny.
I thought I heard the old man say,
Whiskey for my Johnny.
We are bound away this very day,
Whiskey, Johnny.
A dollar a day is a white man's pay,
Whiskey for my Johnny.

Oh, whiskey killed my sister Sue,
Whiskey, Johnny,
And whiskey killed the old man, too,
Whiskey for my Johnny.
Whiskey 's gone, what shall I do?
Whiskey, Johnny,
Oh, whiskey 's gone, and I 'll go too,
Whiskey for my Johnny."

"Belay your maintopsail halliards." "Aye, aye, sir." And so the canvas is set fore and aft, topsails, topgallantsails, royals, and skysails, flat as boards, the inner and outer jibs are run up and the sheets hauled to windward; the main- and after-yards are braced sharp to the wind, the foretopsail is laid to the mast, and the clipper looks like some great seabird ready for flight. The anchor is hove up to:

"I wish I was in Slewer's Hall,
Lowlands, lowlands, hurra, my boys,
A-drinking luck to the old Black Ball,
My dollar and a half a day."

And while some of the hands bring the anchor to the rail with cat and fish tackle, and:

"A Yankee sloop came down the river,
Hah, hah, rolling John,
Oh, what do you think that sloop had in her?
Hah, hah, rolling John,
Monkey's hide and bullock's liver,
Hah, hah, rolling John,"

the rest of the crew fill away the foreyard, draw away the head sheets, and check in the after yards. As the ship pays off, and gathers way in the slack water, the longshoremen and runners tumble over the side into the Whitehall boats, the crowd at Battery Park gives three parting cheers, the ensign is dipped, and the clipper is on her way to Cape Horn.

CHAPTER VIII

THE CLIPPER SHIP CREWS

THE history of men before the mast on board American merchant ships is not a history of American sailors, for strictly speaking there have never been any American merchant sailors as a class; that is, no American merchant ship of considerable tonnage was ever manned by native-born Americans in the sense that French, British, Dutch, Norwegian, Swedish, Spanish, or Danish ships are manned by men born in the country under whose flag they sail. Neither have Americans ever followed the sea all their lives before the mast, as do men of the nations named. Some of the small Salem ships and perhaps a few of the Nantucket whalers of a century ago may possibly have carried entirely American crews, but if so, the men did not remain long in the forecastle.

The ship *George,* 328 tons, built at Salem in 1812 and owned by Joseph Peabody, is a case in point. She was known as the "Salem frigate," and made many successful voyages to Calcutta. Of this ship's sailors, during her long and prosperous career, forty-five became captains, twenty chief mates, and six second mates. One of her Salem crew, Thomas M. Saunders, served as boy, ordinary seaman, able seaman, third, second, and chief mate on board of her, and finally, after twelve East India voyages, became her captain. This ship was a fair sample of many American vessels of that period, but probably no ship of similar or greater tonnage in the merchant service of any other nation can show such a brilliant record for her men before the mast.

The demand for crews for the California clippers brought together a miscellaneous lot of men, some good and some bad, some accustomed to deep-water voyages to India and China, and some only to European ports, while others were not sailors at all, and only shipped as such for the sake of getting to California. The majority were of course from the general merchant service of the time.

During the first half of the nineteenth century, American ships trading upon long voyages to China and India carried crews composed chiefly of Scandinavians—splendid sailormen who could do any kind of rigging work or sail-making required on board of a ship at sea and took pride in doing it well, and who also had sufficient sense to know that discipline is necessary on shipboard. These Scandinavians, who were as a rule fine seamen, clean, willing, and obedient, were the first and best class among the men of whom the clipper ship crews were composed. A vessel with a whole crew of these strong, honest sailors was a little heaven afloat.

Then there were the packet sailors, a different class altogether, mostly "Liverpool Irishmen," a species of wild men, strong, coarse-built, thick-set; their hairy bodies and limbs tattooed with grotesque and often obscene devices in red and blue India ink; men wallowing in the slush of depravity, who could be ruled only with a hand of iron. Among themselves they had a rough-and-ready code of ethics, which deprived them of the pleasure of stealing from each other, though it permitted them to rob and plunder shipmates of other nationalities, or the ship and passengers. So, too, they might not draw knives on each other, being obliged to settle disputes with their fists, but to cut and stab an officer or shipmate not of their own gang was regarded as an heroic exploit.

With all their moral rottenness, these rascals were splendid fellows to make or shorten sail in heavy weather on the Western Ocean, and to go aloft in a coat or monkey jacket in any kind of weather was regarded by them with derision and contempt. But making and taking in sail was about all that they could do, being useless for the hundred and one things on shipboard which a deep-water sailor was supposed to know, such as rigging work, sail-making, scraping, painting, and keeping a vessel clean and shipshape. The packets had all this work done in port, and never looked so well as when hauling out of dock outward bound; whereas, the China and California clippers looked their best after a long voyage, coming in from sea with every ratline and seizing square, the sheer poles coach-whipped, brass caps on the rigging ends and lanyard knots, and the man-ropes marvels of cross pointing, Turks' heads, and double rose knots.

The packet sailors showed up at their best when laying out on a topsail yardarm, passing a weather reef-earing, with their Black Ball caps, red shirts, and trousers stowed in the legs of their sea boots along with their cotton hooks and sheath knives, a snow squall whistling about their ears, the rigging a mass of ice, and the old packet jumping into the big Atlantic seas up to her knightheads. These ruffians did not much care for India and China voyages, but preferred to navigate between the dance-halls of Cherry Street and the grog-shops of Waterloo Road and Ratcliffe Highway. As has often been said, they worked like horses at sea and spent their money like asses ashore.

When the California clippers came out, these packet rats, as they came to be called aboard the deep-water ships—men who had never before had the slightest idea of crossing the equator if they could help it,—were suddenly possessed with the desire to get to the California gold mines. They, with other adventurers and blacklegs of the vilest sort, who were not sailors but who shipped as able seamen for the same reason, partly composed the crews of the clipper ships. The packet rats were tough, roustabout sailormen and difficult to handle, so that it was sometimes a toss-up whether they or the captain and officers would have charge of the ship; yet to see these fellows laying out on an eighty-foot main-yard in a whistling gale off Cape Horn, fisting hold of a big No. 1 Colt's cotton canvas mainsail, heavy and stiff with sleet and snow, bellying, slatting, and thundering in the gear, and then to hear the wild, cheery shouts of these rugged, brawny sailormen, amid the fury of the storm, as inch by inch they fought on till the last double gasket was

Clipper-Ship Captains

Josiah P. Creesy — H. W. Johnson

fast, made it easy to forget their sins in admiration of their splendid courage.

Then there were Spaniards, Portuguese, Chinamen, Frenchmen, Africans, Russians, and Italians from the general merchant service, many of whom were excellent seamen and some of whom were not; and lastly came the men of various nationalities who were not sailors at all nor the stuff out of which sailors could be made, and who had no business to be before the mast on board of a ship. Many of these men had served their time in the penitentiary and some should have remained there. These impostors increased the labor of able seamen who were compelled to do their work, and endangered the safety of the ship so unfortunate as to have them among her crew.

With such barbarians the New England captains from the yellow sands of Cape Cod and the little seaports along the Sound, and from the rocky headlands of Cape Ann and the coast of Maine, were often called upon to handle the clipper ships. There were, as has been said, a large number of respectable, hard-working, Scandinavian sailors, some of whom became captains and mates, as well as from four to eight smart American boys aboard each ship who looked forward to becoming officers and captains.

The clipper ship captains had the reputation of being severe men with their crews, but considering the kind of human beings with whom they had to deal, it is difficult to see how they could have been anything else, and still retain command of their ships. Taken as a class, American sea-captains and mates half a century ago were perhaps the finest body of real sailors that the world has ever seen, and by this is meant captains and officers who had themselves sailed before the mast. They enforced their authority by sheer power of character and will against overwhelming odds of brute force, often among cut-throats and desperadoes. They were the first to establish discipline in the merchant service, and their ships were the envy and despair of merchants and captains of other nations. Intrepid and self-reliant sailors, they are justly entitled to the gratitude of mankind. No doubt there were instances of unnecessary severity on board the American clipper ships; they were exceptional, and the provocation was great; but it would be difficult to cite a case of a sailor being ill-used who knew and performed the duties for which he had shipped, for captains and officers appreciated the value of good seamen, and took the best care of them.

The abuses from which sailors in those days suffered, were not when at sea or on board ship. It was the harpies of the land who lay in wait like vultures, to pollute and destroy their bodies and souls—male and female land-sharks, who would plunder and rob a sailor of his pay and his three months' advance, and then turn him adrift without money or clothes. It made no difference to these brazen-hearted thieves—and the women, if possible, were worse than the men—whether a sailor was bound round the Horn in midwinter or to the East Indies in midsummer; they saw to it that he took nothing away with him but the ragged clothes he stood in, and perhaps a ramshackle old sea chest with a shabby suit of oilskins, a pair of leaky sea boots, a bottle or two of Jersey lightning, and two or three plugs of tobacco chucked into it. These vice-hardened men and women of various nationalities were permitted to work their abominable trade unmolested, almost within the shadow of church spires and Courts of Justice in the chief seaports of the United States. The destitute condition in which men were put on board of American ships became so common that clothing and other necessaries were provided for them in what was known as the slop chest, in charge of the steward, with which all ships bound upon distant voyages were supplied, and from which the crew received whatever they required at about one half the cost extorted by the slop shops on shore. This arrangement was necessary, as otherwise, in many instances, the men would not have had sufficient clothing to stand a watch in cold or stormy weather.

American sea-captains were often compelled to take these outcasts as they found them, because they could get no other men. They provided them with better food than they had ever seen or heard of on board vessels of their own countries, supplied them with clothes, sea boots, sou'westers, oilskins, and tobacco, restored them to health, paid them money which many of them never earned, and for the time being, at least, did their utmost to make men of them. If any one imagines that this class of sailors ever felt or expressed the least gratitude toward their benefactors, he is much mistaken. Let him picture to himself these creatures in their watch below, laying off in their frowzy berths or sitting around their dirty, unkempt forecastle on their chests—those who happen to own them—smoking their filthy clay pipes, amid clouds of foul tobacco smoke, reeking in the stench of musty underclothing, mouldy sea boots, and rancid oilskins, rank enough to turn the stomach of a camel, or any other animal than man. The noxious air is too much for the sooty slush lamp that swings uneasily against the grimy bulkhead; it burns a sickly blue flame with a halo of fetid vapor; while the big fat-witted samples of humanity in the bunks and on the sea chests cheerfully curse their captain up-hill and down dale as their natural enemy, but are never tired of yarning about their "shore friends." They recall the attractive qualities of such characters as Dutch Pete, One-thumbed Jerry, and Limerick Mike—sleek, smooth-tongued boarding-house runners who have practised upon the vices of these same men, robbed them of their advance wages, drugged and shanghaied them without clothing or tobacco. Then these stupid fellows will yarn about the enticing charms of such "real ladies" as Big Moll, Swivel-eyed Sue, or French Kate, and the comfort and hospitality of the establishments over which these hussies preside. But let the boatswain come along and knock three times on the forecastle door with his brawny fist, and sing out, "Now then, get out here and put the stun'sails on her," and these hulky brutes will tumble over each other to get on deck, for they know that they will be beaten and booted if there is any hanging back.

Unfortunately, this was the only way to deal with this type of men on shipboard. They were amenable to discipline only in the form of force in heavy and frequent doses, the theories of those who have never commanded ships or had experience in handling degenerates at sea to the contrary notwithstanding. To talk about the exercise of kindness or moral suasion with such men, would be the limit of foolishness; one might as well propose a kindergarten for baby coyotes or young rattlesnakes.

One does not like to dwell upon these depressing phases of human nature in connection with the graceful, yacht-like clipper, perhaps the most beautiful and life-like thing ever fashioned by the hand of man. It is therefore pleasant to record that there were many American clipper ships with crews that were for the most part decent, self-respecting men, who kept themselves, their clothes, and their forecastles clean and sweet. Of course, these men would have their grog and sweethearts on shore, and their quiet growl at sea—the birthright of all good sailormen; but they required no urging beyond a word of encouragement to do their work on deck and aloft quickly and well. Such a crew would not live with men who were unclean in their speech and habits, and would compel such human nuisances to pick up their traps and take themselves out under the topgallant forecastle to get along as best they might; but it was a great hardship when good seamen found themselves among a crew composed chiefly of these poor enough sailors but proficient blackguards and bullies.

In those days there was a class of persons who

did their utmost to degrade an honorable profession by calling themselves lawyers. The ports of New York and San Francisco were the scenes of their most lucrative exploits. When a ship arrived, these fellows would waylay the sailors and follow them to dance-halls, gin-mills, and other low resorts, worming their way into the confidence of the too easy mariners by fairy tales and glittering prospects of large sums of money to be recovered as damages from their late captains, until they succeeded in extracting a narrative of the last voyage, including alleged grievances. They would then libel the ship and commence legal proceedings against the captain and officers. These cases would be tried before juries of landsmen who, having no practical knowledge of sailors or of the usages of the sea, frequently awarded damages, though in many cases the captain and officers were able to disprove false complaints or to justify their actions upon the ground of necessity in maintaining proper discipline. It is perhaps needless to say that of the damages recovered not one penny was ever handled by the aggrieved sailor, for the guiding principle of the sea lawyer's career being the resolve never to part with his client's money, these fellows literally made their clients' interests their own. Sailors themselves used to laugh and joke about the bare-faced yarns which they had spun under oath in court and got greenhorn juries to listen to and believe; but they did not laugh and joke about their lawyers, whom they regarded with contempt. One of the most insulting epithets which a sailor could apply to another was to call him a "sea lawyer," and there

David S. Babcock

George Lane

Clipper-Ship Captains

was a particularly ravenous species of shark which used also to be known as the "sea lawyer."

At one time this abuse of the law became such a powerful instrument of extortion that captains and officers, innocent of any wrong, unless the protection of life and property be regarded as wrong, were compelled to leave their ships in the harbor of New York before they hauled alongside the wharf, in order to escape prosecution, and were made to appear like criminals fleeing from justice. This cannot be considered a very cheerful welcome home after a voyage round the globe. Yet it compares not unfavorably with the reception sometimes accorded the returning traveller nowadays—at the hands of officers of the law empowered to collect "protective" duties on personal effects.

After a while this nefarious trade, by which shipowners, captains, officers, and crews were alike defrauded, perished by its own rapacity; but the attitude of the United States Government of half a century ago in permitting her splendid American merchant captains and officers to be subjected to gross indignities, and the foreign seamen sailing under her flag to be robbed and shipped away without their knowledge or consent, must ever remain a blot upon the page of American maritime history.

Those well-intentioned philanthropists who had an idea that sailors were being ill-treated on board American ships, and who wasted sympathy upon a class of men most of whom required severe discipline, might have been better employed had they exerted their energies toward purging the seaports of the country of the dens of vice and gangs of robbers that infested them, though this might not have been so romantic as a sentimental interest in the welfare of the sailor when encountering the supposed terrors of the deep. As a matter of fact, the lives, limbs, and morals of sailors at that period were very much safer at sea than they were on land.

It is refreshing to turn to one man, at least, who knew and understood sailors, and who in early life had himself been a sailor. This was the Rev. Edward Thompson Taylor, known upon every sea with respect and affection as "Father Taylor." In 1833 the Seaman's Bethel was erected in North Square, Boston, and there Father Taylor presided for some forty years. During that time he did an enormous amount of good, both among sailors themselves, to whom he spoke in language which they could understand and feel, and by drawing the attention of influential men and women to the lamentable condition of the life of sailors when on shore, not only in Boston, but in all the great seaports of the United States. For many years the Seaman's Bethel was one of the most interesting sights of Boston, and all classes were attracted there by the novel and picturesque earnestness and eloquence of Father Taylor. Distinguished visitors were usually taken there or went of their own accord, to listen to the words of this inspired seaman, and many of them have recorded their impressions. Harriet Martineau, J. S. Buckingham, M. P., Charles Dickens, Frederika Bremer, John Ross Dix, Mrs. Jameson, Catherine Sedgwick, and Walt Whitman all testified to the wonderful power of this homely, self educated Methodist preacher.

Lauchlan McKay

Philip Dumaresq

Clipper-Ship Captains

Father Taylor had little to say about the treatment of sailors on shipboard, for he knew that they were treated with humanity and according to their deserts, but he did have a great deal to say about their life and vile associations on shore; he once prayed with unconscious humor, "that Bacchus and Venus might be driven to the ends of the earth and off it." He possessed a marvellous power of description, and perhaps no poet or painter has more vividly portrayed the ever-changing moods of the ocean. He used these superb sea pictures as metaphors and illustrations. I have a clear remembrance of some of them and recall them with gratitude, but no words of mine can convey an adequate impression of their beauty and grandeur; his was a genius that eludes description.

It was once said of Father Taylor that he hated the devil more than he loved God, but I think whoever said this could not have understood him, for the affection, tenderness, and substantial help which Father Taylor lavished upon God's children, afflicted in body and mind, knew no bounds. At the same time he knew the men whom it was his mission to rescue, and often when denouncing their follies and vices his words fell hot as burning coals. He detested shams in any form, and was swift to detect them in sailors as well as in others.

In those days there was far too much ignorant sentimentality bestowed upon seamen and their affairs, too much

"Poor child of danger, nursling of the storm,
Sad are the woes that wreck thy manly form."

Sad enough, no doubt, to the captain of a clipper ship bound round Cape Horn, compelled to stand by and see his canvas slatting to pieces in the first bit of a blow outside Sandy Hook, because he was cursed with a crew unable or unwilling to handle it. But this seldom happened more than once aboard of an American clipper in the fifties, for such a crew was taken in hand and soon knocked into shape by the mates, carpenter, sailmaker, cook, steward, and boatswain. Belaying pins, capstan-bars, and heavers began to fly about the deck, and when the next gale came along the crew found that they could get aloft and make some kind of show at stowing sails, and by the time the ship got down to the line, they were usually pretty smart at handling canvas. As the clipper winged her way southward, and the days grew shorter, and the nights colder, belaying pins, capstan bars, and heavers were all back in their places, for system, order, and discipline had been established. When the snow-squalls began to gather on the horizon, and the old-time clipper lifted her forefoot to the first long, gray Cape Horn roller, with albatross and Cape pigeons wheeling and screaming in her wake, the mate, as he stood at the break of the quarter-deck in his long pilot-cloth watch-coat, woollen mittens, sea boots, and sou'wester, and sung out to the boatswain to get his men along for a pull on the weather braces, felt with pride that he had something under him that the "old man" could handle in almost any kind of weather—a well-manned ship.

In those days of carrying canvas as long and

sometimes longer than spars and rigging would stand, with only brawn, capstans and watch tackles to handle it, the crew was a far more important factor on board a sailing ship than in the present era of steel spars, wire rigging, double topsail, and topgallant yards, donkey engines and steam winches. Indeed, all the conditions were quite different from anything known at the present time and required a type of men, both forward and aft, that do not sail upon the ocean to-day.

CHAPTER IX

CALIFORNIA CLIPPERS OF 1850 AND THEIR COMMANDERS —MAURY'S WIND AND CURRENT CHARTS

AT the time of the discovery of gold in California, American ship-builders were well prepared for the work that lay before them. The clippers already built furnished valuable experience, for they had attracted much attention, and their models and construction were almost as well known to ship-builders throughout the country as to those from whose yards they had been launched. It was found that the clippers were much easier in a sea-way than the old type of vessel; they labored and strained less, and in consequence delivered their cargoes in better condition. When driven into a heavy head sea, they would bury their long, sharp bows in a smother of foam and drench the decks fore and aft with flying spray; but at a speed that would have swamped the full-bodied, wall-sided ships and made them groan in every knee, timber, and beam.

The superiority of the clippers in speed was even more marked in the average length and regularity of their voyages than in their record passages; they could be depended on not to make long passages; with their sharp lines and lofty canvas they were able to cross belts of calm and light winds much more quickly than the low rigged, full-bodied ships, while in strong head winds there was no comparison, as the sharper ships would work out to windward in weather that held the old type of vessels like a barrier, until the wind hauled fair or moderated. In a word, the clippers could go and find strong or favorable winds while the full-bodied ships were compelled to wait for them.

It must be admitted that some remarkably fast passages were made by the old full-built American vessels. We have seen Captain Waterman's record with the *Natchez,* and other cases of this kind might be cited; but they prove nothing beyond the fact that with a fair wind and enough of it, other things being equal, a well-handled, full-modelled ship is about as fast as a clipper; also that single passages except as between vessels sailing together, are not the most reliable tests of speed. A number of passages by the same vessel, or a record of best days' runs, afford a more accurate means of arriving at a just estimate of speed.

The first California clippers, thirteen in number, were launched during the year 1850, the *Celestial,* 860 tons, built by William H. Webb and owned by Bucklin & Crane, of New York, being the first to leave the ways. She was soon followed by the *Mandarin,* 776 tons, built by Smith & Dimon for Goodhue & Co., of New York, and the *Surprise,* 1361 tons, owned by A. A. Low & Brother; *Game-Cock,* 1392 tons, owned by Daniel C. Bacon, Boston, and the barque *Race Horse,* 512 tons, owned by Goddard & Co., Boston, all built by Samuel Hall at

East Boston. The *Witchcraft,* 1310 tons, was built at Chelsea by Paul Curtis, for S. Rogers & W. D. Pickman, of Salem; the *John Bertram,* 1080 tons, by R. E. Jackson at East Boston, for Glidden & Williams, of Boston; the *Governor Morton,* 1318 tons, by James M. Hood at Somerset, for Handy & Everett, of New York; the *Sea Serpent,* 1337 tons, by George Raynes at Portsmouth, New Hampshire, for Grinnell, Minturn & Co., of New York; the *Eclipse,* 1223 tons, by J. Williams & Son at Williamsburg, for T. Wardle & Co., of New York; the *Seaman,* 546 tons, by Bell & Co., at Baltimore, for Funck & Meincke, of New York; the *White Squall,* 1118 tons, by Jacob Bell, for W. Platt & Son, of Philadelphia, and the *Stag-Hound,* 1535 tons, by Donald McKay at East Boston, for Sampson & Tappan and George B. Upton, of Boston.

The *Celestial* was a remarkably good-looking ship and much sharper than any vessel built by Mr. Webb up to that time. She carried long, slender spars, with plenty of canvas, and proved a very fast and able ship.

The *Mandarin,* also a fine-looking ship, was intended by her builders to be an improved *Sea Witch,* and although she made some excellent passages, she never came up to the older vessel in point of speed; the *Sea Witch* was her builders' masterpiece, and they, like many others, found her a difficult ship to improve upon.

The *Surprise* was one of the most successful clipper ships ever constructed, and proved a mine of wealth for her owners. She was fully rigged on the stocks, with all her gear rove off, and was

The "Surprise"

launched with her three skysail yards across and colors flying, which attracted a multitude of people. They rather expected to see her capsize, and were no doubt highly delighted to find that nothing unusual happened as she glided swiftly down the ways, or at that critical instant when her hull was still partly supported on the land and partly on the waves, or when she swung to her anchors on even keel, with the beautiful skyline of Boston of half a century ago outlined in the distance.

Mr. Hall was a master ship-builder and had figured the weights, displacement, and stability of his ship with the same exactness with which an astronomer foretells the transit of a planet; yet with all the anxiety incident to experiments of this kind, he had found time for plans of a less serious nature. He had a pavilion erected in order that the mothers, wives, sisters, and daughters of the men who had built this beautiful ship might look with comfort upon the crowning scene of their kinsmen's labors, and after the ship was safely afloat, all were invited to a luxurious lunch served upon long tables in the mould loft, which was gaily decorated with flags. There the master foreman of the yard presided, while Mr. Hall entertained personal friends, whom he had asked to see the launch, at his own hospitable home.

The *Surprise* measured: length 190 feet, breadth 39 feet, depth 22 feet with 30 inches dead-rise at half floor. Her main-yard was 78 feet long from boom-iron to boom-iron, and her mainmast was 84 feet from heel to cap, with other spars in proportion. She was beautifully fitted throughout, was painted black from the water-line up, and carried a finely carved and gilded flying eagle for a figure-head, while her stern was ornamented with the arms of New York. She was manned by a crew of 30 able seamen, 6 ordinary seamen, 4 boys, 2 boatswains, a carpenter, a sailmaker, 2 cooks, a steward, and 4 mates, and was commanded by Captain Philip Dumaresq, who had gained a high reputation while in command of the *Antelope, Akbar,* and *Great Britain.*

Captain Dumaresq was born at Swan Island, near Richmond, on the Kennebec River. His father had settled there on an estate which came to him through his mother, who before her marriage was the beautiful Rebecca Gardiner, of Gardiner, Maine, and a daughter of the Rev. John Sylvester Gardiner, the first rector of Trinity Church, Boston. Unlike most American boys, who used to go to sea, young Dumaresq had no special desire for a life upon the ocean, but was sent on a voyage to China by his parents, under the advice of a physician, on account of his delicate health. He soon grew robust, and at the age of twenty-two took command of a vessel, afterwards becoming one of the most celebrated and widely known of all the American clipper ship captains.

When the *Surprise* arrived at New York to load for San Francisco, the New York *Herald* declared that she was the handsomest ship ever seen in the port, and a large number of persons gathered to see her placed at her loading berth by the steamer *R. B. Forbes,* which had towed her round from Boston.

The *R. B. Forbes* at that time, so to speak, was a well-known character about Massachusetts Bay, and no marine function seemed quite complete without her presence. She was generally on hand at launches, regattas, and Fourth of July celebrations, with a jolly party of Boston underwriters and their friends on board, accompanied by a band of music and well-filled hampers of refreshments. Her hull was painted a brilliant red up to the bulwarks, which were black, while the deck fittings, houses, and the inside of the bulwarks were a bright green. Altogether, with a rainbow of bunting over her mastheads, the brass band in full blast, and champagne corks flying about her deck, she contributed liberally to the gayety of many festive occasions. She was also usually the first to introduce a new-born ship to the end of a manila hawser, and for several years she towed most of the eastern-built clippers to their loading berths at Boston or New York.

But these were only the odd jobs at which she put in her time when not engaged in her more serious work of salvage operations, for she was the best equipped and most powerful wrecking steamer on the Atlantic coast, and saved much valuable property abandoned to the Boston Underwriters, for whom she was built by Otis Tafts at East Boston in 1845. She was 300 tons register, and was one of the few vessels at that date constructed of iron and fitted with a screw propeller, her engines and boilers being designed by the renowned Ericsson. Her commander, Captain Morris, not only was a very able wreck master, but did a great deal by experiment and observation to solve the intricate problems relating to the deviation of the magnetic needle on board of iron vessels, and was one of the few reliable authorities of his day upon this important subject. At the outbreak of the Civil War in 1861, the *R. B. Forbes* was purchased by the United States Government, but before the end of the war she was wrecked and became a total loss near Hatteras Inlet. It is hardly necessary to mention that this vessel was named in honor of that noble seaman, Captain Robert Bennett Forbes, whose acts of kindness and humanity were so many that a book might well be devoted to a record of them.

The *Witchcraft* was a very beautiful ship, and was commanded by Captain William C. Rogers, a son of one of the owners, for whom she was built. Captain Rogers was born at Salem in 1823 and had made several voyages as supercargo on board of different ships to Calcutta and Canton. He was a man of unusual ability, and although he never sailed before the mast, or as officer of a ship, he had acquired a knowledge of seamanship and navigation which enabled him to become one of the most famous among the younger clipper ship captains. He was a rare example of a gentleman who went to sea for the pure love of it, who enjoyed dealing with the useful realities of life, and liked a real ship with real sailors on board of her, and a real voyage of commerce profitable to mankind, in preference to an aimless life of luxury and pleasure.

During the Civil War Captain Rogers was one

of the twelve naval commanders appointed by Act of Congress, and he commanded the U. S. clipper barque *William G. Anderson,* which mounted six thirty-two pounders and a long rifled gun amidships, and carried a crew of one hundred and ten men. While in command of this vessel, Captain Rogers captured the Confederate privateer *Beauregard,* Captain Gilbert Hays, one hundred miles east-northeast of Abaco in the Bahamas, November 12, 1861. He also commanded the U. S. gunboat *Iuka,* and in her rendered valuable service to his country during the remainder of the war. He subsequently married a granddaughter of Nathaniel Bowditch, the illustrious navigator.

The *John Bertram* was an extremely sharp ship, and was the pioneer of Glidden & Williams's line of San Francisco clippers. She was named for Captain Bertram, one of Salem's most famous seamen and merchants, and was for several years commanded by Captain Landholm.

The *Sea Serpent* was the first clipper ship built by Mr. Raynes, and was a slender, rakish, handsome-looking craft, comparing favorably with the New York and Boston clippers of that year. She was commanded by Captain Williams Howland, a seaman of experience and ability, who was born at New Bedford in 1804. In 1833 he took command of the *Horatio,* then a new ship and afterwards famous, on her first voyage from New York to China, and remained in her for about ten years. He subsequently commanded the packet ships *Ashburton, Henry Clay, Cornelius Grinnell,* and the *Constantine.* Captain Howland was a gentleman of much dignity, who usually wore kid gloves when he came on deck and seldom gave his orders to any one but the officer of the watch. He had the reputation of being an A1 seaman and navigator.

The *White Squall* was another handsome clipper, very similar in construction and design to the *Samuel Russell* and *Oriental* from the same yard. Although but little more than eleven hundred tons register, this ship cost when ready for sea with one year's stores and provisions on board the sum of $90,000, and her freight from New York to San Francisco on her first voyage amounted to $70,000. She was commanded by Captain Lockwood, and her measurements were: length 190 feet, breadth 35 feet 6 inches, and depth 21 feet.

The *Stag-Hound,* at the time of her launch was the largest merchant ship ever built, though during the nine years that the Cunard Company had been running mail steamers across the Atlantic, the tonnage of American packet ships had steadily increased. In 1846, as we have seen, Donald McKay had built the *New World* of 1404 tons, and in 1849 William H. Webb launched the *Albert Gallatin* of 1435 tons, so that the *Stag-Hound,* 1535 tons, was not a very much larger vessel; but she was of a decidedly different design, having less beam and seventeen feet more length than either of these packets. She attracted much attention and many persons came to see her while she was building. A throng estimated at from twelve to fifteen thousand gathered about the shipyard at noon on December 7, 1850, to witness her launch. The weather was bitterly cold, with drift ice in the harbor and snow

The "Stag-Hound"

lying deep on the ground. It was feared that the launch might have to be postponed on account of the tallow freezing on the ways, but when she had settled in her cradle and everything was ready, a gang of men came from the forge bearing cans filled with boiling whale oil, which they poured upon the ways. When the word was given to knock away the dog shores, the vessel moved rapidly down the smoking ways and plunged into the gray, icy waters of the harbor, amid shouts and cheers from a shivering crowd, while the bells of Boston rang out mellow and clear, on the calm, frosty air, in welcome to the largest merchant ship afloat.

Launches were not then regarded as social functions, although some of the most prominent families in New York and Boston, who were interested in shipping, attended them, and a pavilion was usually erected where they might picnic comfortably and enjoy themselves. It was also not customary in those days for women to name ships, but the ceremony, which was simple and effective, was usually performed by the foreman of the yard from which the ship was launched. On this occasion, when the *Stag-Hound* began to move along the ways, the foreman had a black bottle of Medford rum somewhere about, which he seized by the neck and smashed across her forefoot, at the same time, in the excitement of the moment, shouting out, "*Stag-Hound,* your name's *Stag-Hound!*" and thus brought the ceremony to a close. This vessel measured: length 215 feet, breadth 40 feet, depth 21 feet, with 40 inches dead-rise at half floor. Her main-yard was 86 feet and her mainmast 88 feet in length. She was commanded on her first voyage by Captain Josiah Richardson, and carried a crew of 36 able seamen, 6 ordinary seamen, and 4 boys. When she arrived at New York in tow of the *R. B. Forbes,* to load for San Francisco, the ship fanciers of South Street were for once in their lives of one mind, and their opinion seems to have been that the *Stag-Hound* came pretty near being the perfection of the clipper ship type.

Each one of the clippers of 1850 proved a credit to the yard from which she was launched, and nearly all of them made the passage from New York or Boston to San Francisco in less than one hundred and ten days. This is an exceedingly good record, although the passage from New York has been made by two vessels, the *Flying Cloud* and the *Andrew Jackson,* in a few hours less than ninety days. In Appendix II. will be found the names of ships that made this passage in one hundred and ten days or less, with the dates of their arrivals at San Francisco, for the years 1850–1860. While this list includes almost all of the extreme clippers, still there were a number of ships that gave proof by their other records of being fast and ably commanded, and yet failed to come within the limit of one hundred and ten days.

As most persons are aware, foreign vessels have never been allowed to engage in the United States coasting trade, also that the voyage between Atlantic and Pacific ports of the United States has always been regarded as a coasting voyage. The California clippers therefore had no foreign competitors to sail against, but the racing among themselves was sufficiently keen to satisfy the most enthusiastic lover of sport, while China and Australia voyages afforded opportunities for international rivalry.

The only clipper ship to make the voyage to San Francisco prior to 1850 was the *Memnon,* under Captain George Gordon, which arrived there July 28, 1849, after a record passage of one hundred and twenty days from New York. The first contest of clippers round Cape Horn took place in 1850, between the *Houqua, Sea Witch, Samuel Russell,* and *Memnon,* old rivals on China voyages, and the new clippers *Celestial, Mandarin,* and *Race Horse.* All of these vessels had their friends, and large sums of money were wagered on the result, the four older ships, especially the *Sea Witch,* having established high reputations for speed. The *Samuel Russell* was commanded by Captain Charles Low, previously of the *Houqua,* while the *Houqua* was now commanded by Captain McKenzie; Captain Gordon was again in the *Memnon,* and Captain George Fraser, who had sailed with Captain Waterman as chief mate, commanded the *Sea Witch.*

The *Samuel Russell* arrived at San Francisco May 6, 1850, after a passage of 109 days from New York, thus knocking 11 days off the record, and her friends and backers felt confident that this passage could not be surpassed, at all events not by any of the clippers of that year. This opinion was in a measure confirmed when the *Houqua* arrived on July 23d, 120 days from New York, but on the following day the *Sea Witch* came romping up the bay, 97 days from Sandy Hook, reducing the record by another 12 days. This passage astonished every one, even her warmest admirers, and well it might, for it has never been equalled by a ship of her tonnage and not often excelled even by larger vessels. This performance of the *Sea Witch* was the more remarkable as she had rounded Cape Horn during the Antarctic midwinter.

The remainder of the fleet arrived in the following order: *Memnon,* September 27th, 123 days; *Celestial,* November 1st, 104 days; *Race Horse,* from Boston, November 24th, 109 days; and the *Mandarin,* November 29th, 126 days from New York. These were all fine passages, especially when we consider that none of the vessels was over 1100 tons register. The records show that from June 26 to July 28, 1850, seventeen vessels from New York and sixteen from Boston arrived at San Francisco, whose average passages were 159 days, so that even the *Mandarin's* passage of 126 days was very fast by comparison. We must remember also that none of these vessels had the advantage of using Maury's Wind and Current Charts, as at that time sufficient material had not been collected to perfect them.

Navigators of all nationalities are deeply indebted to Lieutenant Matthew Fontaine Maury, U. S. N., for it was his mind that first conceived the idea of exploring the winds and currents of the ocean. Lieutenant Maury was a Virginian by birth, and in 1825 at the age of nineteen, entered the United State Navy as a midshipman on board the frigate *Brandywine.* In 1830 he was appointed sailing master of the sloop of war *Falmouth,* and ordered to the Pacific station. At this time, being anxious to make a rapid passage round Cape Horn, he searched in vain for information relating to the winds and currents. His attention was thus directed to this subject, and it was upon this voyage that he conceived the design of his celebrated Wind and Current Charts. He also began at this time to write papers for the *American Journal of Science* which attracted much attention, and on his return he published a *Treatise on Navigation* which was made a text-book for the pupils of the Naval Academy at Annapolis.

In 1842 Lieutenant Maury was placed in charge of the Depot of Charts and Instruments at Washington, which afterwards became the National Observatory and Hydrographic Office. Here he devoted his attention to collecting and converting into systematic tables the valuable data contained in the old log-books of the United States warships, which he found stowed away as so much rubbish, and which had narrowly escaped being sold for junk. At the same time he presented a paper to the National Institute, recommending that all merchant ships be provided with charts of sailing directions, "on which should be daily registered all observable facts relating to the winds, currents, and other phenomena of importance and interest, for the foundation of a true theory of the winds."

A general use of these charts would have constituted one of the greatest exploring expeditions ever devised, but for a time it met with much opposition. Lieutenant Maury's first convert was Captain Jackson of the Baltimore ship *D. C. Wright,* trading to Rio Janeiro, who made rapid voyages with the aid of the Wind and Current Charts furnished by Lieutenant Maury. Soon there were many followers among American sea-captains, who gave their earnest co-operation and received great benefits in return, since all who kept Maury's Log, as it was called, were entitled to a copy of the Sailing Directions.

In 1856 the captains and officers of a fleet of no less than a thousand merchant ships, sailing under the United States flag upon every sea and ocean, were recording daily and almost hourly observations of the winds and currents. Under the British flag were to be counted the whole Navy of Great Britain and over one hundred merchantmen; under the flag of Holland, two hundred and twenty-five merchant ships and those of the Royal Navy. Besides these there were the ships of France, Spain, Portugal, Italy, Belgium, Prussia, Denmark, Sweden, Norway, Russia, Chili, Bremen, and Hamburg, all co-operating and assisting this great scientist in his noble work.

Maury's *Physical Geography of the Sea* (1853), the first work of the kind which appeared, ran through twenty editions and was translated into French, Dutch, Swedish, Spanish, and Italian. This book treats of the clouds, winds, and currents of the ocean in a scientific yet attractive manner, dispelling the last of the sea myths which for ages had been the delight of poets and the terror of sailors, and in their stead relating a story of scientific discovery of greater wonder and beauty than any fable.

Maury's researches had, however, a very practical side to them. Hunt's *Merchants' Magazine* for

Matthew Fontaine Maury

May, 1854, states that on the outward passages alone from New York to California, Australia, and Rio Janeiro, American ships, through the use of Maury's Sailing Directions, were saving in time the sum of $2,250,000 per annum, and it is probable that could an estimate have been made of the saving in time to all of the ships using the Sailing Directions, the total amount must have considerably exceeded $10,000,000 per annum.

It should be remembered that this result had been accomplished without expenditure of money, beyond the moderate salaries of Maury and his staff of assistants, and the insignificant cost of printing the blank log-books, charts, and sailing directions.

Sea-captains of all nations regarded Lieutenant Maury as a wise counsellor and faithful friend, while France, Holland, Sweden, Spain, Italy, Russia, Prussia, Austria, Portugal, and Sardinia, all either conferred upon him orders of knighthood or struck medals in his honor.

In 1861, Lieutenant Maury resigned the office of Chief Superintendent of the National Observatory and Hydrographic Office, deeming it his duty as a Virginian to take the side of his State at the outbreak of the Civil War. Upon this occasion he received letters of invitation from the Grand Duke Constantine offering him residence in Russia and every facility for continuing his scientific researches. A similar offer was made by Prince Napoleon on behalf of France, and also by the Archduke Maximilian of Austria. In 1866 a pecuniary testimonial was presented to Lieutenant Maury at Willis's Rooms, London, where he was entertained by English naval officers and scientific men of the highest distinction, Sir John Parkington being chairman. England, France, Russia, and Holland contributed 3000 guineas, a substantial token of their esteem and gratitude for his labors in the service of mankind.

On one occasion Secretary of the Navy, Graham, wrote to Lieutenant Maury as follows:

"Indeed, I doubt whether the triumphs of navigation and the knowledge of the sea, achieved under your superintendence of the Observatory, will not contribute as much to an effective Naval Service and to the national fame as the brilliant trophies of our arms."

Maury died in 1873, in his sixty-seventh year, an American scientist whose life was devoted to discovering the secrets of the sea, and to the welfare of seamen, irrespective of rank or nationality. In lamenting his death, the Senate of Virginia closed its resolutions with this eulogy:

"An honor to Virginia, an honor to America, and an honor to civilization, and in gratefully recognizing this we do but honor ourselves."

CHAPTER X

CALIFORNIA CLIPPERS OF 1851 AND THEIR COMMANDERS—A DAY ON BOARD THE "WITCH OF THE WAVE"

A LITTLE more than sixty thousand tons of shipping had been launched from the shipyards in and near New York during the year 1850, and over thirty thousand tons were still under construction there when the year closed, while the total tonnage of vessels built in the United States that year was 306,034 tons.

At this period the California clippers increased rapidly in size. Ships of a new type from 1500 to 2000 tons register, of which the *Stag-Hound* was the pioneer, were now being built, and ship-builders were called upon to deal with the problem of fitting wooden spars and hemp rigging that would stand the stress and strain of the enormous amount of canvas that these powerful vessels were expected to carry. The rigging and handling of this new type of long-limbed clipper, with her unexplored peculiarities, gave ship-builders and sea-captains some serious thinking and the ship lovers of South Street something to talk about and argue over.

Thirty-one California clippers were launched during the year 1851, and almost all the large shipyards along the Atlantic seaboard were represented by one or more. Donald McKay built the *Flying Cloud, Flying Fish,* and *Staffordshire;* William H. Webb, the *Challenge, Invincible, Comet, Gazelle,* and *Sword-Fish;* Fernald and Pettigrew, of Portsmouth, the *Typhoon;* Jacob A. Westervelt & Sons, the *Hornet* and *N. B. Palmer;* George Raynes, the *Wild Pigeon* and *Witch of the Wave;* Smith & Co., of Hoboken, the *Hurricane;* Perrin, Patterson & Stack, of Williamsburg, the *Ino;* Briggs Bros., of South Boston, the *Northern Light* and *Southern Cross;* Hood & Co., of Somerset, the *Raven;* J. O. Curtis, of Medford, the *Shooting Star;* J. Williams, the *Tornado,* Isaac Taylor, of Medford, the *Syren;* Trufant & Drummond, of Bath, the *Monsoon,* and Jacob Bell, the *Trade-Wind.*

It would be impossible to name the handsomest of these ships, for while they were all of the same general design, each possessed her special type of beauty; and beauty, as we all know, is elusive, depending largely on fashion and individual taste. In order to attract the favorable attention of shippers and to secure the highest rates of freight, it was necessary that these ships should be handsome as well as swift. Ship-owners were content to spend large sums of money, not only upon refined decoration, which was but a small portion of the expense, but also in carefully selected woods, such as India teak and Spanish mahogany for deck fittings, and in the finest shipwright's and joiner's work about the decks, which were marvels of neatness and finish.

Ship-builders certainly had every incentive to exercise their best skill upon these vessels; they received pretty much their own prices for building them, and each ship, as she sailed out upon the ocean, held in her keeping the reputation of her builder, to whom a quick passage meant fame and fortune. Six of the clipper ships launched in 1851, the *Flying Cloud, Comet, Sword-Fish, Witch of the Wave, Ino,* and *Northern Light,* established speed records that have not yet been broken, and as time rolls on, the probability that they ever will be, becomes less and less.

The *Flying Cloud* was originally contracted for by Enoch Train, the good friend of Donald McKay, but while on the stocks she was sold to Grinnell, Minturn & Co., under whose flag she sailed for a number of years. Mr. Train used to say that there were few things in his life that he regretted more than parting with this ship. She was 1783 tons register, and measured: length 225 feet, breadth 40 feet 8 inches, depth 21 feet 6 inches, with 20 inches dead-rise at half floor. Her main-yard was 82 feet and her mainmast 88 feet in length, and like all the large clippers of her day, she carried three standing skysail yards; royal, topgallant and topmast studdingsails at the fore and main, square lower studdingsails with swinging booms at the fore; single topsail yards, with four reef bands in the topsails; single reefs in the topgallant sails, and topsail and topgallant bowlines.

She was commanded by Captain Josiah Perkins Creesy, who was born at Marblehead in 1814. Like most boys who were brought up along the coast of Massachusetts Bay, he began his career by being skipper and all hands of a borrowed thirteen-foot dory, with the usual leg-o'-mutton sail, and steered by an oar over her lee gunwale. In these dories water was carried in a strong earthen jug with a stout handle to which a tin drinking-cup was usually attached, while a wooden dinner-pail, such as the Gloucester fishermen used in those days, contained provisions. When the rode line was coiled down clear with the killick stowed away forward, and the dinner-pail, wooden bailer, and water jug had been made fast with a lanyard to the becket in the stern sheets, the famous Cape Ann dory was about ready for sea.

Joe Creesy was a genuine boy, large and strong for his age, freckled, good-tempered, and fond of rowing, sailing, and fishing. When he got to be thirteen or fourteen years old, he used to get some one to lend him a dory, and in this, during his summer vacation, he would make short cruises to Beverly and sometimes to the neighboring port of Salem. Here he would loiter about the wharves, watching an Indiaman discharge her fragrant cargo, or perhaps some ship fitting out for another voyage to India or China; and he would gaze up in wonder and admiration at the long tapering masts, with their lofty yards and studdingsail booms, and what appeared to him to be a labyrinth of blocks and slender threads. The ships' figureheads, especially those representing warriors and wild animals, pleased Joe mightily, and the spare spars, gratings, capstans, boats, guns, and shining brass work, all delighted his heart. Occasionally he would behold a sea-captain who had really sailed to Calcutta and

Canton, and the bronzed mariner was to him a being quite apart from other mortals.

At that time Salem retained much of the spicy, maritime flavor of the olden days, and these pleasant summer cruises to the old seaport naturally captivated the boy's imagination, until he yearned for the time when he, too, might stand upon the quarter-deck in command of a noble ship. It would, of course, have been sinful to keep a boy like this on land, so he was permitted to follow his inclination and ship before the mast on board of a vessel bound for the East Indies. He advanced steadily through all the grades on shipboard, and became a captain at twenty-three.

When Captain Creesy was appointed to command the *Flying Cloud,* he was well known in New York, as he had commanded the ship *Oneida,* for a number of years in the China and East India trade, and bore a high reputation among ship-owners and underwriters, many of whom were his personal friends and associates.

The *Flying Fish* was owned by Sampson & Tappan, who, with George B. Upton, were the leading Boston ship-owners of their day, and between them owned the largest and finest clipper ships belonging to that port. These firms were composed of men in the prime of life, who enjoyed owning fast and handsome vessels. They cared for nothing but the best in design, construction, and equipment, and fitted out their ships with spare gear, stores, and provisions upon a most generous scale. The *Flying Fish* was 1505 tons register and measured: length 198 feet 6 inches, breadth 38 feet 2 inches, depth

22 feet, with 25 inches dead-rise at half floor. Her commander, Captain Edward Nickels, had sailed out of Boston for a number of years in command of the ship *John Quincy Adams,* and was a fine seaman and navigator. He was fond of entertaining his friends while in home and foreign ports, and his jolly little lunches and dinners were regarded as models of refined hospitality on shipboard. Commander John A. H. Nickels, U. S. N., is a son of Captain Edward Nickels.

Mr. Webb's *Challenge,* a still larger merchantman than had yet been constructed, was regarded with pride by the shipping men of New York. The *Challenge* registered 2006 tons, and measured: length 230 feet 6 inches, breadth 43 feet 6 inches, depth 27 feet 6 inches, with 42 inches dead-rise at half floor. Her mainmast was 97 feet and main-yard 90 feet in length, and the lower studdingsail booms were 60 feet long; with square yards and lower studdingsails set, the distance from boom end to boom end was 160 feet. She carried 12,780 running yards of cotton canvas, which was woven especially for her by the Colt Manufacturing Company. Her mainsail measured: 80 feet on the head, 100 feet on the foot, with a drop of 47 feet 3 inches, and 49 feet 6 inches on the leach. She had four reefs in her topsails, and single reefs in her top-gallant sails, and carried skysails, studdingsails, and ringtail. She was owned by N. L. & G. Griswold, of New York, and was commanded by Captain Robert H. Waterman, late of the *Sea Witch.*

The *Invincible,* owned by J. W. Phillips and others, of New York, was 1767 tons register, and measured: length 221 feet, breadth 41 feet 6 inches, depth 24 feet 10 inches. She was commanded by Captain H. W. Johnson, a gentleman who possessed a merry wit and a vivid imagination. Some of his experiences by land and sea, as related by himself, were certainly startling, and he told them with a minuteness of detail and an earnestness of manner that carried conviction equal to the most realistic illusions of the drama. There was one story about a mutiny on board the British brig *Diadem*, of which vessel Johnson said he was second mate. This craft carried a Lascar crew, and was in the Bay of Bengal, bound from Calcutta to Hong-kong with a cargo of opium, when a mutiny broke out in which all hands took part with such ferocious valor that the second mate and the serang, both badly wounded, were the only survivors.

The listeners are shown the dead bodies of Europeans and Asiatics, lying about the blood-stained deck under the fierce rays of the southern sun, and we breathe the tainted air, while chattering cormorants and screeching fishhawks tear the thin clothing of the corpses into shreds and fight with claw and beak over the decaying flesh. Johnson and the serang, so widely separated by blood, language, and religion, now united by a bond of common suffering, help each other to crawl into the caboose for shelter from the heat and from the birds of prey. Now we hear the gentle chafing of the gear aloft, and the lazy slatting of the sails, as the brig rolls upon the long, glassy swell; we see the sun sink beyond the ocean's rim in a glory of gold and purple that illumines the zenith and turns the sea into a lake of fire; and we feel the benediction of the cool twilight and whispering breeze.

In the silence of the night, the two men, weak from loss of blood, drag themselves aft to the deserted cabin; Johnson lowers himself down the companion and gropes his way to the pantry, where he finds food to share with his companion. In the captain's cabin he finds a decanter of brandy and a tumbler in the rack at the foot of the berth; he fills the glass and pours the spirit down his parched throat to brace his shattered nerves, then fills the glass again and takes it to the serang, but the faithful follower of Mahomet refuses to lift it to his burning lips. We live with them as they work their little vessel back to the muddy waters of the Hooghly and sight a pilot brig lying at anchor on her station, and their joy is ours when the pilot, with his leadsman, servant, and boat's crew, comes on board. Again these unfortunate men, haggard and still suffering from their wounds, are being tried in an Anglo–Indian Court of Justice under a charge of murder on the high seas, and we hear the judge pronounce their solemn sentence of death.

The scenes to which I have referred were so real that it seemed as if Johnson, while describing them, must have believed this story himself, and it was interesting to note the effect upon those who heard it for the first time, when, after giving a circumstantial account of the miraculous escape of the serang and himself from the Calcutta prison during the night before they were to be hanged, he would cheerfully remark, "Well, now, I call that a pretty good yarn to spin out of nothing." Then some one, perhaps a lady, might say, "Why, Captain Johnson, is it not true?" and he would smile pleasantly and reply, "True? Why bless your soul, I never heard of a brig called the *Diadem*, and never was in Calcutta in my life." He had a number of these stories, and in China we never tired of listening to them.

Captain Johnson was an uncommonly able man and a most agreeable companion. He remained in command of the *Invincible* for several years, and in the early sixties he took in succession three frail wooden side-wheel river steamboats, the *Fire Dart*, *Fire Cracker*, and *Fire Queen*, from New York round the Cape of Good Hope to China, with no accident or mishap—a remarkable achievement. In 1866, Captain Johnson was the navigator, but not in command, of the yacht *Vesta* in her race with the *Henrietta* and *Fleetwing* across the Atlantic.

The *Comet* was 1836 tons register, and measured: length 229 feet, breadth 42 feet, depth 22 feet 8 inches. She was owned by Bucklin & Crane, of New York, and was commanded by Captain E. C. Gardner, late of the *Celestial*, in whose hands she gained a high reputation for speed.

The *Sword-Fish* was owned by Barclay & Livingston, of New York, and was 1036 tons register; length 169 feet 6 inches, breadth 36 feet 6 inches, depth 20 feet. Although not so extremely sharp as the larger ships built by Mr. Webb during that year, she was quite as handsome, and while commanded by Captain Babcock she eclipsed them all in speed.

Captain David Sherman Babcock, brother-in-law of Captain N. B. Palmer, was born at Stonington in 1822, and came of a distinguished family, his father being Major Paul Babcock and his grandfather Colonel Harry Babcock of Revolutionary fame. He received the usual New England school education of those days, which appears to have been a sufficient equipment for some of the most useful men that the United States has yet produced.

As a boy David developed a strong desire for a seafaring life, which cannot be wondered at, as at that period Stonington and the neighboring town of Mystic were flourishing seaports, whose ships sailed to every quarter of the globe, and whose jovial mariners kept the social atmosphere well charged with shadowy visions of strange lands, ancient temples, pagodas, palms, and coral isles lying in distant tropical seas. The departure of a ship with colors flying, the crisp, incisive orders of her captain and mates, and the clomp, clomp, clomp, of the windlass pawl, the songs of the sailors heaving up anchor, the hum of the running gear as it rendered through the blocks, and the music of their straining sheaves to the last long pulls on sheets and halliards, were a more potent means of recruiting bright, young boys, soon to become mates and captains of American ships, than all the press-gangs that were ever heard of.

So it came about that young Babcock, at the age of sixteen, was allowed to ship as boy before the mast with Captain Nat Palmer on board the *Hiber-*

nia, and later he sailed again with Captain Palmer as an officer on board the *Garrick.* After making voyages to India and China on board of various ships, he was appointed at the age of twenty-five to command the ship *Charlestown* on a voyage to Callao and Lima. In 1850, Captain Babcock married Charlotte, the youngest daughter of Joseph Noyes, of Stonington, and W. I. Babcock, the well-known naval architect and engineer, who first introduced the scientific construction of steel vessels on the Great Lakes, is their son.

The *Typhoon* was owned by D. & A. Kingsland, of New York, and was commanded by Captain Charles H. Salter, who was born at Portsmouth in 1824, and an ancestor of his, Captain John Salter, commanded a vessel in the European trade during Colonial times, and for generations the Salters had sailed out of Portsmouth in command of ships. Captain Charles Salter went to sea at an early age, and at twenty-two commanded the ship *Venice* and later the *Samuel Badger.*

The *Typhoon* was 1610 tons register, and measured: length 225 feet, breadth 41 feet 6 inches, depth 23 feet. She was fully rigged on the stocks and was launched with skysail-yards aloft and colors flying. Before loading for San Francisco she was sent by her owners to Liverpool and made the passage from Portsmouth during the month of March in 13 days, 10 hours from wharf to dock. She frequently ran 15½ knots by the log on this passage, her best day's run being 346 miles. At Liverpool she attracted much attention, as she was not only the first American clipper, but also the largest merchant ship that had ever been seen at that port.

The *N. B. Palmer* was 1490 tons register, and measured: length 214 feet, breadth 39 feet, depth 22 feet. She was owned by A. A. Low & Brother, and was commanded by another brother, Captain Charles Porter Low. He was born at Salem in 1824, and when a child removed with his parents to Brooklyn. At any early age he manifested a decided liking for ships and the society of sailors, and much against the wishes of his parents, he determined to go to sea. In 1842 he shipped as boy before the mast on board of the *Horatio,* with Captain Howland and made the round voyage to China. He made a voyage to Liverpool with Captain Griswold in the *Toronto* as ordinary seaman, and was an able seaman on board the *Courier* to Rio Janeiro. He then sailed as third, second, and chief mate of the *Houqua,* with the brothers, Captain Nat, Alexander, and Theodore Palmer, and at the age of twenty-three took command of that ship. As we have seen, he also commanded the *Samuel Russell* on her first voyage to San Francisco.

The *N. B. Palmer* was perhaps the most famous ship built in the Westervelt yard. In China she was known as "the Yacht," and with her nettings in the tops, brass guns, gold stripe, and her lavish entertainments on the Fourth of July and Washington's Birthday, she well deserved the title. Her captain was a princely host, as well as a thorough seaman, and a fine navigator. A full-rigged model of the *N. B. Palmer* was exhibited at the Crystal Palace, London, in 1851, and attracted much attention as a fine example of the American clipper-ship type.

The *Hurricane* was owned by C. W. & H. Thomas, of New York, and registered 1607 tons. She had the reputation of being the sharpest ship ever built at or near New York, and she carried plenty of canvas, with Cunningham's rolling topsails, being one of the first American vessels so fitted. Across the lower part of her foretopsail she carried her name painted in large black letters that could be read much further than any signals and looked very smart and shipshape. Her commander, Captain Samuel Very, was born at Salem in 1815, and was a son of John Crowninshield Very, a mariner who had sailed on many a brave Salem ship. Among other experiences, he was one of the survivors of a shipwreck in mid-ocean during the year 1810, when he was picked up by a passing vessel after twenty-three days in an open boat. Admiral Samuel W. Very, U. S. N., is a son of Captain Samuel Very, and was born at Liverpool while the *Hurricane* lay in the Mersey.

The *Northern Light,* of 1021 tons register, measured: length 180 feet, breadth 36 feet, depth 21 feet 6 inches. She was a very sharp ship below the water-line, with 40 inches dead-rise at half floor, and full, powerful lines above water and on deck. She was built by the Briggs Brothers at South Boston, and owned by James Huckins of Boston. Mr. Huckins was a jolly, kind-hearted gentleman whom every one liked. His house-flag was a white field, swallowtail, with a blue star in the centre, and when he took his two sons into partnership, he placed two exceedingly small blue stars in the upper and lower luff of the flag, as he remarked, "to represent their interest in the business." This, however, was his joke, as he was most liberal in every way. After this ship had made her celebrated record passage from San Francisco to Boston, Mr. Huckins usually closed his discussions upon the speed of clipper ships by saying, "Well, anyway, none of them can beat my *Northern Light.*"

The *Trade Wind* measured: length 248 feet, breadth 40 feet, depth 25 feet, and was 2030 tons register, being 24 tons larger than the *Challenge.* Those two ships were the largest clippers that were ever built at or about New York, and with the exception of the *Ocean Monarch,* a packet ship of 2145 tons register, built by William H. Webb in 1856, were the largest sailing ships ever constructed at that port. The *Trade Wind* was an exceedingly sharp and handsome ship, and attracted a great deal of attention. It was estimated that more than thirty thousand persons gathered about Jacob Bell's shipyard at the foot of Houston Street, East River, one bright morning in August of that year to see her launched. She was owned by W. Platt & Son, of Philadelphia, and was commanded by Captain W. H. Osgood, late of the ship *Valparaiso.*

The *Nightingale,* one of the most beautiful clippers launched in 1851, was not built for the California trade, but was originally intended for a yacht. This ship was constructed by Samuel Hanscom, at Portsmouth, with the intention of carrying passengers to the World's Fair, held in London during that year, and was fitted with extensive and

The "Nightingale"

luxurious accommodations for that purpose, her between-decks being given up to large saloons and staterooms. It was proposed, after her arrival at London, to exhibit her in the Thames as a model American clipper ship, and no expense or skill was spared to make her a worthy representative. She was 1066 tons register, length 178 feet, breadth 36 feet, depth 20 feet, with 36 inches dead-rise at half floor.

Unfortunately, when the *Nightingale* was nearly completed, and ready for launching, her owners fell short of money. Mr. Hanscom, however, carried out his contract, and the ship was finished and then put into the hands of Governor Goodwin, of Portsmouth, to dispose of, each sub-contractor agreeing to accept his *pro rata* share of the proceeds. She was taken to Boston and there attracted the attention of Sampson & Tappen, who were so well pleased with the ship that they gladly paid the sum of $75,000 for her. This left the sub-contractors, such as sparmakers, sailmakers, riggers, and blockmakers, an additional profit beyond their contract, and Mr. Hanscom also realized a larger amount than he would have received under the original contract. So great was the excitement over the news from California, and so keen the demand for clippers at this time, that almost any of them could have been sold for a substantial advance upon their contract price. Those were the palmy days of the ocean carrying trade, and at no period before, or since, have ships yielded such golden harvests to their builders and owners.

The *Witch of the Wave* registered 1494 tons, and measured: length 202 feet, breadth 40 feet, depth 21 feet, with 40 inches dead-rise at half floor. Her mainmast was 90 feet and her mainyard 81 feet in length. Though built at Portsmouth, she was owned by Captain John Bertram and Alfred Peabody, of Salem, and was the pride of that ancient seaport. It was usual in those days for owners to entertain on board their ships when favorable opportunity offered, so the trip of the *Witch of the Wave* from Portsmouth to Salem to obtain her register was made an occasion of festivity.

The first of May was the day selected, but lowering clouds and squalls of wind and rain decided Captain Bertram to postpone the cruise until more favorable weather, and those of his guests who had appeared upon the scene were rewarded by an opportunity to examine the ship at their leisure. They found her a very handsome vessel, with grace and beauty in every line and curve of her hull. Her decks were remarkably clear, with plenty of room for working ship, and the between-decks had more than ample head room and were well ventilated. Her figurehead represented a young woman partially clad in gossamer drapery of white and gold, with one shapely arm extended and her small bare feet lightly stepping upon the crest of a wave, while the stern was ornamented with a seashell in which a child was being drawn by dolphins. These designs were executed by John W. Mason, of Boston, and were of decided artistic merit. The cabins and staterooms were finished in the most luxurious manner, the wainscot of the main cabin being of rosewood, birdseye maple, satin and zebra wood, exquisitely polished, with cornices and mouldings of white and gold.

After an inspection of the ship lunch was served, and Ephraim F. Miller, Collector of the Port of Salem, proposed the following toast: "Success to the newest and youngest of the Salem Witches. She perhaps includes in her composition an equal amount of craft with her unfortunate predecessors. Had they possessed a proportional share of her beauty, we are confident that the sternest tribunal before which any of them were arraigned, would never have had the heart to subject a single one to the trial to which their successor is designed—the Trial by Water." This sentiment was received with applause by the company, who then separated, some returning to Salem by train, while others remained over night, to be ready for the next day in case the weather improved. In the evening the Raynes Mansion was the scene of generous hospitality.

During the night the sky cleared, the sun came up warm and bright with a pleasant northwesterly breeze, and the early morning found Portsmouth in a state of bustle and excitement. Wagons laden with hampers, bags, and boxes of good things, with plenty of ice to keep them cool, were unloaded alongside the ship, and presently the *R. B. Forbes* appeared steaming up the river with a big bone in her teeth, the embodiment of energy and strength. The morning train came in, bringing a large number of men and women, from Boston, Salem, and Newburyport, who, with the Portsmouth guests, made a distinguished company of more than two hundred persons.

At about eleven o'clock, everything being ready, the *Witch of the Wave,* with colors flying and the Boston Cadet Band on board playing "The Star-Spangled Banner," was towed out into the stream amid the shouts and cheers of a multitude of people, who thronged the wharves and shipyards along the river. After passing through the Narrows and rounding New Castle Point, the *R. B. Forbes,* which had been towing alongside, took her hawser out ahead and shaped a course for Cape Ann, which brought the wind well over the starboard quarter. The breeze had freshened, though the sea was still quite smooth, and this, with the clear, blue sky and bright sunshine, made a day altogether too fine to be spent on shore.

Many of those on board were interested to see what effect some canvas would have on the new clipper, so Mr. Raynes said to Captain Bertram that he thought it might perhaps be a good plan to set some sail, "just to assist the tow-boat a little." Captain Bertram, with a twinkle in his eye, said he thought so, too, and gave orders to loose the topsails, jib, and foretopmast staysail. The *Witch of the Wave* had a crew of Portsmouth riggers, shipped by the run to Boston, and it did not take them long to put the topsails on her. As soon as the yards were braced, she began to dart through the water like a fish, and soon ranged up on the weather beam of the *R. B. Forbes,* the hawser towing between them with the bight skipping along among the blue waves in showers of sparkling spray.

On board the *R. B. Forbes* the safety valve was lifting, with steam at thirty pounds pressure murmuring in protest to the breeze. There was great joy on board the *Witch of the Wave,* with clapping of hands and waving of handkerchiefs, while the band struck up "A Life on the Ocean Wave." The log was hove, and she took nine and one half knots off the reel. The topsail yards were then lowered on the caps, and the reef tackles hauled out, yet with only this small canvas, the *R. B. Forbes* did not have much towing to do.

After rounding Thacher's Island, a banquet was served on tables in the between-decks, which were decorated with the ensigns of all nations, and at the close of the entertainment speeches were made by E. H. Derby, a grandson of Salem's great merchant of that name, Charles H. Parker, Henry N. Hooper, and the Hon. Charles W. Upham; then the following resolution was adopted with hearty cheers:

"Ship *Witch of the Wave,*
"Off Salem Light, May 2, 1851.

"At a meeting of invited guests, held this afternoon, it was unanimously

"*Resolved*—That the ladies and gentlemen here assembled gratefully acknowledge the courtesy, kindness, and generous hospitality of Captain John Bertram and the other owners of the *Witch of the Wave,* on this festive day, and tender their best wishes for the success of this noble vessel.

"E. H. Derby, *Chairman.*

"Charles H. Parker, *Secretary.*"

After this, Jonathan Nicholas, of Salem, recited the following impromptu lines:

"I wonder what 's the dreadful row
They 're kicking up in Portsmouth now!
The people running up and down
Crying 'All Salem 's come to town!'

Clear the track, the ship is starting!
Clear the track, the ship is starting!
Clear the track, the ship is starting!
And Portsmouth hearts are sad at parting.

"They say a man came down to-day
To carry the *Witch of the Wave* away;
And the people think he ought n't oughter
Just because he 's been and brought her.

"They called it rainy yesterday,
But I know better, anyway;
'T was only Portsmouth people crying
To see the good ship's colors flying!

"But Captain B. said, 'Hang the sorrow!
The sun is bound to shine to-morrow.'
And when he speaks it 's no use talking—
So the clouds and the blues, they took to walking.

"And so to-day the sun shines bright,
And Salem sends her heart's delight;
And the good ship flies, and the wind blows free,
As she leaps to her lover's arms—the sea!

"They have crowded her deck with the witty and
wise,
The saltest wisdom and merriest eyes;
And manned her yards with a gallant crew
That it tickles her staunch old ribs to view.

"They say she 's bound to sail so fast
That a man on deck can't catch the mast!
And a porpoise trying to keep ahead,
Will get run over and killed stone dead.

"Then here 's a health to the hands that wrought
her,
And three times three to the mind that thought
her
For thought 's the impulse, work 's the way
That brings all Salem here to-day.

"Clear the track, the ship is starting!
Clear the track, the ship is starting!
Clear the track, the ship is starting!
And Portsmouth hearts are sad at parting."

Repeated rounds of applause greeted this effusion, and the company went on deck where music called the dancers to their feet. The wind had died out, and as the sun began to set in the west, the *Witch of the Wave* anchored in Salem harbor. The day's pleasure was brought to a close by a portion of the company singing these lines of Whittier's that had been set to music for the occasion:

"God bless her wheresoe'er the breeze
Her snowy wings shall fan,
Beside the frozen Hebrides
Or sultry Hindostan!

"Where'er, in mart or on the main,
With peaceful flag unfurled,
She helps to wind the silken chain
Of commerce round the world.

"Her pathway on the open main
May blessings follow free,
And glad hearts welcome back again
Her white sails from the sea!"

The guests were landed in boats at Phillips's wharf, in time to reach their homes by the early evening trains, and on the following day the *R. B. Forbes* towed the *Witch of the Wave* to Boston, where she loaded in Glidden & Williams's Line for San Francisco, under the command of Captain J. Hardy Millett.

CHAPTER XI

CALIFORNIA CLIPPER PASSAGES OF 1851

EACH of the clippers had her devoted admirers, who gave tangible proof of loyalty by investing money liberally in support of their belief in her speed. At that period the merchants and ship-owners of Boston used to meet "on 'change" in front of the old Merchants' Exchange in State Street, and before going home to their comfortable two o'clock dinners, these old-time gentlemen would lay many a quiet wager upon the *Northern Light, Flying Fish, Witch of the Wave, Raven, John Bertram, Shooting Star,* or *Game Cock* as to their relative speed and the length of their passages from Boston to San Francisco.

In New York the Astor House was the meeting-place of merchants, ship-builders, and sea-captains, who carried on endless arguments concerning the merits of the clipper ships, their builders, owners, and captains, and discussed the latest shipping news with untiring earnestness. These men knew whereof they spoke, for almost any evening there was sufficient capital represented by ship-owners to pay for half a dozen clippers, and the men were there also who could build and navigate them. Occasionally an argument would reach a point of animation where something had to be done, and one might hear a remark very much like this: "No, no, Henry, I can't do that, but I will lay five dollars at one to three on the *Challenge* against the fleet, bar one, or the same even on the *Flying Cloud* against the *N. B. Palmer.*" These were pleasant evenings, gay with the clink of mugs and glasses and the murmur of small talk and laughter rippling among wreaths of smoke from fragrant Havanas, until, at a little before ten, Michael, the venerable barkeeper would announce, "Gentlemen, I will take the last orders of the evening; we close in ten minutes."

The interest in clippers was not confined to seamen and capitalists, for when the mail steamer from Aspinwall was reported toiling up the bay, there would be a large number of persons patiently waiting on the wharf, who were not expecting friends among the passengers or crew, but who had come to hear the latest news, then five or six weeks old, of arrivals of clipper ships at San Francisco.

The first clipper to arrive at San Francisco from New York in 1851 in less than 110 days was the *Seaman,* a smart little Baltimore ship of 546 tons. She made a fine passage of 107 days, arriving on March 11th.

The second to arrive was the *Surprise.* A merchant of San Francisco wagered heavily on her beating the passage of the *Sea Witch*—97 days—of the year before, and as the time limit grew near he began to feel rather nervous. On the morning of her ninety-sixth day out, March 19th, he thought if the *Surprise* was going to win his money for him it was about time for her to do it, so he mounted his horse and rode over to the North Beach to get a glimpse of her if she was in sight. He found the weather thick outside and so returned, but he had not reached his counting-room before the *Surprise* had passed the Golden Gate. And by noon, Captain Dumaresq was with his friends on shore, 96 days from New York. The *Surprise* had sailed 16,308 miles since leaving Sandy Hook, and had reefed topsails but twice. It should not, however, be supposed that she had not had plenty of wind, for it was usually blowing hard when Captain Dumaresq began to think of taking in his topgallantsails, to say nothing of reefing topsails. A list of her cargo on this voyage filled a manifest twenty-five feet long, and her freight amounted to the sum of $78,000.

The *Sea Serpent* arrived on May 17th, after putting into Valparaiso for repairs, as she had lost spars and sails off Cape Horn. She had made the passage in 115 days, deducting her delay at Valparaiso. This was the first of a series of disasters which befell the clippers that year, and which proved pretty clearly that their power of carrying canvas had been underestimated. It became quite evident that these ships could stand stouter spars and rigging, and indeed required them.

The *Eclipse,* Captain Hamilton, also went into Valparaiso with the loss of some of her spars and sails, and allowing for her loss of time in port, made the passage from New York to San Francisco in 112 days, arriving May 20th, with the remarkable run of 63 days from New York to Valparaiso to her credit. Captain Hamilton was not only an accomplished mariner, but a most delightful companion, and he had many friends in San Francisco, some of whom gave a dinner at the Niantic Hotel in honor of his arrival on this occasion. When the proper moment came, one of the party proposed the health of Captain Hamilton, and this is the way he did it:

"Gentlemen! I give you the shipper-clips—the clippy—sh—the, gentlemen, I give you the—the slipper." Here he paused, steadied himself by the table edge, bowed with great dignity, and began again very slowly: "Gentlemen!—I—give—you—the—ship—*E—clipse,* and her gallant cap'n Hamilton," and then with an at-peace-with-all-the-world grin, this disciple of Silenus subsided.

The Niantic had a curious history, even for a San Francisco hotel. This refuge for the traveller, or rather a portion of it, had originally been the British ship *Niantic* which arrived at Valparaiso from Liverpool just as the California gold fever was at its height. She was bought by a Chilean merchant and started for Panama, where she loaded a cargo of tropical fruits and two hundred and forty-eight passengers, and arrived at San Francisco, July 5, 1849. Most of the fruit had either been devoured by the passengers or become so decayed that it was thrown overboard, and as soon as the anchor was down, the captain and all hands cleared out for the mines, leaving the ship to take care of herself.

After some months of neglect, she was bought

by a real estate speculator, who hauled her broadside to on the beach, at what was then the foot of Clay Street, and turned her into a warehouse. By degrees the old craft found herself embedded in some ten or twelve feet of sand and mud at a considerable distance from the water-front, but she made more money for her owner here than at any other time in her career, until one of the periodical fires swept away her top sides. The rest of her hull, which being below ground had escaped destruction, became the cellar of the Niantic Hotel, erected over her remains, and had the reputation of being the only tight and dry cellar in the neighborhood.

In the course of time the Niantic Hotel was torn down to make room for a more substantial building, and upon clearing away the débris to secure a more solid foundation, thirty-five baskets of champagne were discovered hidden away among the floor timbers of the old hull, where they had remained unmolested for some twenty-one years. So faithfully had the wine been bottled and so dry had been its resting-place, that there was not a speck of rust on the wires securing the corks, and the labels were as fresh as the day they were put on, while the wine was found to have retained much of its original sparkle and *bouquet*. It was the then celebrated Jacquesson Fils brand, which at the time of its arrival might easily have been sold for $25 a bottle. I am not sure that it did not sell at nearly its former value, for almost every one in San Francisco in 1870 needed at least one bottle with which to celebrate the anniversary of his arrival "in the fall of Forty-nine or the spring of Fifty," and thirty-five baskets would seem a small allowance for that vast and increasing multitude.

The *Stag-Hound* arrived May 26th. She sailed from New York in January, and when six days out in a heavy southeast gale, her maintopmast and three topgallantmasts came down by the run. She was without a maintopsail for nine days and without topgallantsails for twelve days; nevertheless, she crossed the equator 21 days from Sandy Hook, arrived at Valparaiso in 66 days under jury rig, and, allowing for her detention there, reached San Francisco 107 days from New York. Captain Richardson reported that she was a very fast ship in moderate breezes, while in strong winds she frequently logged sixteen and seventeen knots, although her best day's run was only 358 miles.

The *Witchcraft* arrived August 11th. She, too, had suffered aloft and put into Valparaiso for spars and repairs, and, allowing for this delay, she had made the passage from New York in 103 days. The *N. B. Palmer* arrived August 21st in 108 days, and the *Flying Cloud* on August 31st in 89 days—a passage never surpassed and only twice equalled—once three years later by the *Flying Cloud* herself, and once in 1860 by the *Andrew Jackson.*

The *Flying Cloud's* abstract log on this passage is as follows:

Sandy Hook to the equator	21	days.
Equator to 50° S.	25	"
50° S. in the Atlantic to 50° S. in Pacific	7	"
50° S. to the equator	17	"
Equator to San Francisco	19	"
Total	89	"

It was during this passage that the *Flying Cloud* made her famous run of 374 miles, while steering to the northward and westward under topgallantsails, after rounding Cape Horn. This was the fastest day's run, under steam or sail, that had ever been made up to that time, and exceeded by 42 miles the best day's run that had ever been made by a mail steamship on the Atlantic. A few extracts from her log will, I think, be of interest:

"June 6th (three days out from New York). Lost main and mizen topgallantmasts, and maintopsail yard.—June 7th. Sent up main and mizen topgallantmasts and yards.—June 8th. Sent up maintopsail yard.—June 14th. Discovered mainmast badly sprung about a foot from the hounds, and fished it.—July 11th. Very severe thunder and lightning, double reefed topsails, split fore and maintopmast stay sails. At 1 P.M. discovered mainmast had sprung, sent down royal and topgallant yards and studding sail booms off lower and topsail yards to relieve strain.—July 13th. Let men out of irons in consequence of wanting their services, with the understanding that they would be taken care of on arriving at San Francisco. At 6 P.M., carried away the maintopsail tye and band round mainmast.—July 23d. Cape Horn north five miles. The whole coast covered with snow.—July 31st. Fresh breezes, fine weather, all sail set. At 2 P.M. wind southeast. At 6 squally; in lower and topgallant studding sails; 7, in royals; at 2 A.M. in foretopmast studding sail. Latter part, strong gales and high sea running. Ship very wet fore and aft. Distance run this day by observation is

374 miles. During the squalls 18 knots of line was not sufficient to measure the rate of speed. Topgallantsails set.—August 3d. At 3 P.M. suspended first officer from duty, in consequence of his arrogating to himself the privilege of cutting up rigging, contrary to my orders, and long-continued neglect of duty.—August 25th. Spoke barque *Amelia Packet,* 180 days from London for San Francisco.—August 29th. Lost foretopgallant mast. —August 30th. Sent up foretopgallant mast. Night strong and squally. Six A.M. made South Farallones bearing northeast ½ east; took a pilot at 7; anchored in San Francisco harbor at 11:30 A.M. after a passage of 89 days, 21 hours."

An analysis of this remarkable log shows that during twenty-six consecutive days the *Flying Cloud* had sailed a distance of 5912 miles, an average of 227 miles a day, or within a fraction of 9½ knots, and for four consecutive days 284, 374, 334, 264—a total of 1256, or 314 miles per day, an average speed of 13½ knots. This splendid passage of the *Flying Cloud* reduced by one quarter the clipper-ship record of 120 days made by the *Memnon* two years before, and established a new record that stands to-day.

This grand ocean exploit was celebrated in San Francisco with rejoicing, as every American in the town felt, now that the voyage round Cape Horn had been made in three months, that he was nearer to his old home in the East; while in the Atlantic seaports the news was received with enthusiasm, and was regarded by the press not only as a personal victory for the owners, builder, and captain of the *Flying Cloud,* but as a triumph of the United States upon the sea. One of the New York papers [1] in the course of an editorial remarked: "Such a passage as this is more than a local triumph, and inures to the reputation not alone of the builder of the ship and her enterprising owners, but of the United States. It is truly a national triumph, and points clearly and unmistakably to the preeminence upon the ocean which awaits the United States of America. The log of the *Flying Cloud* is now before us. It is the most wonderful record that pen ever indited, for rapid as was the passage, it was performed under circumstances by no means the most favorable."

The *Challenge* arrived October 29th, 108 days from New York—a fine passage, certainly, but not what her friends had hoped or expected. She had on this voyage a large but very poor crew—incompetent and mutinous—indeed, some of them were among the most desperate characters that ever sailed out of the port of New York. It was only after the ship had passed Sandy Hook and the pilot had been discharged that Captain Waterman began fully to realize what a gang of ruffians he had to deal with. He seriously considered taking the ship back to New York for another crew, and a less resolute man probably would have done so; but he realized that it would mean a heavy expense to the owners, as each of the crew had received three month's advance wages, which would have to be paid over again to another crew, besides other expenses and loss of time and disappointment to the

[1] *New York Commercial,* October 8, 1851.

shippers of cargo, so he decided to protect every one but himself and kept the ship on her course.

The crew of the *Challenge* consisted of 56 men before the mast, supposed to be able seamen, and 8 boys. Of the men in the forecastle only two were Americans, the remainder representing most of the maritime countries of Europe. So soon as Captain Waterman decided to continue the voyage, he made his plans quickly. After giving some orders to Mr. Douglas, his chief officer, he called all hands aft and manufactured a speech in which, among other things he said that the men would find that they were on board of a good comfortable ship, with plenty to eat and very little work to do; but when the officers gave them orders they must obey willingly and quickly; that he hoped none of them had brought spirits or weapons on board, as such things were apt to make trouble at sea. This camp-meeting discourse occupied perhaps fifteen or twenty minutes, during which the mates, carpenter, sailmaker, and boatswain were employed in the forecastle breaking open chests and boxes, emptying bags, and gathering up bottles of rum, knuckle-dusters, sling-shots, bowie-knives, and pistols which they threw over the side. After the watches were chosen, each man was made to lay his knife on the main hatch, where the carpenter broke the point of the blade off square.

It was found that only six men among the crew could steer the ship properly; these were made quartermasters and did nothing else during the passage except to lend a hand making and taking in sail. Fully one half of the crew who had shipped as able seamen were not sailormen at all, but blacklegs of the vilest type, who had taken this means of getting to the California gold mines. It also developed that many of the men had contracted a loathsome disease, most difficult to cure at sea, and at one time seventeen of the crew were laid up and off duty. Captain Waterman had the sailroom turned into a sick bay, but although these men received every care, five of them died, and eight were still in their berths when the *Challenge* arrived at San Francisco.

For some time after sailing from New York, Captain Waterman and his officers were always armed when they came on deck, but after a while the crew appeared to be in such good shape that this precaution gradually became neglected, until, one morning off Rio Janeiro, while Captain Waterman was taking his sights, he heard shouts for help from the main deck. He at once laid down his sextant and hurried forward to find the mate, Mr. Douglas, with his back to the port bulwark just abaft the main rigging, defending himself with bare fists from four of the crew armed with knives, who were attacking him. As Captain Waterman ran along the main deck he pulled a heavy iron belaying pin out of the rail, and using this with both hands as a club, he dealt a terrific blow on the skull of each of the would-be assassins, which laid them out on deck—two of them dead. Mr. Douglas had received no less than twelve wounds, some of them of a serious nature; indeed, he barely escaped with his life. From that time the officers always carried arms, and there was no further trouble with the crew.

Off Cape Horn three men fell from aloft, one of whom was drowned while two struck the deck and were killed. The bodies of the men who died were sewn up in canvas with holystones at their feet, and were buried in the sea. Captain Waterman read the funeral service over their remains, but the ship was not hove to as the braces were never allowed to be started except when absolutely necessary, owing to the difficulty and danger of handling the yards with such an inferior crew. The bodies of the two men who attempted to murder the chief officer were taken from where they fell and lowered into the sea. Many years afterward Captain Waterman told me that he could not bring himself to read the Christian burial service over these corpses, but that he gave the crew permission to take the bodies forward, and offered them canvas, holystones, and a prayer-book with which to hold their own service, but none of the crew would volunteer to bury these men.

The *Challenge* had moderate winds the whole passage, excepting a succession of westerly gales off Cape Horn, and with her wretched crew besides, there was really no opportunity properly to test her speed. Her best day's run was only 336 miles, with the wind abeam and skysails set. She was 55 days from Sandy Hook to Cape Horn, thence 34 days to the equator in the Pacific, and 19 days from the equator to San Francisco. The great wonder is, not that Captain Waterman made such a fine passage, but that he succeeded in getting his ship to San Francisco at all.

Soon after the *Challenge* rounded to and let go

anchor, in San Francisco Bay, she was boarded by a throng of crimps and runners who at once took the crew and their dunnage ashore. There was nothing unusual in this, for it happened nearly every day, captains and mates being powerless to prevent it. A gang of longshoremen would then be sent aboard at wages of from $3 to $5 an hour each, to heave up anchor, put the ship alongside the wharf, stow sails and clear up the decks. As these prosperous sons of toil were never in much of a hurry, it usually required from four to five hours to finish up these jobs, and meant a heavy expense to the ship-owner for work that should have been done by the crew.

When the crew of the *Challenge* got on shore, some of them had terrible tales to tell about their hardships and privations during the voyage; how they had been nearly starved to death; how some of the crew had starved to death or been murdered, and their bodies hove overboard like dead rats, and how six men had been shot from the mizzentopsail yard in a gale of wind off Cape Horn. According to these blatant imposters, no such floating hell as the *Challenge* had ever before set sail upon the ocean, and as for Captain Waterman, he was a blood-thirsty, inhuman navigator, the like of whom had never been seen or heard of, since the days when Noah put his ship ashore among the mountains of Ararat. All this was, of course, profitable material for journalists, one impetuous knight of the pen actually proposing that Captain Waterman should be burned alive, until finally the publisher of this attack became frightened for his own safety, as he had incited the most dangerous set of men, perhaps, that ever existed in any seaport—ticket-of-leave from Australia, cut-throats from New Mexico, and drainings from the social gutters and cesspools of European ports.

At this moment San Francisco happened to be in one of the numerous stages of reform through which that amazing city has passed. It had recently emerged from a reign of lawlessness and mob rule under the guidance of a Vigilance Committee, and while this admirable body of citizens was not yet disbanded, it had in a measure relaxed its grasp upon public affairs. Now, a number of the newly-converted thugs, murderers, and outlaws of the town, whose necks had narrowly escaped the hangman's noose, formed themselves into a new "Vigilance Committee," to deal with Captain Waterman and the officers of the *Challenge*. These outcasts, crafty and unscrupulous as they were, possessed neither the courage nor the mental capacity to carry out their own plans. They accordingly called a public meeting, held somewhere among the sandhills, at which it was decided to "execute" Captain Waterman and his officers "on sight," and then burn or scuttle the vessel at her wharf. Naturally, the real Vigilance Committee were the first to learn of these proceedings, and at once took the captain and officers under their protection, holding themselves in readiness to scatter the mob should this measure become necessary.

The crowd that gathered at the sandhills consisted of two or three hundred men who had lately been hunted from one end of San Francisco to the

The "Challenge"

other, and had prudently kept themselves stowed away in order to escape the righteous wrath of the Vigilance Committee. One can scarcely conceive anything more grimly grotesque than the spectacle of these inexperienced reformers, in their red flannel shirts and black slouched hats with pistols and bowie-knives stuck in their leather belts, and trousers tucked into the tops of their cowhide boots, the odor of the gin palace and dance-hall clinging to their unwashed skins and clothing, as they wended their way to Pacific Wharf, where the *Challenge* lay moored, and demanded that Captain Waterman and his officers be delivered over to them for purposes of justice.

As might have been expected, these gentlemen had vanished and no one but a few members of the Committee knew where they were. So finding that Captain John Land had been placed in command of the ship, the mob seized this venerable seaman, and for more than an hour wrangled among themselves as to whether they should shoot, drown, or hang him in place of Captain Waterman. They, however, concluded to hold him as a hostage, and walked their white-haired prisoner up to the office of Alsop & Co., the agents of the *Challenge.* By this time, the crowd had been considerably augmented and numbered about two thousand men, who filled the air of California Street with yells, curses, lewd jests, and ribald songs. They again demanded from the agents that their intended victims be given up, and six of the ringleaders forced their way with crowbars and axes into the house of Alsop & Co. At this point the bell of the Monumental Fire Engine House began to toll—the well-known signal that called the Vigilance Committee to arms—and long before the Marshal had finished reading the Riot Act, the mob had dispersed with alacrity.

Captain Waterman was not the man to submit quietly to such attacks upon his character and conduct, and he at once offered to meet any charge that might be brought against him before a proper legal tribunal. When no one appeared, he demanded that a full investigation be made into the facts of the voyage of the *Challenge*. It then appeared, from the testimony of a portion of the crew, that a large number of the men who had shipped in New York as able seamen were grossly incompetent and desperately mutinous; that the food had been of the best, in fact, the same quality of beef, pork, and flour that had been used in the cabin had also been served to the crew without stint, and that no more punishment had been inflicted by the officers than was necessary to maintain proper discipline for the safety of the ship and her cargo.

It also appeared that from the time the ship sailed from New York until the time of her arrival at San Francisco, Captain Waterman had never been out of his clothes except to change them, and had never slept in his berth, but had taken such rest as he could find upon the the transom in his chart-room near the companionway. He was commended for his skill and courage in bringing his vessel safely into San Francisco without the loss of a spar, sail, or piece of rigging. It is therefore humiliating to record that neither the owners of the *Challenge* nor their underwriters, for both of whom

Captain Waterman had saved thousands of dollars, ever had the courtesy to make the slightest acknowledgment of his services, although they were well aware of their obligation in this matter. It is, however, some consolation to know that he asked and needed nothing at their hands.

As we already have seen, Captain Waterman had taken the Pacific Mail steamship *Northerner* from New York to San Francisco in 1850, and fully intended at that time to retire from the sea. He was then forty-two years old, and had passed thirty-two years upon the ocean; he possessed ample means, with a portion of which he bought four leagues of land in Solano County, California, and it was only at the earnest solicitation of N. L. & G. Griswold, the owners of the *Challenge,* that he consented to take her from New York to San Francisco in this year. He was now free to attend to his own affairs. Together with Captain A. A. Richie, he founded the town of Fairfield, California. In 1852, he was appointed Port Warden and Inspector of Hulls at the port of San Francisco, a position he held for twenty-eight years. He then retired to his farm, where he died in 1884, at the age of seventy-six. Probably no man in California was more widely known or more highly respected.

One of the best ocean races of 1851 was that between the *Raven,* Captain Henry; the *Typhoon,* Captain Salter, and the *Sea Witch,* Captain Frazer. These clippers sailed for San Francisco nearly together: the *Sea Witch* passed out by Sandy Hook on August 1st, followed by the *Typhoon* on August 4th, while the *Raven* passed Boston Light on August 6th. All had able commanders, who carried Maury's wind and current charts to assist them. In this month of light and baffling breezes a quick run to the equator was hardly to be expected, but these clippers threaded their way across the calm belt of Cancer, ran down the northeast trades, and drifted through the doldrums, with surprising speed. The *Sea Witch* still kept her lead at the equator, crossing on August 30th, closely followed by the *Raven* and the *Typhoon,* which crossed together on the 31st, so that the *Raven* had gained four and the *Typhoon* two days on their swift competitor. They all weathered Cape St. Roque and stood away to the southward for a splendid dash of over three thousand miles through the southeast trades and the strong westerly winds further south, all crossing the parallel of 50° S. in the same longitude, 64° W. The *Raven* had gained another day on the *Sea Witch* and these two clippers were now side by side, with the *Typhoon* only two days astern.

Here began one of the keenest races ever sailed upon the ocean. They all stood to the southward with studdingsail booms and skysail yards sent down from aloft, with extra lashings on the boats, spare spars, and skylights, while all hands hardened their hearts for a thrash to windward round Cape Horn. On this desolate ocean the clippers raced from horizon to horizon in heavy westerly gales and a long, fierce, sweeping head sea. For fourteen exciting days and nights, with single-reefed, double-reefed, close-reefed topsails, reefs in and reefs out, their keen, watchful captains made use of every lull and slant to drive their ships to the westward of Cape Horn, across the great, broad-backed, white-crested seas. The *Sea Witch* and *Raven* were having it out tack for tack, sometimes one and then the other gaining an advantage, both carrying sail to the utmost limit of prudence, lifting their long, sharp bows to the wild, surging seas, the cold spray flying across their decks and blue water swirling along their lee waists, each handled with consummate skill, and not a spar carried away or rope parted. The *Typhoon* in hot pursuit, was pressing the two leaders and slowly closing upon them, for her greater length and power helped her here. Finally the *Sea Witch* and *Raven* emerged from this desperate contest side by side, as they had entered it, both crossing latitude 50° S. in the Pacific in fourteen days from the same parallel in the Atlantic. The *Typhoon* had now gained another day, and was within twenty-four hours' sail of each.

Clear of Cape Horn they all went away fast to the northward, rushing through the southeast trades with studdingsails, skysails, water-sails, and ring-tails—every yard of canvass set that would draw. On this stretch to the equator, the *Sea Witch* fairly flew through the water, and crossed in 22 days from 50° S., leading the *Raven* 2 and the *Typhoon* 4 days. They now stood to the northward, close-hauled on the starboard tack, for their final struggle. Here again length and power counted in favor of the *Typhoon*, and she came up with the *Sea Witch* and *Raven*, leading them both into port; the *Raven*, too, for the first time fairly headed the *Sea Witch*. The *Typhoon* glided through the Golden Gate, November

18th, 106 days from Sandy Hook; the *Raven,* November 19th, 105 days from Boston Light, and the *Sea Witch,* November 20th, 110 days from Sandy Hook. Here is a brief abstract from their log-books:

	Raven	*Typhoon*	*Sea Witch*
To the equator in the Atlantic	25 days	27 days	29 days.
From the equator to 50° S.	21 "	23 "	22 "
From 50° S. in the Atlantic to 50° S. in the Pacific	14 "	13 "	14 "
From 50° S. to the equator	24 "	25 "	22 "
From the equator to the Golden Gate	21 "	18 "	23 "
Total	105 "	106 "	110 "

This was a great victory for the *Raven,* the only ship of her tonnage that ever outsailed the *Sea Witch,* to say nothing of vanquishing the large and famous *Typhoon,* a ship more than double her size. It should, however, be remembered with regard to the *Sea Witch,* that she was at that time over five years old, and had led a pretty wild life under Waterman, while she had known no peace with Frazer in command, and had been strained and weakened by hard driving. Moreover, a wooden ship, after five or six years, begins to lose her speed through absorbing water, and becomes sluggish in light airs. In her prime and at her best with Waterman in command, the *Sea Witch* was probably the fastest sailing-ship of her inches ever built.

The California clippers were, of course, racing all the time, against each other and against the record, and the strain upon their captains in driving their ships against competitors whose relative positions were unknown, was terrific. It became a confirmed habit with them to keep their ships going night and day in all weathers and at their utmost speed.

In order to appreciate what a passage of 110 days or less from an Atlantic port to San Francisco really means, we must take a few of the long passages of 1851, made by ships that were not clippers: *Arthur,* from New York, 200 days; *Austerlitz,* Boston, 185 days; *Barrington,* Boston, 180 days; *Bengal,* Philadelphia, 185 days; *Capitol,* Boston, 300 days; *Cornwallis,* New York, 204 days; *Franconia,* Boston, 180 days; *Henry Allen,* New York, 225 days; *Inconium,* Baltimore, 190 days. The logs of these vessels tell of long, weary days and nights of exasperating calms, and dreary, heart-breaking weeks of battle with tempests off Cape Horn.

Some of the vessels built in 1851 did not take part in the races of that year, as they were not launched until too late; and did not arrive at San Francisco before 1852. Those among them which became most famous were the *Hurricane, Comet, Northern Light, Flying Fish, Staffordshire, Trade Wind, Sword-Fish,* and *Shooting Star.* We shall hear of them later.

The record of San Francisco passages for 1851 should not be closed without mention of the pilot-boat *Fanny,* of 84 tons; length 71 feet, breadth 18 feet 4 inches, depth 7 feet 2 inches, built by Daniel D. Kelly at East Boston in 1850. This schooner was commanded by Captain William Kelly, a brother of her builder, and arrived at San Francisco February 18, 1851, 108 days from Boston. She passed through the Straits of Magellan and thus saved a considerable distance; but even allowing for this, her passage was a very remarkable one for a vessel of her tonnage, and reflects much credit upon the skill and courage of her captain and his plucky companions.

CHAPTER XII

AMERICAN COMPETITION WITH GREAT BRITAIN IN THE CHINA TRADE

THE California clippers, after discharging their cargoes at San Francisco, either returned in ballast round Cape Horn, or continued their voyages across the Pacific and loaded cargoes at Asiatic ports for the United States or Great Britain.

Some of the ships which sailed to China from San Francisco, raced across the Pacific in ballast, touching at the Sandwich Islands only long enough to back the main yard off Diamond Head and send the mails ashore with perhaps a missionary or two. In those days the Kanaka maidens used to swim off alongside the ships, and they were probably the nearest approach to mermaids that has ever been known in real life. The *Stag-Hound* made the passage from San Francisco to Honolulu in 9, and the *Flying Cloud* and *Surprise* in 12 days each. The *Flying Cloud* sailed 374 miles in twenty-four hours, the day after leaving San Francisco, with a fresh whole-sail breeze and smooth sea, under skysails and royal studdingsails. The *Southern Cross* made the passage from San Francisco to Hong-kong in 32, and the *Game-Cock* in 35 days, the run of the *Game-Cock* from Honolulu to Hong-kong in 19 days being most remarkable. When these and other fast American vessels loaded again in China for English ports, they, of course, added to the competition from which British ships were already suffering.

We have seen how the *Oriental* brought a cargo of tea from China to England in 1850, and what interest her appearance excited in London. She was soon followed by the *Surprise, White Squall, Sea Serpent, Nightingale, Argonaut, Challenge,* and other clipper ships built for the California trade. These American clippers received from £6 to £6, 10s freight per ton of forty cubic feet, with immediate despatch, while British ships were loading slowly at £3, 10s per ton of fifty cubic feet. The American ships made fine passages and delivered their teas in excellent condition; but what especially appealed to the Briton was the fact that they had cleared more than their original cost and running expenses on this, their first voyage.

An able English writer,[1] referring to the American clippers engaged in the China tea-trade at this period, remarks: "This new competition proved for a time most disastrous to English shipping, which was soon driven out of favor by the lofty spars, smart, rakish-looking hulls, and famed speed of the American ships, and caused the tea-trade of the London markets to pass almost out of the hands of the English ship-owner. British vessels well manned and well found are known to have lain in the harbor of Foo-chow for weeks together, wait-

[1] William John, in an article on clipper ships in *Naval Science*, vol. ii. (1873), p. 265.

ing for a cargo, and seeing American clippers coming in, loading, and sailing immediately with full cargoes, at a higher freight than they could command.

"This soon became a matter of serious moment, and the arrival of these vessels in the Thames caused great excitement, and aroused no small amount of curiosity and criticism. Even the attention of the Government became attracted towards them, and draughtsmen were sent from the Admiralty to take off the lines of two of the most famous—the *Challenge* and the *Oriental*—when they were in Messrs. Green's drydock."

This state of affairs could not, of course, continue without further arousing British ship-owners and builders to the danger of their position. Here was not one vessel, but a fleet of American clippers bringing cargoes from China at double the rates of freight that British ships could command, and unless some measures were adopted to check this invasion no one could predict where it might end. That British merchants paid so liberally to get their teas to a home market was certainly not because they cherished any special affection for American ships or their owners. They would have been quite as willing to pay British clippers the same freights, had there been any such to receive them, or even Chinese junks, provided the service could have been performed by them as quickly and as well. So we find the British ship-owners and builders of that period forced to exert their finest skill and most ardent energy.

The firm of Jardine, Matheson & Co., of London

and China, were the owners of the first clipper ship built in Great Britain. This vessel was the *Stornoway,* 506 tons, launched from the yard of Alexander Hall & Co., at Aberdeen, toward the close of 1850 for the China trade. It will be recalled that this firm had built the clipper schooner *Torrington,* for the same owners, four years before. The new ship was named for Stornoway Castle, Lewis, one of the Hebrides Isles, which was then owned by Sir James Matheson, and to which he retired after his long and successful career as ship-owner and merchant in the China trade.

It cannot be said that the *Stornoway* was a copy of any American model, as a comparison of dimensions will clearly show. Comparing her measurements with those of the American clipper barque *Race Horse,* of 512 tons register, built by Samuel Hall at East Boston in the same year, we find:

	Length	Breadth	Depth
Stornoway	157 ft. 8 in.	25 ft. 8 in.	17 ft. 8 in.
Race Horse	125 ft.	30 ft.	16 ft.

Thus the *Stornoway,* while she exceeded the *Race Horse* by 32 feet 8 inches in length and by 1 foot 8 inches in depth, yet had 4 feet 4 inches less breadth; and here began a contest, which extended over so many years, of breadth against length and depth. There can be no doubt that the *Stornoway* with more beam and the *Race Horse* with more length and depth, would have been faster, but at the same time considerably larger vessels.[1]

[1] The various systems of calculating the tonnage of vessels which were in force in Great Britain prior to 1854,

The "Stornoway"

The *Stornoway* was commanded by Captain Richard Robinson, and on her first voyage she made the passage from the Downs to Java Head in 80 days, to Hong-kong in 102 days, and from Hong-kong to London in 103 days. These were at that time the quickest passages between these ports that had ever been made by a British vessel.

In 1851 Alexander Hall & Co. built the China tea-clipper *Chrysolite,* of 471 tons, for Taylor & Potter of Liverpool; length 149 feet 3 inches, breadth 29 feet, depth 17 feet. As will be seen this vessel approached more nearly the proportions of the *Race Horse,* having 8 feet 5 inches less length than the *Stornoway,* with 3 feet 4 inches more breadth, and 8 inches less depth. She made her first passage from Liverpool to Canton, under the command of Captain Anthony Enright, in 102 days, and came home in 104 days. She also made the

---

(see Appendix iv.,) gave the breadth measurement a preponderating influence upon the result, and as taxation, port, and light dues, etc., were based upon the registered tonnage of a vessel, there was economy in decreasing the breadth of a vessel at the expense of the other dimensions. Ship-builders and owners in England showed a much greater tendency to profit by this feature of the law than did those in the United States, where substantially the same system was in force. In this country some very narrow vessels were built for the New Orleans and West India trade, in the period 1820–1845, but it was found that the saving in taxation did not pay for using such an undesirable type of vessels, so they were given up. As a rule, American owners and builders preferred to build vessels of a type which they regarded as the best for speed and for the trade in which they were engaged, without regard for the tonnage laws.

passage from Liverpool to Java Head in 80 days, her best day's run being 320 miles.

The very keen rivalry between the British and American clipper ships engaged in the China trade at this time, seems to have been stimulating to the imagination. W. S. Lindsay, in his *History of Merchant Shipping* (vol. iii., p. 291), relates an interesting story of one of the early races, and as I wish to do the narrative full justice, I give it in Mr. Lindsay's own words:

"Mr. T. C. Cowper, of Aberdeen, himself a member of a well-known ship-building firm in Aberdeen, who had spent some time in China at the period to which I refer, and to whom I am much indebted for the information connected with our struggles to maintain our position in that trade, gives the following graphic description of his voyage home in the *Ganges,* Captain Deas, belonging to Leith, one of the vessels we had sent forth after the repeal of our Navigation Laws, to compete with the Americans in that trade: 'We loaded,' he says, 'new teas at Wampoa, and sailed on the first of September, 1851. Two of the fastest American clippers, the *Flying Cloud* and *Bald Eagle,* sailed two or three days after us. A great deal of excitement existed in China about the race, the American ships being the favorites. The southwest monsoon being strong, the *Ganges* made a rather long passage to Anjer, but when we arrived there we found that neither of our rivals had been reported as having passed. We arrived in the English Channel on the evening of the 16th of December. On the following morning at daylight we were off Portland, well inshore and under short sail, light winds from the north-east, and weather rather thick. About 8 A.M. the wind freshened and the haze cleared away, which showed two large and lofty ships two or three miles to windward of us. They proved to be our American friends, having their Stars and Stripes flying for a pilot. Captain Deas at once gave orders to hoist his signals for a pilot also, and as, by this time, several cutters were standing out from Weymouth, the *Ganges,* being farthest inshore got her pilot first on board. I said that I would land in the pilot-boat and go to London by rail, and would report the ship that night or next morning at Austin Friars. (She was consigned to my firm.) The breeze had considerably freshened before I got on board the pilot cutter, when the *Ganges* filled away on the port tack, and Captain Deas, contrary to his wont, for he was a very cautious man, crowded on all small sails. The Americans lost no time and were after him, and I had three hours' view of as fine an ocean race as I can wish to see; the wind being dead ahead, the ships were making short tacks. The *Ganges* showed herself to be the most weatherly of the three; and the gain on every tack inshore was obvious, neither did she seem to carry way behind in fore reaching. She arrived off Dungeness six hours before the other two, and was in the London docks twenty-four hours before the first, and thirty-six hours before the last of her opponents.' "

It is always unpleasant to spoil a really good story, but in this instance I feel constrained to point out that the *Flying Cloud* arrived at San Francisco on August 31, 1851, after her famous passage of 89 days from New York; it is therefore difficult to understand how she could have sailed from Wampoa on the Canton River on or about September 1st of that year, as stated by Mr. Cowper; while the *Bald Eagle* was not launched until 1852.

On January 3, 1852, the *Illustrated London News*, which then, as now, had many readers in the United States, published a portrait of the *Chrysolite* accompanying an article in which it was stated that both the *Chrysolite* and the *Stornoway* had beaten the *Oriental* and the *Surprise*, and that the *Chrysolite* had completely beaten the *Memnon* during a race in the Gaspar Straits. This article excited a good deal of interest in the United States, and it caused the formation by a number of high-spirited young merchants and ship-owners at Boston of a society called the American Navigation Club, which consisted of Daniel C. Bacon, President; Thomas H. Perkins, John P. Cushing, William H. Bordman, John M. Forbes, Warren Delano, and Edward King. In due time they issued the following challenge, which was published in all the leading shipping papers of Great Britain in September, 1852, and was copied into *Bell's Life*, at that period the great sporting publication of England:

"The American Navigation Club challenges the ship-builders of Great Britain to a ship-race, with cargo on board, from a port in England to a port in China and back. One ship to be entered by each party, and to be named within a week of the start. These ships to be modelled, commanded, and officered entirely by citizens of the United States and Great Britain, respectively. To be entitled to rank A 1 either at the American offices or at Lloyd's. The stakes to be £10,000 a side, satisfactorily secured by both parties, to be paid without regard to accidents, or to any exceptions, the whole amount forfeited by either party not appearing. Judges to be mutually chosen. Reasonable time to be given after notice of acceptance to build the ships if required, and also for discharging and loading cargo in China. The challenged party may name the size of the ships, not under 800 nor over 1200 American registered tons; the weight and measurement which shall be carried each way; the allowance for short weight or over-size. Reference may be made to Messrs. Baring Bros. & Co. for further particulars.

"DANIEL C. BACON, *President*."

A few weeks later, on October 10, 1852, the following comment appeared in *Bell's Life:*

"It will be remembered early in the past month there was wafted across the broad Atlantic, from the American Navigation Club, a challenge to the ship-builders of Great Britain, which created no little interest, and which after the defeat, then just accomplished, of the magic yacht *America* by one of our own little island craft, gave rise to no inconsiderable speculation as to what might be the result of an acceptance of Brother Jonathan's proposal. . . . The Club by the last clause of their terms held themselves at liberty to withdraw the challenge should it not be accepted within thirty days. The limit of the time is now expiring, and it is with no little disappointment that a letter received from the head of the eminent banking house of Baring & Co., was received in Boston a short time since, when it was found that he had nothing like an acceptance of the challenge to communicate to the American Club, but that, on the contrary, he had to report no inquiry as to the proposition. As a sort of enticement, however, to our ship-builders, the President of the American Navigation Club, Mr. D. C. Bacon, is authorized, should the present challenge not be accepted within thirty days, to allow the British vessels a start of fourteen days before the departure of the American craft. And also to allow us a crew picked from seamen experienced in voyaging between English and Chinese ports, while their own crew is to be composed of American seamen and officers whose experience is limited in sailing between China and English ports. The Americans, under the new conditions, are willing to augment the stake to £20,000, or any higher sum than the £10,000 of the present conditions most agreeable to us, but the last amount to be the minimum. The Americans want a match, and it reflects somewhat upon our chivalry not to accommodate them."

The London *Daily News* also published a leader in which it urged the importance to Great Britain of making good her claim to maritime supremacy by accepting the challenge and winning the race; but in spite of all that was said the challenge was not accepted. Had it been, Captain Dumaresq would have commanded the American ship, and Lieutenant Maury was to have prepared special wind and current charts for his assistance. As nearly all the American clippers had been constructed for the California trade, it is probable that for an important race of this nature, two ships would have been built especially for the China trade, and very likely by Donald McKay and Samuel Hall, as the *Flying Cloud, Flying Fish, Stag-Hound, Game-Cock,* and *Surprise* had already placed these two in the front rank of clipper ship-builders. No reason was ever given for the non-acceptance of the challenge, though the inference seems obvious.

It would, however, be a mistake to suppose that the *Stornoway* and *Chrysolite* were not fast vessels; for they were probably the two fastest ships sailing under the British flag at that time, and were ably commanded, and on a China voyage, which is very different sailing from a San Francisco or Australian passage, would have given any ship afloat a run for her owner's money. The fitful uncertainty of the monsoons in the China seas, with an occasional typhoon thrown in, has always rendered the voyages to and from China rather unsatisfactory tests of speed, and in this respect not to be compared with those to Australia or to San Francisco.

The *Stornoway* and *Chrysolite* were soon followed by other British clipper ships, among them the *Abergeldie,* of 600 tons register, built by Walter Hood & Co., of Aberdeen, in 1851. This vessel was named for an estate that adjoins Balmoral, at that time under a forty years' lease to Prince Albert, and carried a figurehead of His Royal Highness in full Highland costume.

In 1852, Richard Green, of London, built the *Challenger,* of 699 tons. This ship, owned by W. S. Lindsay, of London, was constructed with the avowed purpose of beating the *Challenge* of New York. A comparison of the dimensions of this ship and those of the *Sword-Fish,* 1036 tons, is interesting.

	Length	Breadth	Depth
Challenger	174 ft.	32 ft.	20 ft.
Sword-Fish	169 ft. 6 in.	36 ft. 6 in.	20 ft.

The *Challenger* was commanded by Captain Killick, who made eight China voyages in her, the best passage home being 105 days. Although she was never directly matched with her American rival, they both took part in an informal race from China in 1852, while the challenge of the Navigation Club was pending. The passages of the seven vessels, four American and three British, were as follows:

Witch of the Wave....	Canton to Deal.......	90	days.
Challenge.............	Canton to Deal.......	105	"
Surprise...............	Canton to Deal.......	106	"
Stornoway............	Canton to Deal.......	109	"
Chrysolite.............	Canton to Liverpool...	106	"
Nightingale...........	Shanghai to Deal.....	110	"
Challenger.............	Shanghai to Deal.....	113	"

It is only fair to state that the *Witch of the Wave,* commanded by Captain Millett, sailed from

Canton, January 5th, in the height of the northeast monsoon, and made the run, remarkable even at that season of the year, of 7 days 12 hours from Canton to Java Head, while the three British clippers, *Stornoway, Chrysolite,* and *Challenger,* sailed later with a moderate monsoon, and the *Challenge, Surprise,* and *Nightingale* later still, when the monsoon was less favorable. The rate of freight this year was £8 per ton, the highest that was ever paid.

This race, if so it can be called, resulted in "win, tie, or wrangle" as it was claimed, for one reason or another, by every vessel engaged in it, and ended by Sampson & Tappan, of Boston, offering to match the *Nightingale* for £10,000 against any ship, British or American, for a race to China and back. The rivalry of the American clipper ships among themselves was as keen as with those of Great Britain, and this challenge was intended for the Navigation Club, of Boston, of which Sampson & Tappan were not members, and for New York as well, quite as much as for the British clippers; but it found no response from either side of the Atlantic.

The *Nightingale* was owned by Sampson & Tappan for a number of years, during which she made some exceedingly fast passages, under the command of Captain Samuel Mather. Among them were the passage from Portsmouth, England, to Shanghai, against the northeast monsoon, in 106 days in 1853; and during the year 1855 a passage from Shanghai to London in 91 days, and from Batavia Roads to London in 70 days, an average of 197 miles per day, her best day's run being 336 miles.

The *Surprise* proved one of the most successful

American clippers in the China trade. After her first voyage she was for a number of years commanded by the captains Charles Ranlett, father and son, and in their hands made many fine passages —she made eleven consecutive passages from China to New York in 89 days or less, six from Hong-kong, and five from Shanghai, the best being 81 days from Shanghai, in 1857. Among other fast passages from Canton to New York may be mentioned those of the *Stag-Hound* 85, 91, and 92 days; *Flying Cloud,* 94 and 96 days; *N. B. Palmer,* 84 days; *Comet, Panama,* and *Hurricane,* each 99 days; *Sword-Fish,* 80 days; *Sea Serpent,* 88 days; *Vancouver,* 96 days; *Mandarin,* 89 days; but I am unable to find that Captain Waterman's passage of 77 days in the *Sea Witch* in 1848, and 78 days in the *Natchez* in 1845, from Canton to New York, have ever been beaten. In 1854 the *Comet* made a record passage of 84 days from Liverpool to Hong-kong, an average of 212 miles per day, and in the same year the *Typhoon* made the run from the Lizard to Calcutta in 80 days.

In Great Britain the *Cairngorm,* of 1250 tons register, was built in 1853 by Alexander Hall & Co., and owned by Jardine, Matheson Co. Between 1853 and 1856 came the *Crest of the Wave, Norma, Flying Dragon, Formosa,* and *Spirit of the Age,* built by John Pile of Sunderland, and the *Lord of the Isles* (iron) by John Scott & Co., of Greenock. The ship last named registered 770 tons, measured: length 190 feet 9 inches, breadth 27 feet 8 inches, depth 18 feet 5 inches, and was an extremely sharp and handsome, though a very wet ship. It used to be said that Captain Maxton, her commander, drove her into one side of a sea and out the other; at all events, she was generally known among sailormen as the "Diving Bell."

The British clippers of this type, which was extremely sharp and narrow, very nearly held their own against the American ships, and it is much to be regretted that there never was a fair and square race between them; for no British and American clipper ships ever sailed from China near enough together to afford a satisfactory test of speed.

The *Lord of the Isles* made the remarkable run from Shanghai to London in 1855 during the northeast monsoon of 87 days. In 1856 she sailed against the American clipper barque *Maury,* commanded by Captain Fletcher, from Foo-chow to London, both carrying new teas. In this year a premium of £1 per ton on the freight was offered for the first ship home during the season. The reward was offered without regard to the length of the passage, and was intended to encourage quick despatch in loading as well as fast sailing. The *Lord of the Isles* finished loading and sailed four days ahead of the *Maury.* Both vessels arrived in the Downs on the same morning and passed Gravesend within ten minutes of each other, the *Maury* leading, but Captain Maxton, having the smartest tug, succeeded in getting his ship first into dock, and so won the prize. The *Maury* was an exceedingly pretty barque of about 600 tons, built by Roosevelt & Joyce, and owned by A. A. Low & Brother. She was a very similar vessel to the barques *Fairy, Penguin,* and *Benefactor,* by the same builders, all engaged in the

China trade. The *Lord of the Isles* was the only tea-clipper built of iron at that time. It was found that she sweated her tea cargoes, though otherwise they were delivered in excellent condition, and she was certainly a very fast vessel.

At this period (1853–1856) British iron ships, both sail and steam, were coming into favor for other trades, but their introduction had been slow. It is not easy at the present time to realize the difficulties attending the building of the first iron vessels. The rolling of iron plates to a uniform thickness was a matter requiring great care and skill, and a number of years elapsed before plates exceeded or even reached ten feet in length; then bending the frames and riveting the plates were difficult processes, only learned through much trial and experiment. In the early days, when an iron ship was completed, her owner's troubles had only begun. Finding a composition that would prevent fouling and at the same time not destroy the plates; the adjustment of compasses, and devising effective means of ventilation, were all matters that required years of investigation and labor, to say nothing of the prejudice against iron vessels, which time and experience alone could overcome. Yet it was the skilful use of this stubborn metal in the construction of ships, together with wise legislation, that enabled Great Britain to regain her empire upon the sea.

CHAPTER XIII

CALIFORNIA CLIPPERS OF 1852—THE "SOVEREIGN OF THE SEAS"

AS one by one the California clippers came home from Asiatic ports or round Cape Horn from San Francisco in 1852, it was found that almost all of them needed a pretty thorough overhauling aloft. The masts, spars, and rigging of the *Flying Cloud* were fine examples of the skill of her sailors in clapping on fishings, lashings, stoppers, and seizings, while her topmast fids, crushed and broken, were taken up to the Astor House and exhibited to the admiration of the town. Her owners, Grinnell, Minturn & Co., had her log from New York to San Francisco printed in gold letters on white silk for distribution among their friends, and Captain Creesy fled to his home in Marblehead in order to escape notoriety.

The *Sea Serpent, Eclipse,* and *Stag-Hound* were in much the same condition aloft as the *Flying Cloud,* while the *Witchcraft,* on the voyage from San Francisco to Hong-kong had lost her main and mizzen masts with all sails and rigging attached, during a severe typhoon in the China Sea. The *Tornado,* commanded by Captain O. R. Mumford, bound from San Francisco to New York, had lost her bowsprit with the foremast and sprung her mainmast, when to the westward of Cape Horn. It required fourteen days to complete the jury rig at sea, after which she sailed to New York, a distance of 8000 miles, in 51 days. In acknowledgment of Captain Mumford's services on this occasion, the New York, Sun, Astor, and Mercantile Insurance Companies presented him with a costly solid silver service, which was made by Ball, Black & Co., and exhibited in the window of their store on the corner of Murray Street and Broadway.

All of these ships were rerigged in New York with stouter spars and rigging than they originally carried, and much valuable experience was gained by sparmakers and riggers as to the requirements aloft of these large, powerful clippers, while their captains had at the same time become better acquainted with their peculiarities. The great difficulty was to get a large ship, say from 1600 to 2000 tons, that would sail fast in moderate winds. If she had canvas enough to drive her along in a light breeze, the chances were that in a gale something was bound to carry away aloft. The utmost skill and judgment were required to rig and to handle these heavily masted ships with wooden spars and hemp rigging.

The great race to San Francisco in 1852 was between the *Sword-Fish* of New York and the *Flying Fish* of Boston, both extreme clippers and built respectively by William H. Webb and Donald McKay. The *Flying Fish* sailed from Boston November 11, 1851, and on the same day the *Sword-Fish* passed Sandy Hook. Large sums were wagered upon the result. Captain Nickels of the *Flying Fish* and Captain Babcock of the *Sword-Fish* were both young and skilful commanders, and it was believed by their friends that each would send his ship along at her utmost speed. The *Flying Fish* made an excellent run of 19 days to the equator, leading the *Sword-Fish* by four days. From the equator to 50° S., the *Flying Fish* was 26 and the *Sword-Fish* 22 days, so that they passed that parallel on the same day. They raced round Cape Horn, part of the time side by side, the *Flying Fish* making the run from 50° S. in the Atlantic to 50° S. in the Pacific in 7 and the *Sword-Fish* in 8 days. From this point the *Sword-Fish* came up and steadily drew away. She made the run to the equator in 19 days, leading the *Flying Fish* by 3 days, and from the equator to San Francisco in 20 days, gaining on this stretch another 3 days, and arrived at San Francisco February 10, 1852, after a splendid passage of 90 days 16 hours from New York. The *Flying Fish* arrived on the 17th, or 98 days from Boston. The *Sword-Fish* was regarded by many as the fastest and handsomest ship built by William H. Webb; and her passage of 90 days, the second best ever made from New York to San Francisco, and within one day of the record, together with many other fast passages, among them her record run of 31 days from Shanghai to San Francisco in 1855, an average of 240 miles a day, certainly places her at or very near the head of the list of clippers launched from this famous yard.

Some of the other notable passages of this year were made by the *Sovereign of the Seas* and *Comet*, each 102 days; *Sea Witch* 108 days from New York; *Staffordshire* 101 days, and *John Bertram* and *Shooting Star* each 105 days from Boston.

The *Flying Cloud,* on this, her second voyage from New York, arrived at San Francisco September 6, 1852, 113 days from New York. She had, for her, a long run of 30 days to the equator; and when she was off the coast of Brazil, running before a light northerly wind under skysails and royal studdingsails, with the weather clew of her mainsail hauled up: as Captain Creesy was taking his noon observation, a large clipper ship was reported about six miles ahead, under the same canvas but almost becalmed. She was soon recognized by Captain Creesy and his officers as the *N. B. Palmer.* The *Flying Cloud* carried the breeze until about two o'clock, when she also ran into the calm, and signals were exchanged. Captain Low, of the *N. B. Palmer,* reported with pardonable pride, that he had sailed from New York eight days after the *Flying Cloud,* and had found good winds to the equator; indeed, a few days after sailing he had made 396 miles in twenty-four hours.

As may be imagined, Captain Creesy was somewhat chagrined, but at all events, here at last were the ships about whose speed there had been so much discussion, side by side on blue water, and soon there would be a chance to find out which was the faster of the two. As there was every indication of a southerly breeze, both ships took in their studdingsails, rigged in the booms, and got ready for the new wind, with a pull on sheets and halliards fore and aft. The *Flying Cloud* had a fine crew, and in after years Captain Creesy in describing this race said that, "They worked like one man, and that man a hero."

At about four o'clock there was a faint southerly air with a few cat's-paws, and soon the breeze came up from the south in a dark-blue line across the horizon. Both ships felt it at the same moment, and braced their yards on the starboard tack sharp by the wind, which soon freshened to a fine whole-sail breeze. The *Flying Cloud* now began to draw away. At daylight the next morning, the *N. B. Palmer* was hull down to leeward, and by four o'clock in the afternoon was no longer in sight. Both ships had strong westerly gales off Cape Horn, and the *Flying Cloud* led her rival into San Francisco by twenty-three days.

It is only fair to say, however, that the *N. B. Palmer* lost five days through putting into Valparaiso to land two of her crew, and as it turned out, to ship seventeen men to replace deserters. One of the two men landed had shot and wounded the mate, and the other, known as "Doublin Jack," had knocked the second mate down with a handspike. Captain Low put both these men in irons, triced them up in the mizzen rigging, and gave them each four dozen lashes of ratline stuff, which they had well earned. Captain R. B. Forbes, one of the most humane and kind-hearted of men, declared in an address before the Boston Marine Society in 1854, that he regarded "the abolition of the power of flogging refractory seamen as having been injudicious"; and I think that most men who had experience in handling the crews of merchant ships on the high seas in those days will be inclined to agree with him.

The demand for new clipper ships had by no means abated in 1852, and thirty-three California clippers were launched in this year. Donald McKay built the *Sovereign of the Seas, Bald Eagle,* and *Westward Ho;* William H. Webb, the *Flying Dutchman;* Samuel Hall, the *Polynesia, John Gilpin, Flying Childers,* and *Wizard;* Jacob A. Westervelt, the *Golden City, Golden State,* and *Contest;* Jacob Bell, the *Messenger* and *Jacob Bell;* Paul Curtis, the *Golden West, Queen of the Seas, Cleopatra,* and *Radiant;* J. O. Curtis, the *Phantom* and *Whirlwind;* Jabez Williams, the *Simoon;* R. E. Jackson, the *Winged Racer;* Fernald & Pettigrew, the *Red Rover.*

Undismayed by difficulties as to spars and rigging that beset the minds of other ship-builders, Donald McKay resolved in this year to build a still larger clipper than had yet appeared. This ship was the *Sovereign of the Seas,* of 2421 tons register, and when she was launched in June, 1852, the bells that had welcomed the *New World* and *Stag-Hound* as the largest merchant ships afloat, again rang out a joyous greeting to this noble clipper, as she glided smoothly and swiftly into the blue waters of Boston harbor.

The *Sovereign of the Seas* measured: length 258 feet, breadth 44 feet, depth 23 feet 6 inches, with 20 inches dead-rise at half floor. It is interesting to note that each one of Mr. McKay's clippers had less dead-rise than her predecessor. The *Stag-Hound* had 40 inches dead-rise at half floor with slightly convex water-lines; the *Flying Cloud* and *Staffordshire* 30 inches with concave water-lines and shorter but sharper ends. The *Sovereign of the Seas* had the longest and sharpest ends of any vessel then built, and combined the grace and beauty of the smaller ships with immense strength and power to carry sail.

She had a crew of 105 men and boys, consisting of 4 mates, 2 boatswains, 2 carpenters, 2 sailmakers, 3 stewards, 2 cooks, 80 able seamen, and 10 boys before the mast. She was commanded by Captain Lauchlan McKay, who was born at Shelburne, Nova Scotia, in 1811, being one year younger than his brother Donald. Like him, he went to New York, served an apprenticeship there with Isaac Webb, and after becoming a master shipwright, was appointed carpenter of the U. S. frigate *Constellation,* in which he served four years. Admiral Farragut was a young lieutenant on board this ship at the same time. In 1839 Captain McKay published a work on naval architecture, and soon after, in company with his brother Hugh, opened a shipyard at Boston. Here they did repairing, and in 1846 built the bark *Odd Fellow,* in which Lauchlan sailed as captain. In 1848 he commanded the ship *Jenny Lind,* and made some excellent passages in her. When he took command of the *Sovereign of the Seas,* Captain McKay was in his forty-first year, and of gigantic build and strength.

The *Sovereign of the Seas* sailed from New York for San Francisco, August 4, 1852, a poor season of the year for a rapid run to the equator, but she crossed 25 days out from Sandy Hook, making a run which had never been bettered in the month of August, and only twice equalled—once by the *Raven* from Boston in 1851 and once by the *Hurricane* from New York in 1853. She was 23 days from the equator to 50° S., and 9 days from 50° S. in the Atlantic to the same parallel in the Pacific. After rounding Cape Horn, she carried away her fore- and maintopmasts and foreyard, and it required fourteen days to rerig her, during which time she was kept on her course, and made the run from 50° S. to the equator in the remarkable time, considering her disabled condition, of 29 days. She went thence to San Francisco in 17 days, which is the record for the month of November, and her total run from New York to San Francisco was 103 days.

Had the *Sovereign of the Seas* not been dismasted, it is reasonable to suppose that she would have equalled the fastest run from 50° S. to the equator in the month of October, which is 19 days, made by the *Ocean Telegraph* in 1855. This would have reduced her passage to 93 days; still, as it stands, her passage of 103 days has never been equalled by a vessel sailing from New York for San Francisco in the month of August. Captain McKay received much credit for rerigging his ship at sea and not putting into Valparaiso, and was presented with a very beautiful silver dinner service by the New York Board of Marine Underwriters.

This was the only passage made by the *Sovereign of the Seas* between New York and San Francisco. She carried on this voyage 2950 tons of cargo, and her freight amounted to $84,000; a portion of the

The "Sovereign of the Seas"

cargo, consisting of flour, sold in San Francisco at $44 per barrel.

She cleared from San Francisco in ballast for Honolulu, and there loaded a cargo, or rather several cargoes, of sperm oil which had been landed by American whale-ships in the Pacific, and sailed for New York, February 13, 1853. She had light and variable winds to the equator, her day's runs ranging from 89 to 302 miles, and she made this stretch from Honolulu in 8 days. On February 27th, she was off the Navigator or Samoan Islands, and one cannot help thinking of the delight it would have given Robert Louis Stevenson if he could have looked upon this giant clipper flying southward under her white cloud of canvas, and with what magic words he would have made her name immortal.

On March 4th, the *Sovereign of the Seas* sprung her foretopmast, and although it was fished on the 6th, it was a source of anxiety for the remainder of the passage, and Captain McKay, mindful of his recent experience in these seas, carried sail with a considerable caution. Nothing of special interest occurred until March 15th, when the first strong westerly gales were felt, and a series of remarkable day's runs was begun. Up to noon on March 16th, she had sailed from her position at noon the day before, 396 miles; on the 17th, 311 miles; on the 18th, 411 miles, and on the 19th, 360 miles, a total of 1478 miles in four days. During these four days, she made 34° 43′ of longitude eastward, which with the difference in time gives an average of 15½ knots, or an average of a fraction over 378 miles for each twenty-four hours. In the 11 days from March 10th to the 21st, she made the remarkable run of 3562 miles, and as she made during this time 82° 24′ of longitude, her average allowing for difference in time, was 13¾ knots, or 330 miles each twenty-four hours.

During her great run on the 18th of 411 miles, she made 10° 30′ of longitude, which reduced her sea day to 23 hours 18 minutes, and shows an average speed of 17 2/3 knots, or 424 miles in twenty-four hours. On this day her log records: "Strong northwest breezes and rough sea." It seems extremely improbable that she could have maintained uniform speed of 17 2/3 knots throughout the twenty-four hours, but at times her speed probably slackened to 15 or 16 knots. If this supposition is correct, it follows that her speed must at times have exceeded 17 2/3 knots in order to account for this average. In the absence of any data on this point, which is much to be regretted, it seems probable that she must have sailed at a speed of not less than 19 knots during a portion of these twenty-four hours, and perhaps 20 knots. After rounding Cape Horn she had light and moderate winds, her best day's run being only 286 miles, and she arrived off Sandy Hook May 6, 1853, after a passage of 82 days from Honolulu.

She sailed again from New York for Liverpool, June 18th, passing Sandy Hook at 6:30 P.M., sighted Cape Race in Newfoundland at 6 A.M. on the 24th, was off Cape Clear in Ireland at 6 A.M. on June 30th, took a pilot at 2 P.M. July 2d, and anchored in the Mersey at 10:30 P.M. that day, having made the entire run from dock to anchorage in 13 days 22 hours and 50 minutes. This must be regarded as a most remarkable passage for the season, and has never been equalled by a sailing vessel during the month of June. Her best day's run was on June 28th, 344 miles, by the wind, under single-reefed topsails, and on the 30th, 340 miles with skysails and royal studdingsails set. The Cunard S.S. *Canada* sailed from Boston on the same day that the *Sovereign of the Seas* sailed from New York, and a comparison of their logs published at the time shows that in five days, June 25–30th, the ship outsailed the steamer by 325 miles, and that the best run of the *Canada* during this passage was only 306 miles.

On this voyage her builder, Donald McKay, was a passenger on board the *Sovereign of the Seas,* and he passed most of his waking moments on deck, watching her movement through the water and observing the various strains on her spars and rigging. When he returned home, Enoch Train asked him what he thought of the ship, and Mr. McKay replied, "Well, she appears to be a pretty good ship, but I think I can build one to beat her"; and eventually he did so.

Mrs. Donald McKay sailed with her husband on this voyage and took a keen interest in everything that went on aboard ship. Although this was a summer passage, nevertheless, there was enough rough weather to bring out the splendid sea-going qualities of the vessel, and to Mrs. McKay, who, it is a pleasure to record, is still living, the vivid picture of this thoroughbred clipper wrestling with the winds and waves has always remained one of the exciting experiences of her life.

All of the American clippers made good passages home from China to Atlantic ports in 1852, though no record was broken. The run of the *Shooting Star,* 83 days from Canton to Boston, was the best of the year.

It was during the passage from Canton to New York in this year that Captain Creesy of the *Flying Cloud* had the unusual experience of perusing his own obituary in mid-ocean. It appears that after passing Java Head, and when his vessel was well across the Indian Ocean, she fell in with a ship outward bound, and in exchange for chickens, fruits, and vegetables from Anjer, received newspapers from New York, one of which contained the following somewhat startling announcement:

"Captain Creesy of the ship *Flying Cloud.*—It will be seen by the telegraph news in another column that this gallant sailor is no more. Two days after sailing from San Francisco, bound to China, he died, and the ship proceeded in charge of the mate; he was a native of Marblehead, and about forty-six years of age. For many years, he commanded the ship *Oneida* in the China trade, and was distinguished for the rapidity of his passages. In the *Flying Cloud,* he made the shortest passage on record to San Francisco, and eclipsed the finest and most costly merchant ship in the world,[1] and yet this crowning triumph of his life was attended with many disasters to his spars and sails; still, he pressed on, disdaining to make a port short of

[1] The *Challenge.*

his destination. In every scene of a sailor's life 'with skill superior glowed his daring mind'—his dauntless soul 'rose with the storm and all its dangers shared.' But now he rests from his toils, regardless of his triumphs. Peace to his manes."

It was found that this news originated in New Orleans, having been telegraphed from there to New York, and although no explanation of the blunder was ever made, it at all events relieved Captain Creesy of an annoying lawsuit. It will be remembered that in August, 1851, on the passage to San Francisco, his first officer was put off duty soon after rounding Cape Horn, "in consequence of his arrogating to himself the privilege of cutting up rigging." This was a more serious offence than perhaps appears at first sight, as the *Flying Cloud* was badly crippled aloft, and was a long way from the nearest ship chandler's store, while Captain Creesy needed every fathom of rope on board for preventers and lashings. In due time, the mate turned up in New York and got in tow of a philanthropic legal "gent," who paid his board and lodging while awaiting the arrival of the *Flying Cloud* in order to prosecute Captain Creesy; but when they learned that he was supposed to be dead, the mate was shipped off to sea again, while the sea-lawyer friend lost no time in making fast to his three months' advance.

CHAPTER XIV

CALIFORNIA CLIPPERS OF 1853

DURING the year 1853, twenty ships arrived at San Francisco from Atlantic ports, chiefly New York, in 110 days or less, showing the high standard of efficiency that had been reached. The best passages of the year were made by the *Flying Fish,* 92 days; *John Gilpin,* 93 days; *Contest,* 97 days; *Oriental* 100 days; *Trade Wind,* 102 days; *Westward Ho,* 103 days; *Phantom,* 104 days; *Sword-Fish, Hornet,* and *Flying Cloud,* each 105 days; and *Sea Serpent,* 107 days. The *Comet* arrived on January 17th, after a passage of 112 days from Boston. While off Bermuda she encountered a heavy southwest gale, and was laying to under close-reefed fore- and maintopsails and foretopmast staysail, when the wind suddenly shifted into the southeast and blew with terrific force, carrying away the foretopmast stays, sending the foretopmast over the side, and making junk of the two topsails. Captain Gardner had a good crew, and so soon as the weather moderated, he rerigged his ship at sea, and took her into San Francisco as noted, in 112 days.

Racing had now become close and exciting, and the fleet was so large that it was not uncommon

The "Comet"

for two or three ships to be in company at sea, each striving to outsail the others. As we have seen, the *Flying Fish* won the race this year, and from one of the finest fleets of clippers that ever sailed from New York. The match between her and the *John Gilpin* was exceedingly close, and taken altogether was one of the best ever sailed upon this famous ocean course, the Derby of the sea. It was Samuel Hall against Donald McKay, Justin Doane against Edward Nickels, and all against the fleet.

The *John Gilpin* sailed out past Sandy Hook, October 29, 1852, followed by the *Flying Fish* on November 1st, and before the green Highlands of Neversink had disappeared below the horizon both ships were under a cloud of canvas. The *Flying Fish* fanned along through the doldrums and crossed the equator 21 days from Sandy Hook, leading the *John Gilpin* by one day. From the line to 50° S., the *John Gilpin* made the run in 23 days, passing the *Flying Fish* and getting a clear lead of two days. The *Flying Fish* did some fine sailing here; dashing through the Straits of Le Maire, she came up alongside the *John Gilpin* just off the Horn, and Nickels, ever famous for his jovial good-cheer, invited Doane to come aboard and dine with him, "which invitation," the *John Gilpin's* log-book ruefully records, "I was reluctantly obliged to decline." This is perhaps the only instance of an invitation to dine out being received off Cape Horn. Few men have had the opportunity to extend such unique hospitality and certainly none could do so more heartily and gracefully than the famous commander of the *Flying Fish.* His vessel made the run from 50° S. in the Atlantic to 50° S. in the Pacific in 7 days, leading her rival by two days. From this point to the equator, the *Flying Fish* was 19 and the *John Gilpin* 20 days. From here the *John Gilpin* showed remarkable speed, making the run to San Francisco in 15 days, a total of 93 days, closely followed by the *Flying Fish,* 92 days from Sandy Hook. Their abstract logs are as follows:

	Flying Fish	*John Gilpin*
Sandy Hook to the equator.......	21 days	24 days.
Equator to 50° S................	27 "	23 "
50° in the Atlantic to 50° S. in Pacific	7 "	11 "
To the equator..................	19 "	20 "
Equator to San Francisco........	18 "	15 "
Total	92 "	93 "

When we reflect that this match was sailed over a course of some 15,000 miles, and that the difference of time was only twenty-four hours, one is impressed with the perfection to which the models of the vessels had been brought, as well as the exactness of the data relating to the winds and currents that had been gathered and reduced to a system by Maury, and with the skill of their captains, who were guided by his charts and sailing directions. The average difference of sailing between these two ships was less than six seconds per mile over the entire distance. Few races over thirty-mile courses have been sailed by yachts more evenly matched.

No racing yachts have ever been handled with greater care and skill than were these clipper ships over courses of thousands of miles. It was the custom for the captains to change their clothes at eight o'clock in the evening and at the same time in the morning, the exceptions being in thick and stormy weather, when they would not be out of their clothes perhaps for two or three days at a time. The officers and men of the watch below were expected to be ready to tumble out on deck at a moment's notice to make or to shorten sail. The "old man" was very likely to appear on deck at any moment, night or day, which kept the officers in a high state of watchfulness. This was the only way in which these ships could be sailed and make the passages they did.

Another splendid match of this year, sailed to the eastward round the Horn, was that between the *Northern Light* and the *Contest.* The *Contest* was built by Jacob A. Westervelt and commanded by Captain William Brewster, of Stonington, and was one of the fastest ships owned by A. A. Low & Brother. She sailed from San Francisco for New York, March 12, 1853, followed by the *Northern Light* on the 13th, bound for Boston. Off Cape Horn, the *Northern Light* came up with and signalled the *Contest,* and from there led her home by three days, the *Northern Light* being 76 days 5 hours to Boston Light, while the *Contest* was 80 days to Sandy Hook. In 1854 the *Comet* made the passage from San Francisco to New York in 76 days, these being the record passages from San Francisco to Atlantic ports.

On this famous passage the *Northern Light* made the run from San Francisco to Cape Horn in 38 days, and was off Rio Janeiro in 52 days, thence to Boston Light in 24 days. Her best day's run was 354 miles. She made the round voyage to San Francisco and return, including detention in port, in exactly seven months. Captain Hatch, her commander, was a thorough clipper ship captain, who never allowed his ship to suffer for want of canvas, and on this passage he brought his vessel across Massachusetts Bay before a fresh easterly breeze, carrying her ringtail, skysails, and studding-sails on both sides, alow and aloft, until she was off Boston Light—a superb marine picture, and one seldom seen by landsmen even in those days.

No more beautiful sight can be imagined than a morning at sea, with these magnificent vessels racing in mid-ocean, perhaps two or three of them in sight at once; the sun rising amid golden clouds; the dark blue sea flecked with glistening white caps; long, low black hulls cleaving a pathway of sparkling foam; towering masts, and yards covered with snowy canvas which bellies to the crisp morning breeze as if sculptured in marble; the officers alert and keen for the contest; the African cook showing his woolly head and grinning, good-natured face out through the weather door of the galley, while the wholesome odor of steaming coffee gladdens the hearts of officers and men. And after all, when has anything ever tasted half so refreshing as a tin pot of hot coffee, sweetened with molasses, under the lee of the weather bulwark, in the chill dawn of the morning watch?

The third mate walks over to the lee side and knocks the ashes out of his pipe against the rail, and as the sparks fly far to leeward, like falling stars among the foaming waves, he sings out, "Turn to there forward and wash down decks; boatswain, take a pair of those gulpins and rig the head pump; the rest of you get the gear triced up." The watch, with sand, buckets of water, and brooms, bare-footed and with trousers rolled up to their knees, begin to scrub and scrub and scrub. Then when the sun has dried out ropes and canvas, the gear is swayed up fore and aft, with watch tackles on the chain topsail sheets, and a hearty:

"Way haul away,
Haul away the bowline,
Way haul away, Haul away, Joe!"

The halliards are led along the deck fore and aft in the grip of clean brawny fists with sinewy arms and broad backs behind them, the ordinary seamen and boys tailing on, and perhaps the cook, steward, carpenter, and sailmaker lending a hand, and all hands join in a ringing chorus of the ocean, mingling in harmony with the clear sky, indigo-blue waves, and the sea breeze purring aloft among the spars and rigging:

"Oh, poor Reuben Ranzo,
Ranzo, boys, O Ranzo,
Oh, Ranzo was no sailor,
Ranzo boys, O Ranzo.
So they shipped him aboard a whaler,
Ranzo boys, O Ranzo,

And he could not do his duty,
Ranzo boys, O Ranzo.
So the mate, he being a bad man,
Ranzo boys, O Ranzo,
He led him to the gangway,
Ranzo boys, O Ranzo,
And he gave him five-and-twenty,
Ranzo boys, O Ranzo,
But the captain, he being a good man,
Ranzo boys, O Ranzo,
He took him in the cabin,
Ranzo boys, O Ranzo,
And he gave him wine and whiskey,
Ranzo boys, O Ranzo,
And he learned him navigation,
Ranzo boys, O Ranzo,
And now he 's Captain Ranzo,
Ranzo boys, O Ranzo."

Finally the mate's clear, sharp order comes: "Belay there; clap a watch tackle on the lee fore brace." "Aye, aye, sir!" And so every sheet, halliard, and brace is swayed up and tautened to the freshening breeze. The gear is coiled up, the brass-work polished until it glistens in the morning sun, the paintwork and gratings are wiped off, decks swabbed dry, and the pumps manned to another rousing chanty:

"London town is a-burning,
Oh, run with the bullgine, run.
Way, yay, way, yay, yar,
Oh, run with the bullgine, run."

The "old man" gets his morning sights, the log is hove, the wheel and watch are relieved at eight bells, and the clipper is ready for another day of stress and strain.

Mornings like these bring keen appetites to officers and men, so the watch below sit about on their chests in the forecastle or on the fore hatch and dive into the mess kid with knives and spoons. It may be a chunk of salt pork or cold salt beef, or what Rufus Choate, in one of his flights of forensic eloquence, described as the "nutritious hash," "succulent lob-scouse," or "palatable dandy funk," with plenty of hard tack in the bread barge, and all washed down with unlimited coffee. Not quail on toast or devilled kidneys, to be sure, but good substantial seamen's food, upon which a man can work better at sea, grow stronger, and become less tired than on any other.

In the old days captains used to lay in large stocks of chickens, eggs, etc., for their crews at Anjer Point, but before the ship was half-way across the Indian Ocean, the men would begin to crow in the dog watch, and come aft in a body, asking that their salt junk might be restored to them. In those days, as now, salmon were plentiful in California, but their introduction on board the clipper ships failed to tempt the appetites of sailormen when off soundings. They said they liked salt junk a good deal better. Besides, it gave them something to growl about—for sailors knew how to curse junk according to traditions approved by generations of jackies, but when it came to chickens and salmon they were at a loss for sufficiently vigorous and appropriate expletives to express their disgust. There used to be a yarn about an old shellback who, in a cross-examination, was asked by a smart Boston lawyer whether the crew did not have enough to eat. The mariner replied, "Well, yes, your honor, there was enough of it, such as it was"; and upon further inquiry as to the quality of the food, he answered, "Now, you see, sir, it was like this: the food was good enough, what there was of it." And this summed up a sailor's idea of food and pretty much everything else, in those days.

The building of clipper ships in the United States reached its zenith in 1853. In that year forty-eight clippers were added to the California fleet, and the wild excitement of building, owning, and racing these splendid ships was at its height. Every one who had capital to invest wanted one, or at least shares in one, and the ship-building yards were taxed to their utmost capacity. It should be remembered also that there was a great deal of other ship-building going on in the United States besides the clippers, and that captains, officers, and crews for such a large number of vessels were by no means easy to obtain.

In this year Donald McKay built the *Empress of the Seas* and *Romance of the Seas;* William H. Webb, the *Fly Away, Snap Dragon,* and *Young America;* Jacob A. Westerwelt, the *Cathay* and *Sweepstakes;* Samuel Hall, the second *Oriental,* the *Amphitrite,* and *Mystery;* Greenman & Co., the *David Crockett;* Roosevelt & Joyce, the *David Brown;* John Currier, the *Guiding Star;* Thomas Collier, the second *Panama;* J. W.

The "Young America"

Cox, the *Red Gauntlet;* Briggs Brothers, the *John Land* and *Golden Light;* and Toby & Littlefield, the *Morning Star*—all beautiful ships, the pride of their owners and captains.

The *Romance of the Seas,* owned by George B. Upton, of Boston, was the last extreme clipper ship built by Donald McKay for the California trade. She was a beautiful vessel, with extremely fine lines, heavily sparred, and proved an exceedingly fast ship in moderate weather. Captain Dumaresq was in command on her first voyage to San Francisco. She was 1782 tons register; length 240 feet, breadth 39 feet 6 inches, depth 29 feet 6 inches. The *Sweepstakes,* owned by Grinnell, Minturn & Co., and designed by Daniel Westervelt, a son of Jacob A. Westervelt, was a very sharp and handsome ship, and was the last extreme clipper built in the Westervelt yard. She made three passages from New York to San Francisco averaging 106 days. Captain George Lane, who commanded her for a number of years, was subsequently a commander in the Pacific Mail between San Francisco and China, and later became the agent of the company at Hong-kong.

The *Young America,* the last extreme clipper built by William H. Webb, was owned by George Daniels, of New York, and for several years was commanded by Captain David Babcock. This ship was 1962 tons register; length 236 feet 6 inches, breadth 42 feet, depth 28 feet 6 inches. She proved an excellent and fast vessel. Among her many fine passages may be mentioned: from New York to San Francisco, 103, 107, 110, 112, 117, and 116 days, and from San Francisco to New York, 92, 97, 85, 101, 103, and 83 days; San Francisco to Liverpool, 103 and 106 days; Liverpool to San Francisco, 117, 111, and 99 days; and twenty consecutive passages from New York to San Francisco averaging 117 days. Her best performance, however, was from 50° S. in the Atlantic to 50° S. in the Pacific, in the record time of 6 days. She, too, was an exceedingly handsome ship, and was Mr. Webb's favorite among all the splendid ships constructed by him. After thirty years' continuous service in the San Francisco trade, during which she is said to have rounded Cape Horn over fifty times, she was finally sold to a firm in Austria, upon condition that her name should be changed. She then became known as the *Miroslav* and foundered with all hands in 1888, while bound from Philadelphia to a European port.

CHAPTER XV

THE "GREAT REPUBLIC" AND THE "DREADNOUGHT"

TWO other ships built in 1853 deserve notice here, though they were not constructed for the California trade. They were Donald McKay's *Great Republic* and the famous packet ship *Dreadnought.*

For some time Mr. McKay had contemplated building a ship for the Australian trade, but failing to find any one to join in the undertaking, and stimulated by the success of the *Sovereign of the Seas,* he resolved to build her for himself. This vessel was the *Great Republic,* the largest extreme clipper ship ever built. She attracted universal attention from the fact of her being by far the largest merchant ship constructed up to that time, and also, among those interested in shipping, on account of the excellence of her construction and her majestic beauty.

This vessel was 4555 tons register, and measured: length 335 feet, breadth 53 feet, depth 38 feet. She had four decks, the upper or spar deck being flush with the covering board and protected by a rail on turned oak stanchions. She carried a fifteen horse-power engine on deck to hoist the yards and to work the pumps, this being the first time an engine was put aboard a sailing ship for these purposes. She had four masts with Forbes's rig [1] on the fore-, main-, and mizenmasts, the after- or spankermast being barque-rigged.

October 4, 1853, was a proud day for Boston. Business was suspended, and the schools were closed in order that every one might have an opportunity to see the launch of the *Great Republic.* People flocked from far and near. It was estimated that thirty thousand persons crossed by ferry to East Boston, while Chelsea Bridge, the Navy Yard at Charlestown, and the wharves at the north end of

[1] Forbes's rig was invented by Captain R. B. Forbes, and was first put on the topsail schooner *Midas* in 1841, afterwards on the auxiliaries *Edith, Massachusetts,* and *Meteor;* ships, *R. B. Forbes, Lintin, Flying Childers, Aurora, Cornelius Grinnell,* and probably others. In this rig the topmast was fidded abaft the lowermast head, and the lower topsail yard hoisted on the lowermast head from the eyes of the lower rigging to the cap. The lower topsail had two reefs with reef-tackles, buntlines, and clewlines, as in the single topsail rig. The upper topsail hoisted on the topmast and had the same gear as the lower topsail. Sometimes the topmast was fidded before the lower masthead, and then the lower topsail yard hoisted on the doubling of the topmast. This rig was an improvement upon the single topsail rig, but was eventually superseded by Howes's rig, which was invented by Captain Frederic Howes, of Brewster, Massachusetts, who in 1853 first put it on the ship *Climax,* of Boston, which he commanded. Captain Howes took out a United States patent for his rig in 1854. In this rig, the lower topsail yard is slung by a truss at the lower mast cap; indeed, Howes's rig is the double topsail rig of the present day, though one does not often hear the name of Captain Howes in connection with it.

the city were thronged by at least as many more. The shipping at the Navy Yard was gayly dressed with bunting, and the harbor was filled with steamers and pleasure boats crowded with people. It was a beautiful day, with a clear blue sky, bright sunshine, and a gentle westerly breeze.

All the staging used in the construction of the ship had been removed, leaving her in full view as she rested upon the ways. Her long black hull had no ornament except a beautifully carved eagle's head where the sweep of her raking stem and the sharp lines of her bow intersected, and across her handsome stern the American eagle with extended wings, under which her name and port of hail were carved in plain block letters. She had the same graceful sheer, finely formed midship section, and beautifully moulded ends that had been seen in this yard in the *Stag-Hound, Flying Cloud, Bald Eagle, Westward Ho, Flying Fish,* and *Sovereign of the Seas,* only on a much larger scale; indeed, from end to end she looked the out-and-out clipper. Spars were erected at the mast partners, and from the main she carried a long coach-whip pennant and a large white flag with the arms of the United States in the centre; from the other three spars she flew large United States ensigns, and from a staff on her bowsprit, the Union Jack.

The sun gleamed and sparkled upon her smooth, bright yellow-metal sheathing, when at twelve o'clock the signal was given and the shores fell, to the wild chorus of topmauls, so well known in every Atlantic port fifty years ago. She moved slowly at first; then, gathering way, fairly leaped into the sea, amid smoke and fire from the burning ways, the roar of artillery, the music of bands, and the cheers of the vast multitude. So swiftly did she leave the ways that two anchors and the powerful steamer *R. B. Forbes* barely succeeded in bringing her up, close to Chelsea Bridge. The *Great Republic* was named by Captain Alden Gifford, who performed the ceremony by breaking a bottle of Cochituate water over her bow as she began to move along the ways. This was an innovation that created much comment at the time, and was permitted by Mr. McKay in deference to the wishes of Deacon Moses Grant and a number of energetic Boston women who were pushing the temperance movement and desired to advertise their wares.

During the afternoon she was towed under the shears at the Navy Yard to receive her masts, yards, and rigging, and the work of fitting them was done under the supervision of Lauchlan McKay, her captain. As no vessel before or since ever had such enormous spars, their dimensions are interesting enough to be given in full:

Masts	Diameters Inches	Lengths Feet	Mastheads Feet
Fore	44	130	36
Top	24	76	12
Topgallant	18	28	0
Royal	15	22	0
Skysail	11	19	Pole 12
Main	44	131	36
Top	24	76	12
Topgallant	18	28	0

Masts	Diameters Inches	Lengths Feet	Mastheads Feet
Royal	15	22	0
Skysail	11	19	Pole 12
Mizen	40	122	33
Top	22	69	10
Topgallant	16	22	0
Royal	10	19	0
Skysail	8	15	Pole 8
Yards			**Yardarms**
Fore	26	110	6
Lower topsail	24	90	5
Upper topsail	19	76	4½
Topgallant	15	62	4
Royal	12	51	3½
Skysail	9	40	3
Main	28	120	6
Lower topsail	24	92	5
Upper topsail	19	76	4
Topgallant	15	62	4
Royal	12	51	3½
Skysail	9	40	3
Crossjack	24	90	5
Lower mizentopsail	19	76	4½
Upper mizentopsail	15	62	4
Topgallant	12	51	3½
Royal	9	40	3
Skysail	6	29	2

The spankermast, nowadays called the jigger, was 26 inches in diameter, 110 feet long, including 14 feet head, and the topmast was 40 feet long divided at 15 and 10 feet above the cap, for the gaff-topsail and gaff-topgallantsail. The spanker boom was 40 feet long, including 2 feet end, and the gaff

34 feet, including 8 feet end. The bowsprit was 44 inches in diameter and 30 feet out-board; the jibboom 23 inches in diameter, and 18 feet outside of the cap, and the flying jibboom was 14 feet long including 6 feet end. Her fore and main rigging and fore- and maintopmast backstays were 12½ inch, four-stranded Russian hemp rope, wormed, and served over the eye and over the ends to the leading trucks. The mizen rigging and mizentopmast rigging were of eight-inch rope.

It was Mr. McKay's intention to put the *Great Republic* into the Australian trade in competition with the British clippers that were then coming out, and when her rigging and outfit were completed, she was towed to New York by the *R. B. Forbes* and placed in the hands of Grinnell, Minturn & Co., who began loading her for Liverpool at the foot of Dover Street, East River. Thousands of people came to see this splendid ship, including the Governor of New York, members of the Legislature, and other prominent citizens. The season was favorable for a rapid passage across the Atlantic, and it was confidently predicted that the *Great Republic* would make a record run to Liverpool.

She was nearly ready for sea with all her sails bent below the royals, when, on the night of December 26, 1853, a fire broke out in Front Street, one block from where the vessel lay, and nearly in line with her as the wind was then blowing. At a little past midnight the watchman called the second mate, as sparks were flying across and falling in all directions about the ship. All hands were at once called and stationed with buckets of water in various parts of the ship; men were sent into the fore-, main-, and mizentops, and whips were rove to send up buckets of water. Soon the foresail burst into flames, and one by one the topsails and topgallantsails took fire. Every effort was made to cut the sails from the yards, but the men were driven back exhausted, and the firemen, who by this time had arrived with their engines, refused to work on board or near the ship for fear of falling blocks and gear.

Captain McKay, and Captain Ellis, representing the underwriters, had a hurried consultation, and it was decided, in order to save the hull, to cut away the masts. The fore- and foretopmast stays and rigging were cut and the mast went over the side into the dock; the topmast in falling broke short off and came down, end on, through three decks. The main- and mizenmasts were next cut away, and in falling, crushed boats, deckhouses, and rails, and disabled the steam-engine. At this time the decks were a mass of burning yards, masts, sails, and rigging. The firemen now got to work, and toward morning succeeded in putting out the fire on deck.

The firemen had left, and it was supposed that the hull and cargo were safe, when suddenly smoke was discovered coming from the hold, and it was found that the burning foretopmast in falling through the decks had set fire to the cargo. This fire had gained such headway that it was beyond control; the ship was therefore scutted in three places and sunk ten feet when she took the bottom. Every means was used to extinguish the fire, but she burned for two days until the flames reached the water's edge. After the fire had burned itself out a coffer-dam was built and the wreck floated by means of steam pumps. It was found that a portion of her cargo of grain had swollen to such an extent as to start the knees and beams of the lower hold, and that the hull was otherwise badly strained and buckled. She was therefore condemned and abandoned to the underwriters. The ships *Joseph Walker* and *White Squall* were also destroyed in this fire.

The wreck of the *Great Republic* was subsequently sold by the underwriters to Captain N. B. Palmer and taken to Greenpoint, Long Island, to be rebuilt by Sneeden & Whitlock, and she eventually became the property of A. A. Low & Brother. The rebuilding occupied more than a year, and when the *Great Republic* again appeared, much of the original beauty of her hull had been restored. The spar-deck had not been replaced, but her freeboard was nearly the same, as the height of the bulwarks was only a little below the former upper deck, and the same sheer line had been preserved. Forward, the eagle's head which had been destroyed was replaced by a carved billet head and scrool, and her bow was still exceedingly handsome. A great change had been wrought aloft; her sail plan had been cut down and all of her spars greatly reduced in length—the fore- and mainmasts 17 feet, the fore- and main-yards 20 feet, and all other spars in proportion. She still carried four masts, but her rig had been changed to Howes's double topsail yards.

As rebuilt the *Great Republic* registered 3357 tons, and was still the largest merchant ship of her time,

The "Great Republic"

but her reduced rig required only one half the number of hands to handle it—fifty able seamen and fifteen ordinary seamen and boys. It was for this purpose that her sail plan had been cut down, as freights were beginning to slacken and the tide of economy was setting in. It is to be regretted that she could not have made a few voyages under her original rig, as her performance in strong winds under the reduced rig left little room for doubt that she would have proved, what Mr. McKay intended her to be, the swiftest sailing ship ever built.

The *Great Republic* sailed on her first voyage, February 21, 1855, commanded by Captain Limeburner, and made the run from Sandy Hook to Land's End in thirteen days. On her arrival at London, three days later, she was obliged to lie in the Thames, as no dock was large enough to take her. She was subsequently chartered by the French Government as a troop ship during the Crimean War, and carried 1600 British soldiers from Liverpool to Marseilles. During the Civil War, she was chartered by the United States Government as a troop ship, and was one of the transports in Butler's expedition to Ship Island.

The burning of the *Great Republic* was a severe blow to Donald McKay, from which he never fully recovered, but he soon began to bring out Australian clippers, some of which proved quite as famous as the ships he had previously constructed.

The well-known packet ship *Dreadnought* also came out in 1853. She was built by Currier & Townsend at Newburyport, and was 1413 tons register; length 210 feet, breadth 40 feet, depth 26 feet. This ship was owned by Governor E. D. Morgan, Francis B. Cutting, David Ogden, and others, of New York, who subscribed to build her for Captain Samuel Samuels. He superintended her construction and under his able command she made some remarkably quick voyages between New York and Liverpool, sailing in David Ogden's Red Cross Line, with the *Victory, Racer,* and *Highflyer.*

Captain Samuels was born in Philadelphia in 1823 and went to sea when he was eleven years old, and a narrative of his adventures afloat and on shore is contained in his interesting memoirs entitled, *From the Forecastle to the Cabin,* published in 1887. He was a most amiable and entertaining companion, full of good humor and penetrating wit. He also cherished a belief in the uplifting influence of an enterprising press agent, and perhaps no merchant ship of modern times has been better advertised than the *Dreadnought.* She sailed on her first voyage from New York for Liverpool, December 15, 1853, and from that date until her arrival at New York, January 28, 1855, had made eight passages between New York and Liverpool, the average time of her eastern passages being 21 days 15 hours, and her western passages 24 days 12 hours from dock to dock.

Captain Samuels commanded the *Dreadnought* for ten years, and during that time she made from seventy to eighty passages across the Atlantic, and must have had ample opportunity to make fast voyages and day's runs. The following abstracts from the logs of her best passages are therefore of interest:

She sailed from New York for Liverpool, November 20, 1854; passed Sandy Hook at 6.30 P.M. and ran to noon, November 21st, 120 miles; 22d, 57 miles; 23d, 225 miles; 24th, 300 miles; 25th, 175 miles; 26th, 125 miles; 27th, 250 miles; 28th, 263 miles; 29th, 240 miles; 30th, 270 miles; December 1st, 242 miles; 2d, 222 miles; 3d, 212 miles; 4th, 320 miles. Total 3071 miles. The log records:

At noon on the 4th took a pilot off Point Lynas; was detained eight hours for want of water on the bar; arrived in the Mersey at 10 P. M.; thus making the passage in 14 days 4 hours, apparent time. Deducting eight hours for detention by tide at the bar, and also deducting the difference of longitude, 4 hours and 45 minutes, gives the mean or true time of passage, 13 days 11 hours and 15 minutes. Average speed for the passage, 9½ miles per hour. On this passage, the *Dreadnought* was off Cape Clear, Ireland, in 12 days 12 hours from Sandy Hook.

She sailed from New York, May 4, 1855, and arrived at Liverpool May 20th; passage recorded as 15 days 12 hours.

She sailed from Sandy Hook, January 24, 1856 (time not given), and ran to noon, January 25th, 345 miles; 26th, 312 miles; 27th, 252 miles; 28th, 223 miles; 29th, violent gale, drifted 90 miles west-southwest; 30th, 115 miles; 31st, 212 miles; February 1st, 228 miles; 2d, 208 miles; 3d, 185 miles; 4th, 238 miles; 5th, 252 miles; 6th, 244 miles; 7th, 212 miles; 8th, off Point Lynas. Hove-to until daylight for pilot and tide. Total distance run 3116 miles in 14 days, or an average of 222 miles per day.

The *Dreadnought* sailed from New York, February 27, 1859; at 3 P.M. discharged pilot, and ran to noon, February 28th, 200 miles; wind south to west-northwest, brisk breezes. March 1st, 293 miles; west-northwest fresh breezes. 2d, 262 miles; northwest to north-northwest brisk gales and snow-squalls. 3d, 208 miles; north-northwest to north heavy gales and snow-squalls. 4th, 178 miles; north-northeast to north heavy gales and snow-squalls. 5th, 218 miles; north to north-northeast heavy gales and snow-squalls. 6th, 133 miles; northeast to south light breezes. 7th, 282 miles; south-southeast brisk breezes and clear. 8th, 313 miles; south-southwest to south fresh breezes and clear. 9th, 268 miles; south to southeast brisk gales. 10th, 205 miles; southeast to southwest brisk breezes and squally. 11th, 308 miles; south to southwest strong breeze and squally. 12th, 150 miles; southwest, thick weather. Distance sailed from Sandy Hook to the Northwest Lightship, 3018 miles; passage 13 days 8 hours, mean time.

It was during this passage that the *Dreadnought* is supposed to have made the run from Sandy Hook to Queenstown in 9 days 17 hours, but an analysis of the abstract log shows that 9 days 21 hours after discharging her pilot to the eastward of Sandy Hook she was not within 400 miles of Queenstown.

How this mythical tale originated, is difficult to imagine, but it has been passed along from one scribe to another these many years, until at last it has reached the dignity of an "historical fact," having recently been embalmed in an encyclopedia. Curiously enough, Captain Samuels appears to be

The "Dreadnought"

almost the only person who has written about the *Dreadnought* who does not refer to this fable. In his memoirs, he makes no mention of it.

The best passage to the westward made by the *Dreadnought* was in 1854, when she ran from the Rock Light, Liverpool, to Sandy Hook in 19 days. While it cannot be said that the *Dreadnought* ever made the fastest passage of a sailing vessel between New York and Liverpool, as the records in this respect are held by the *Red Jacket,* Captain Asa Eldridge, from Sandy Hook to the Rock Light, in 13 days 1 hour, in 1854, and by the *Andrew Jackson,* Captain John Williams, from Rock Light to Sandy Hook in 15 days, in 1860, still the uniform speed of the *Dreadnought's* many voyages entitles her to a high place among the celebrated packet ships of the past.

The *Dreadnought* was a strikingly handsome and well-designed, though by no means a sharp ship. Her masts, yards, sails, ironwork, blocks, and standing and running rigging were of the best material and were always carefully looked after. She was a ship that would stand almost any amount of driving in heavy weather, and her fast passages were in a measure due to this excellent quality, though mainly to the unceasing vigilance and splendid seamanship of her commander. She was wrecked in 1869 while under the command of Captain P. N. Mayhew; her crew were rescued after being adrift fourteen days in the boats, but the noble old packet ship went to pieces among the rugged cliffs and crags and roaring breakers of Cape Horn.

CHAPTER XVI

AMERICAN CLIPPERS OF 1854 AND 1855

DURING the year 1854 no less than twenty passages were made from Atlantic ports to San Francisco in 110 days or less. The *Flying Cloud* repeated her famous record passage of 89 days, and was followed by the *Romance of the Seas,* 96 days; *Witchcraft,* 97 days; *David Brown,* 98 days, and *Hurricane,* 99 days. The abstract log of the *Flying Cloud* is as follows:

Sandy Hook to the equator	17	days.
Equator to 50° South	25	"
From 50° South in the Atlantic to 50° South in the Pacific	12	"
To the equator	20	"
To San Francisco	15	"
Total	89	"

On this passage the *Flying Cloud* gave a fine example of her sailing qualities. She sailed eight days after the *Archer,* also an exceedingly fast ship, and led her into San Francisco by nine days. Captain Creesy received a grand ovation on this, his second record passage, and the merchants of San Francisco, always generous and hospitable, vied with each other to do him honor. Upon his return to New

York, a banquet was given him at the Astor House, then the finest hotel in the city, and a splendid service of silver plate was presented to him by the New York and Boston Marine Underwriters.

The *Romance of the Seas* sailed from Boston two days after the *David Brown*, commanded by Captain George Brewster, of Stonington, had passed out by Sandy Hook, but came up with her off the coast of Brazil. From this point they were frequently in company for days together, finally passing through the Golden Gate side by side, March 23, 1854. After discharging their cargoes, they again passed out of the Golden Gate together, this time bound for Hong-kong, and while they were not in company during this passage of 45 days, they anchored in Hong-kong harbor on the same day and almost at the same hour. The log of the *Romance of the Seas* records that skysails and royal studdingsails were set just outside the Golden Gate and were not taken in during the passage until entering the harbor of Hong-kong.

It is difficult to realize the intense interest with which these clipper ship races were regarded in those days; and it is doubtful whether at the present day any branch of sport inspires so much wholesome, intelligent enthusiasm as did these splendid ocean matches of the old clippers.

In this year a change came over the California trade. The wild rush to the mines had subsided, and the markets of San Francisco, while not overstocked, were so sufficiently and regularly supplied as to render great speed in the transportation of merchandise unnecessary; the rates of freight had therefore declined, but were still good. Twenty ships, the last of the extreme clippers, were built in 1854 for the California trade, including some which became celebrated, such as the *Canvasback, Fleetwing, Grace Darling, Harvey Birch, Nabob, Nonpareil, Ocean Telegraph, Rattler, Robin Hood,* and *Sierra Nevada;* but we miss from among the ship-builders of this year the names of Donald McKay, William H. Webb, Samuel Hall, Jacob A. Westervelt, and George Raynes, none of whom brought out California clippers.

Although no more extreme clippers were built for the California trade after 1854, a fine class of ships, known as medium clippers, was constructed, some of which proved exceedingly fast, and remarkable passages continued to be made. Many of these medium clippers would be considered very sharp and heavily sparred vessels at the present time.

The *Sunny South,* of 703 tons register, was one of the prettiest clippers ever launched at New York, and was the only sailing ship built by George Steers, the designer of the yacht *America,* steam frigate *Niagara,* and Collins Line steamship *Adriatic.* She was built for the China trade, was launched at Williamsburg, September 7, 1854; was owned by Napier, Johnson & Co., and was commanded by Captain Michael Gregory. It is a singular fact that while this ship was well known to possess great speed when in company with other clippers, yet she never made a passage worthy of being recorded, and was not a very successful ship financially; although the product of the skill of a designer, who, dying in early manhood, left a name so interwoven with his country's triumphs upon the sea that it can never be forgotten.

In 1859, the *Sunny South* was sold at Havana, her name being changed to *Emanuela.* At that time her royal studdingsail booms and skysail masts and yards were removed. On August 10, 1860, she was seized in the Mozambique Channel flying the Chilian flag, with a cargo of slaves on board, by the British man-of-war *Brisk,* and the following particulars of her capture are given by one of the officers of that vessel:

"At 11:30 A.M. on the 10th of August last, as Her Majesty's ship *Brisk,* Captain De Horsey, bearing the flag of Rear-Admiral the Hon. Sir Henry Keppel, K. C. B., was running to the northward in the Mozambique Channel, a sail was reported as seen from the masthead. Steam was got up without delay, and sail made in chase. It being hazy, the stranger was shortly lost sight of. When the weather had partially cleared the stranger was reported four points on our starboard bow, and the ship's course was altered in that direction. We were now going eleven knots and a half, and the Captain, feeling that it must be something out of the common that would alter bearings at that distance in so short a time, proceeded himself with his glass to the foretopmast head, officers mounting the rigging.

"That a general excitement prevailed was evident from the manner in which our sails were trimmed, taken in, and set again. Hottentots and landsmen, who on other occasions only looked at ropes, now laid hold of them with a will. The

Captain's order from the masthead to keep away two points showed that he had observed something suspicious—in fact, he had noticed a sudden alteration in the course of the chase, and pronounced her to be a long, rakish-looking ship, too large to be a slaver, but thought there was something very suspicious in the sudden alteration of her course, her crowd of sail, and the unusual number of staysails.

"At about 3 P.M. we could see her hull from the deck, and, carrying with us a fresh breeze, while she was in the doldrums, we closed on her rapidly. When within half a mile we hoisted our colors, when every glass was pointed toward her peak, and all sorts of conjectures were made as to what colors she would show. No one could imagine that so large a vessel could be a slaver.

"On closing under her lee, and when within a cable's length, a white package was thrown from her side into the sea; and the experienced then exclaimed, 'A slaver, and there go her papers!' A few minutes more, and we sheered up alongside to leeward of as beautiful model of a ship as ever was seen. Some forty dejected looking individuals, apparently a mixture of all nations, stood on her deck; still no colors, nor did she appear inclined to shorten sail or heave-to. The Captain then determined to run ahead and lower the quarter-boats to drop down and board; and as this manœuvre was being carried out a blank gun caused her to square the mainyard, which she did with studding-sails hanging to the yard, and luffed up into the wind.

The "Brisk" The "Emanuela"

"It was an anxious five minutes to those on board while the boats were away. A small white British ensign run up at her peak showed that she was a prize, and a voice hailed us, 'Eight hundred and fifty slaves on board!'"

In 1855 the California fleet was increased by the building of thirteen medium clipper ships, among which were the *Andrew Jackson, Carrier Dove, Charmer, Daring, Herald of the Morning, Mary Whitridge,* and *Ocean Express.* Only three passages were made from Atlantic ports to San Francisco during this year in 100 days or less; the *Herald of the Morning,* from New York, 99 days; *Neptune's Car,* from New York, and *Westward Ho,* from Boston, each 100 days. Thirteen ships made the passage in over 100 days and less than 110 days; among them being the *Boston Light,* from Boston, 102 days; the *Cleopatra* and *Red Rover,* from New York, each 107 days; the *Flying Cloud,* from New York, and *Meteor* and *Don Quixote,* from Boston, each 108 days; the *Flying Fish,* two passages from Boston in 109 and 105 days, and the *Governor Morton,* from New York in 104 days.

This was Captain Creesy's last voyage in the *Flying Cloud,* and he now retired to his home in Salem until 1861, when he was appointed a Commander in the United States Navy and assigned to the clipper ship *Ino.* She carried a crew of eighty men from Marblehead, and on her second cruise in 1862 made the record run of twelve days from New York to Cadiz. Captain Creesy subsequently commanded the clipper ship *Archer,* and made two voyages to China. He died at Salem in 1871, in his fifty-seventh year. So long as the American clipper ships and their brilliant exploits hold a place in the memory of man, the names of Josiah Creesy and the *Flying Cloud* will be remembered with pride.

The *Mary Whitridge* became one of the most famous of the clippers launched in 1855. She was built in Baltimore, where she was owned by Thomas Whitridge & Co., and was commanded by Captain Robert B. Cheesborough, also of that port. She was 877 tons register; length 168 feet, breadth 34 feet, depth 21 feet. On her first voyage she made the remarkable run of 13 days 7 hours from Cape Charles to the Rock Light, Liverpool. She was engaged for many years in the China trade under the command of Captain Benjamin F. Cutler and bore the reputation of being the finest and fastest ship sailing out of Baltimore.

At this time an important development took place in the California trade. It had been found that the fertile soil of the Pacific slope could be made to yield other treasures than gold, and in May, 1855, the barque *Greenfield,* Captain Follansbee, loaded the first consignment of wheat exported from California, consisting of 4752 bags. She was soon followed by the *Charmer,* commanded by Captain Lucas, which loaded a full cargo of 1400 tons of wheat for New York at $28 per ton freight. The export of wheat in sailing vessels rapidly increased, enabling ships to earn freights out and home, and this continued for many years.

In 1855 Donald McKay built three fine medium

clipper ships, the *Defender, Amos Lawrence,* and *Abbott Lawrence,* which remind us that a number of Boston ships bore the names of her distinguished citizens. There were the *Thomas H. Perkins, Rufus Choate, Starr King, Edward Everett, R. B. Forbes, Enoch Train, John E. Thayer, George Peabody, Samuel Appleton, Robert C. Winthrop, Russell Sturgis,* and perhaps others now forgotten. There were already a ship, a barque, two brigs, and two schooners named the *Daniel Webster,* besides several steamboats and tugs and a pilot-boat; hence, the owners of ships who were desirous of honoring the great statesman were obliged to adopt some other means of expressing their admiration, and since Webster was known as the Defender of the Constitution and also as the Expounder of that document, there were two ships named the *Defender* and the *Expounder.* Some one suggested that the latter ship might, perhaps, have been named in honor of Yankee Sullivan, a noted prize-fighter then retired from the ring.

The *Defender* was 1413 tons register, and carried a splendid full-length figurehead of Daniel Webster. She was owned by D. S. Kendall and H. P. Plympton, of Boston, and was commanded by Captain Isaac Beauchamp.

My object in drawing attention to this vessel is to mention a notable gathering at Mr. McKay's house on the day of her launch, July 27, 1855. The leading merchants of Boston and their families were his guests on that occasion, and speeches were made by the Hon. Edward Everett, ex-Mayor, the Hon. Benjamin Seaver, and Enoch Train. In the course of his address, Mr. Everett remarked: "I was at a loss, I confess, to comprehend the secret of the great success which has attended our friend and host. Forty-two ships, I understand, he has built —all vessels such as we have seen to-day. I do not mean that they were all as large, but they were as well constructed and looked as splendidly, as they rode on the waves. Forty-two vessels![1] No one else, certainly, has done more than our friend to improve the commercial marine of this country, and it has long seemed to me that there was a mystery about it. But since I have been under this roof to-day, I have learned the secret of it—excellent family government, and a good helpmeet to take counsel with and encouragement from. A fair proportion of the credit and praise for this success is, I am sure, due to our amiable and accomplished hostess [Cheers]. I congratulate also the father of our host, the father of such a family. He has, I am told, fourteen sons and daughters, and fifty grandchildren. Nine of the latter were born during the last year. I wish to know, my friends, if you do not call that being a good citizen!"

When the *Abbott Lawrence* was launched, in October of the same year. Mr. McKay was called upon to respond to the toast, "In memory of Abbott Lawrence," and his brief speech has fortunately been preserved:

"Ladies and gentlemen: I regret my inability

[1] Mr. Everett is reported to have said "eighty-two," but if he did so, it was a mistake, for forty-two is the true number.

Donald McKay

to do justice to the name that is honored and respected in every part of the civilized world. My speech is rude and uncultivated, but my feelings, I trust, are warm and true, and could I express those feelings, I would tell you how much I honor the memory of Abbott Lawrence. I know you all honor it, for you all knew him, and to know him was to love him. Love begets love. He loved our common country as a statesman of enlarged and liberal views, and our state and city as the scene of his personal labors. In Massachusetts he commenced his career; here he toiled and triumphed, here he has bequeathed the richest tokens of his love, and here all of him that can die mingles with the soil. He was not only a great man, but a good man. In every relation of life, he was a model for imitation. Ever be his memory green in the hearts of his countrymen. When the ship which bears his name shall have been worn out by the storms and the vicissitudes of the sea, may another, and another, and so on, till the end of time, perpetuate it upon the ocean, for he was the patron and friend of commerce as well as of the other great interests of the state. In conclusion, ladies and gentlemen, I again give you the memory of Abbott Lawrence. May his name and noble example never be forgotten."

This speech seems to me to be most interesting, as showing the natural refinement of a mind destitute of the culture of even a common-school education, or perhaps it would be nearer the truth to say, a mind that had escaped the restraining influence of the pedagogue.

"Yet is remembrance sweet,
  Though well I know
The days of childhood
  Are but days of woe;
Some rude restraint,
  Some petty tyrant sours
What else should be
  Our sweetest blithest hours."

These lugubrious lines found no echo in the early life of Donald McKay, for his boyhood was passed in earnest, healthy toil, and filled with a keen desire for knowledge, while his manhood had known the joy of well-earned success.

After the *Abbott Lawrence,* Mr. McKay built the medium clippers *Minnehaha, Baltic, Adriatic, Mastiff,* and barque *Henry Hill,* all in 1856; the *Alhambra,* 1857; the *Helen Morris,* and second *Sovereign of the Seas,* 1868, and the *Glory of the Seas,* 1869. During the Civil War, he built for the United States Government, the iron gunboat *Ashuelot,* the ironclad monitor *Nausett,* the wooden gunboats *Trefoil* and *Yucca,* and the sloop of war *Adams.* In 1877 he retired to his farm at Hamilton, Massachusetts, and there he died, September 20, 1880, in the seventy-first year of his age.

Donald McKay was a man of untiring energy and industry. He was a rapid and skilful draughtsman and designed and superintended the construction of every vessel that he built. This may also be said of almost every ship-builder of that period, but Mr. McKay's skill, the result of an intuitive perception ripened by experience, gave him a peculiar insight not only into how to create, but into what to create, and it was this genius that made him preeminent as a builder of clipper ships. He was a born artist and his ships were the finest expression of mechanical art. They are entitled to a place in the realm of fine arts far more than much of the merchandise that claims that distinction.

Mr. McKay was of a generous nature, and liberally rewarded the men who assisted him, and he was ever ready to lend a helping hand to those less fortunate than himself. So soon as he began to prosper he sent for his parents and made a new home for them at East Boston, and their comfort and happiness were always his care and greatest pleasure. In his later years he endured misfortune and ingratitude with the same sturdy sweetness and equanimity that he had shown in the days when fortune smiled.

CHAPTER XVII

AUSTRALIAN VOYAGES, 1851–1854

THE years between 1849 and 1856 were perhaps the most prosperous that ship-owners and ship-builders have ever known. The discovery of gold in Australia in 1851 had much the same effect as that in California in 1848, and people flocked to Melbourne from all parts of the world. There was this difference, however, that whereas passengers went to California, after the first rush, by steamers via Panama, and the mails and gold were always transported by this route, all the Australian passengers, mails, and gold were for a considerable period carried by sailing vessels. The extent of this traffic may be judged from the fact that the yield of the gold fields up to December 30, 1852, a little more than a year after their discovery, was estimated at £16,000,000 sterling, or $80,000,000. Prior to 1851 the emigration to the Australian colonies had been about 100,000 persons per annum, while the average between 1851 and 1854 was 340,000 annually. The transportation of these passengers alone required an enormous amount of tonnage, so that the discovery of gold in Australia gave an additional impulse to clipper ship building.

At this time the proper route to ports on that

part of the globe had only just become known, although British ships had been sailing to and from Australia and New Zealand for many years, taking out emigrants and bringing back wool. They usually called at the Cape of Good Hope both outward and homeward bound, this being the route recommended by the Admiralty. One of the most important services rendered by Lieutenant Maury was his careful research in this matter, which resulted in an entire revolution of both outward and homeward tracks. Instead of sailing near the Cape of Good Hope outward bound, he discovered that a ship would find stronger and more favorable winds from 600 to 800 miles to the westward, then continuing her course southward to 48°, she would fall in with the prevailing westerly gales and long rolling seas in which to run her easting down. It was in this region that the Australian clippers made their largest day's runs.

The homeward bound Admiralty track was entirely abandoned by Lieutenant Maury in favor of continuing in the brave west winds, as he called them, round Cape Horn, so that a voyage to Melbourne out and home encircled the globe. By the old routes, vessels were usually about 120 days each way, though sometimes considerably longer. By the tracks which Lieutenant Maury introduced, the outward and homeward voyages were made in about the same time that had formerly been consumed in a single passage, though of course the increased speed of the clipper ships contributed to this result.

The misery and suffering of passengers on board the old Australian emigrant ships before the days of the clippers are difficult to realize at the present time, but there is an account compiled from the report of the Parliamentary Committee appointed in 1844 to investigate the matter, which reads as follows:

"It was scarcely possible to induce the passengers to sweep the decks after their meals, or to be decent in respect to the common wants of nature; in many cases, in bad weather they would not go on deck, their health suffered so much that their strength was gone, and they had not the power to help themselves. Hence the between-decks was like a loathsome dungeon. When hatchways were opened under which the people were stowed, the steam rose and the stench was like that from a pen of pigs. The few beds they had were in a dreadful state, for the straw, once wet with sea-water, soon rotted, beside which they used the between-decks for all sorts of filthy purposes. Whenever vessels put back from distress all these miseries and sufferings were exhibited in the most aggravated form. In one case it appeared that, the vessel having experienced rough weather, the people were unable to go on deck and cook their provisions; the strongest maintained the upper hand over the weakest, and it was even said that there were women who died of starvation. At that time the passengers were expected to cook for themselves, and from their being unable to do this the greatest suffering arose. It was naturally at the commencement of the voyage that this system produced its worst effects, for the first days were those in which the people suffered most from sea-sickness, and under the prostration of body thereby induced, were wholly incapacitated from cooking. Thus though provisions might be abundant enough, the passengers would be half-starved."

In an interesting book entitled *Reminiscences of Early Australian Life,* a vivid description is given of maritime affairs in 1853. The writer, who had arrived at Melbourne in 1840, says that: "Since that time the town of Melbourne had developed from a few scattered and straggling wooden buildings, with muddy thoroughfares interspersed with stumps of gum trees, into a well-built and formed city, with wide, and well-made streets, symmetrically laid out, good hotels, club houses, and Government buildings. Port Phillip Bay, in which two or three vessels used to repose at anchor for months together, was now the anchorage ground of some of the finest and fastest clippers afloat."

At this time (1853) upwards of two hundred full-rigged ships from all parts of the world were lying in the Bay. This writer continues: "After landing their living freight of thousands that were rushing out to the gold fields to seek for gold, and fearing that they might be too late to participate in their reputed wealth, ships now waited for return cargoes, or more probably for crews to take them home, as in many cases all the hands had deserted for the gold fields. On ascertaining that there were two good ships sailing for London, with cargoes of wool and gold-dust, about the same time, or as soon as they could ship crews—one the *Madagascar,* of Messrs. Green & Co.'s line, and the other the *Medway* of Messrs. Tindall & Co.'s line—I proceeded to the office and booked a passage by the *Madagascar*—the passage in those days for a first-class cabin being £80. After paying the usual deposit and leaving the office, I met a friend, who was also homeward bound, and on my informing him that I had booked by the *Madagascar,* he persuaded me to change my ship and go home with himself and others whom I knew in the *Medway,* and upon returning to the office of Green's ship, and stating my reasons for wishing to change to Tindall's ship, they were very obliging, and returned my deposit, stating that they could easily fill up my berth. It was well for me at the time that I changed ships, as the *Madagascar* sailed the same day from Port Phillip Head as we did, with four tons of gold-dust on board; and to this day nothing has ever been heard of her. She either foundered at sea, or, as was generally supposed, was seized by the crew and scuttled and the gold taken off in boats. All must have perished, both passengers and crew, as no tidings of that ill-fated ship ever reached the owners.

"On board the *Medway* there were four tons' weight of gold-dust, packed in well-secured boxes of two hundred pounds each, five of these boxes being stowed under each of the berths of the saloon passengers. Each cabin was provided with cutlasses and pistols, to be kept in order and ready for use, and a brass carronade gun loaded with grape shot was fixed in the after part of the ship, in front of the saloon and pointed to the forecastle—not a man, with the exception of the ship's officers and stewards, being allowed to come aft.

"The character of the crew shipped necessitated

the precautions; for the day previous to the ship's sailing men had to be searched for and found in the lowest haunts and were brought on board drugged and under the influence of liquor, and placed below the hatches. We, the passengers, heaved up the anchor and worked the ship generally until outside of Port Phillip Head, when the men confined below, who were to compose the crew, were brought on deck, looking dazed and confused, any resistance or remonstrance on their part being futile. But those amongst them that were able-bodied seamen were paid in gold, forty sovereigns down, on signing the ship's articles for the homeward voyage.

"Amongst them were useless hands and some of a very indifferent character. Some, no doubt, were escaped convicts, or men who had secreted themselves to evade the police and law; others deserters from ships then laying in the Bay—about forty in all, and in general appearance a very unprepossessing lot. However, there being no help for it, we had but to keep guarded and prepared against the worst; the ship's passengers together with the officers numbering about twenty hands. The captain was an old and well-known sailor of high reputation and long experience; and the ship was well found and provisioned, in anticipation of a long voyage —which it proved to be, extending over four months from the time we left Port Phillip Head until she reached the English coast."

The first clipper ship constructed for the Australian trade was the *Marco Polo,* of 1622 tons; length 185 feet, breadth 38 feet, depth 30 feet. She was built in 1851 by Smith & Co., at St. John, N. B., for James Baines & Co., Liverpool, and was the pioneer clipper of the famous Australian Black Ball Line. The *Marco Polo* was constructed with three decks, and was a very handsome, powerful-looking ship. Above her water-line, she resembled the New York packet ships, having painted ports, and a full-length figurehead of the renowned explorer whose name she bore. Below water she was cut away and had long, sharp, concave ends. Her accommodations for saloon and steerage passengers were a vast improvement upon anything before attempted in the Australian trade.

She sailed from Liverpool for Melbourne, July 4, 1851, commanded by Captain James Nicol Forbes, carrying the mails and crowded with passengers. She made the run out in the then record time of 68 days, and home in 74 days, which, including her detention at Melbourne, was less than a six months' voyage round the globe. Running her easting down to the southward of the Cape of Good Hope, she made in four successive days 1344 miles, her best day's run being 364 miles. Her second voyage to Melbourne was also made in six months out and home, so that she actually sailed twice around the globe within twelve months. To the *Marco Polo* and her skilful commander belongs the credit of setting the pace over this great ocean race-course round the globe.

Her success led to the building of a number of vessels at St. John for British owners engaged in the Australian trade. Among these the most famous were the *Hibernia,* 1065 tons, *Ben Nevis,* 1420 tons, and *Guiding Star,* 2012 tons. In Great Britain also a large number of ships were built for the Australian trade between the years 1851 and 1854. Many of these were constructed of iron, the finest being the *Tayleur,* 2500 tons, which was built at Liverpool in 1853 and was at that time the largest merchant ship that had been built in England. She was a very handsome iron vessel, with three decks and large accommodation for cabin and steerage passengers. This vessel was wrecked off the coast of Ireland on her first voyage to Melbourne when only two days out from Liverpool, and became a total loss; of her 652 passengers, only 282 were saved. Among the many other vessels built in Great Britain during this period were the *Lord of the Isles,* already mentioned in Chapter XII; *Vimiera,* 1037 tons, built at Sunderland; the *Contest,* 1119 tons, built at Ardrossan on the Firth of Clyde; and the *Gauntlet* (iron), 784 tons, and *Kate Carnie,* 547 tons, both built at Greenock. All of these vessels were a decided improvement upon any ships hitherto built in Great Britain, and they made some fine passages, among them that of the *Lord of the Isles,* from the Clyde to Sydney, N. S. W., in 70 days in 1853, but the 68-day record of the *Marco Polo* from Liverpool to Melbourne remained unbroken.

The *Marco Polo* was still a favorite vessel with passengers, which goes to show what a good ship she must have been, in view of the rivalry of newer and larger clippers. She sailed from Liverpool in November, 1853, commanded by Captain Charles McDonnell, who had been her chief officer under

Captain Forbes. The passengers on this voyage, on their arrival at Melbourne, subscribed for a splendid service of silver, to be presented to Captain McDonnell upon his return to England, which bore the following inscription: "Presented to Captain McDonnell, of the ship *Marco Polo,* as a testimonial of respect from his passengers, six hundred and sixty-six in number, for his uniform kindness and attention during his first voyage, when his ship ran from Liverpool to Port Phillip Head in seventy-two days, twelve hours, and from land to land in sixty-nine days." The *Marco Polo* came home in 78 days, but these were the last of her famous passages, as she drifted into the hands of captains who lacked either the ability or the energy, or perhaps both, to develop her best speed—the unfortunate fate of many a good ship.

There were at that time a number of lines and private firms engaged in the Australian trade, the best known being the White Star Line, later managed by Ismay, Imrie & Co., and James Baines & Co.'s Black Ball Line, both of Liverpool. There was keen rivalry between the two, and the *Ben Nevis* and *Guiding Star* had both been built by the White Star in hopes of lowering the record of the *Marco Polo.* By degrees, however, it became apparent that she was an exceptional ship, not likely to be duplicated at St. John, and also that much of her speed was due to her able commanders, while the ships built in Great Britain, though fine vessels, had not come up to the mark in point of speed or passenger accommodations. It was under these circumstances that British merchants and ship-owners began to buy and build ships for the Australian trade in the United States.

The *Sovereign of the Seas* had attracted much attention upon her arrival at Liverpool in 1853, and was almost immediately chartered to load for Australia in the Black Ball Line. It is to be regretted that for some reason Captain McKay gave up charge of the ship and returned to the United States, the command being given to Captain Warner, who had no previous experience in handling American clipper ships, although he proved an extremely competent commander. The *Sovereign of the Seas* sailed from Liverpool September 7, 1853, and arrived at Melbourne after a passage of 77 days. In a letter from Melbourne Captain Warner gives the following account of this passage:

"I arrived here after a long and tedious passage of 77 days, having experienced only light and contrary winds the greater part of the passage—I have had but two chances. The ship ran in four consecutive days 1275 miles; and the next run was 3375 miles in twelve days. These were but moderate chances. I was 31 days to the Equator, and carried skysails 65 days; set them on leaving Liverpool, and never shortened them for 35 days. Crossed the equator in 26° 30', and went to 53° 30' south, but found no strong winds. Think if I had gone to 58° south, I would have had wind enough; but the crew were insufficiently clothed, and about one half disabled, together with the first mate. At any rate, we have beaten all and every one of the ships that sailed with us, and also the famous English clipper *Gauntlet* ten days on the passage, although the *Sovereign of the Seas* was loaded down to twenty-three and one half feet." On the homeward voyage she brought the mails and over four tons of gold-dust, and made the passage in 68 days. On this voyage there was a mutiny among the crew, who intended to seize the ship and capture the treasure. Captain Warner acted with great firmness and tact in suppressing the mutineers and placing them in irons without loss of life, for which he received much credit.

The White Star Line, not to be outdone by rivals, followed the example of the Black Ball and in 1854 chartered the *Chariot of Fame, Red Jacket,* and *Blue Jacket.* These ships, of which the first was a medium clipper and the other two extreme clippers, were built in New England. The *Chariot of Fame* was a sister ship to the *Star of Empire,* 2050 tons, built by Donald McKay in 1853, for Enoch Train's Boston and Liverpool packet line. The *Chariot of Fame* made a number of fast voyages between England and Australia, her best passage being 66 days from Liverpool to Melbourne. The *Blue Jacket* was a handsome ship of 1790 tons, built by R. E. Jackson at East Boston in 1854, and was owned by Charles R. Green, of New York. Her best passages were 67 days from Liverpool to Melbourne and home in 69 days.

The *Red Jacket,* the most famous of this trio, was built by George Thomas at Rockland, Maine, in 1853–1854, and was owned by Seacomb & Taylor, of Boston. She registered 2006 tons; length 260 feet, breadth 44 feet, depth 26 feet; and was designed by Samuel A. Pook, of Boston, who had designed a number of other clipper ships, including the *Challenger*—not the English ship of that name, —the *Game-Cock, Surprise, Northern Light, Ocean Chief, Fearless, Ocean Telegraph,* and *Herald of the Morning.* He also designed several freighting vessels and yachts. It was the custom at that period for vessels to be designed in the yards where they were constructed, and Mr. Pook was the first naval architect in the United States who was not connected with a ship-bulding yard. On her first voyage the *Red Jacket* sailed from New York for Liverpool, February 19, 1854, commanded by Captain Asa Eldridge, and made the passage in 13 days 1 hour from Sandy Hook to the Rock Light, Liverpool, with the wind strong from southeast to west-southwest, and either rain, snow, or hail during the entire run. During the first seven days she averaged only 182 miles per twenty-four hours, but during the last six days she made 219, 413, 374, 343, 300, and 371 miles, an average of a fraction over 353 miles per twenty-four hours.

Captain Eldridge was well known in Liverpool, having, together with his brothers, John and Oliver, commanded some of the finest New York and Liverpool packet ships of their day; he had also commanded Commodore Vanderbilt's steam yacht *North Star* during her cruise in European waters in 1853. He was afterwards lost in command of the steamship *Pacific* of the Collins Line.

The *Red Jacket* attracted a great deal of attention at Liverpool, being an extremely handsome ship—quite as good-looking as any of the clippers built at New York or Boston. For a figurehead she carried a full-length representation of the Indian chief for whom she was named. She made her first voyage from Liverpool to Melbourne in 1854 under command of Captain Samuel Reed in 69 days, and as she received very quick despatch, being in port only 12 days, and made the passage to Liverpool in 73 days, the voyage round the globe, including detention in port, was made in five months and four days. On the homeward passage, bringing home 45,000 ounces of gold, she beat the celebrated *Guiding Star* by 9 days, though she lost considerable time through being among the bergs and field ice off Cape Horn. Upon her arrival at Liverpool the *Red Jacket* was sold to Pilklington & Wilson, of that port, then agents of the White Star Line, for £30,000, and continued in the Australian trade for several years, becoming one of the most famous of the American-built clippers.

The competition of the Black Ball and White Star lines proved of great benefit to both cabin and steerage passengers, as their comfort and convenience became subjects of consideration in a manner unthought of in the old days before the discovery of gold at Bendigo and Ballarat.

The "Red Jacket"

CHAPTER XVIII

AUSTRALIAN CLIPPERS, 1854–1856

IN view of the keen rivalry at this period, James Baines & Co. determined to own the finest and fastest ships that could be constructed, and accordingly placed an order with Donald McKay to build four clipper ships for their Australian line. These vessels were the *Lightning,* 2084 tons; the *Champion of the Seas,* 2448 tons; *James Baines,* 2515 tons; and *Donald McKay,* 2598 tons, all launched in 1854, with the exception of the *Donald McKay,* which was not completed until January, 1855. This firm also bought from Mr. McKay the sister ships *Japan* and *Commodore Perry,* 1964 tons each, while they were on the stocks in course of construction.

These ships designed for the Australian trade were very similar to the later California clipper ships built by Mr. McKay, though with less dead-rise and sharper ends; they were fitted with large accommodation for cabin and steerage passengers; while the *Japan* and *Commodore Perry* were somewhat fuller ships than the others, and were designed with a view to carry large cargoes rather than to attain high speed.

The *Lightning* measured: length 244 feet, breadth 44 feet, depth 23 feet, with 20 inches dead-rise at half floor. She had long, concave water-lines, and at her load-displacement line a chord from her cut-water to just abaft the fore rigging showed a concavity of 16 inches. Her stem raked boldly forward, the lines of the bow gradually becoming convex and blending with sheer line and cutwater, while the only ornament was a beautiful full-length figure of a young woman holding a golden thunderbolt in her outstretched hand, the flowing white drapery of her graceful form and her streaming hair completing the fair and noble outline of the bow. The after body was long and clean, though fuller than the bow, while the stern was semi-elliptical in form, with the plank-sheer moulding for its base, and was ornamented with gilded carved work, though this really added nothing to the beauty of the strong, sweeping outline of her hull.

Aloft the *Lightning* was heavily and strongly rigged. Her main yard was 95 feet in length, and the total height from the deck to the mainskysail truck was 164 feet; her lower studdingsail booms were 65 feet in length; her topsails and topgallantsails were diagonally roped from clews to earings, and her fore and main stays, lower rigging, and topmast stays and backstays were of 11½ inch Russian hemp, with the rest of the standing rigging in proportion. Indeed, her masts and spars were as strongly secured as skill and labor could make them. Evidently, Mr. McKay had grown weary of having his ships go to pieces aloft.

The quarter-deck was 90 feet long, flush with the top of the bulwarks, and protected by a mahogany rail on turned stanchions of the same wood. She had also two large deck-houses, which, together with the between-decks, gave ample passenger accommodation. The quarters for the steerage passengers were comfortably fitted and well ventilated, while the saloons, staterooms, bathrooms, and smoking-room for the cabin passengers were superbly decorated and furnished.

Captain Forbes, late of the *Marco Polo,* was appointed to command the *Lightning,* and came to Boston by one of the Cunard steamers to superintend the outfit of his ship. He brought good letters of introduction, and was well received; indeed, he hardly needed any introduction, as the high reputation he had gained while in command of the *Marco Polo* had preceded him. He made many friends in Boston, especially among the clergy, as he was an enthusiastic churchman, and he found a congenial spirit in Captain Lauchlan McKay, who likewise took a great interest in ecclesiastical affairs. These two mariners became such close friends that Captain McKay consented to accompany Captain Forbes to Liverpool as his companion and adviser, and as we shall presently see, the *Lightning* developed her finest speed in the hands of these experienced and skilful seamen.

The *Lightning* loaded in Train's Line at Constitution Wharf, and sailed for Liverpool, February 18, 1854. The Boston *Daily Atlas* of that date published the following account of her departure:

"At 2 o'clock the *Lightning* hove her anchor up, and at 3 o'clock discharged her pilot off Boston Light. She went down in tow of the steamer *Rescue,* Captain Hennessy, and was piloted by Mr.

E. G. Martin. Before the steamer left her, she set her head sails, fore- and mizentopsails, and had a moderate breeze from west to southwest. She appeared to go at the rate of 6 knots under this canvas, though she draws 22 feet of water, and has only 23 feet depth of hold. We have seen many vessels pass through the water, but never saw one which disturbed it less. Not a ripple curled before her cutwater, nor did the water break at a single place along her sides. She left a wake as straight as an arrow and this was the only mark of her progress. There was a slight swell and as she rose we could see the arc of her forefoot rise gently over the seas as she increased her speed. At 5 P.M., two hours after the pilot left her, the outer telegraph station reported her thirty miles east of Boston Light, with all drawing sails set, and going along like a steamboat. We think her talented designer and builder, Mr. McKay, cannot improve upon her model. Her commander, being a pious man, was attended down the harbor by a select party of brethren and sisters of the church, who at parting gave him their blessing. This is much better than the dram-drinking and vociferous cheering which usually make up the parting scenes of the unregenerated."

The voyage so auspiciously begun proved one of the most remarkable ever made by a ship on the ocean; for before the *Lightning* set her pilot signal off Point Lynas, she had left more miles of salt water astern in twenty-four hours than any vessel that has ever sailed the seas propelled by winds and canvas. From the abstract log, published in the

Liverpool *Albion* soon after her arrival, it appears that she went round the north of Ireland, making the run to Eagle Island in 10 days, and to the Calf of Man, within 80 miles of Liverpool, in 12 days, thence to Liverpool in 13 days 19½ hours from Boston Light. Her day's runs were as follows:

1.—" February 19th. Wind west-southwest, and northwest, moderate; 200 miles.
2.—20th. Wind north-northeast and northeast, strong breezes with snow; 328 miles.
3.—21st. Wind east-southeast with snowstorms; 145 miles.
4.—22d. Wind east-southeast, a gale with high cross sea and rain; 114 miles.
5.—23d. Wind north. Strong gales to east-southeast; ends moderate; 110 miles.
6.—24th. Wind southeast, moderate; 312 miles.
7.—25th. Wind east-southeast and southeast. Fresh breezes with thick weather; 285 miles.
8.—26th. Wind west-southwest, moderate; 295 miles.
9.—27th. Wind west-northwest, moderate; 260 miles.
10.—28th. Wind west and northwest, steady breezes; 306 miles."

[The position at noon on this day was latitude 52° 38′ N., longitude 22° 45′ W., and here began the greatest day's run ever made by a ship under canvas.]

11.—" March 1st. Wind south. Strong gales; bore away for the North Channel, carried away the foretopsail and lost jib; hove the log several times and found the ship going through the water at the rate of 18 to 18½ knots; lee rail under water, and rigging slack. Distance run in twenty-four hours, 436 miles.
12.—2d. Wind south, first part moderate, latter part light and calm.
13.—3d. Light winds and calms.
14.—4th. Light southeast winds and calms; at 7 A.M. off Great Orms Head; 12 M. off the N. W. Lightship."

This was a remarkable passage considering the percentage of easterly winds, though its memorable incident is, of course, the phenomenal run of 436 miles in twenty-four hours, an average of 18½ knots, which entitles the *Lightning* to the proud distinction of being the swiftest ship that ever sailed the seas. There was no ocean steamship of her day that approached her record by less than 100 miles, and another five-and-twenty years passed away before the Atlantic greyhound, the *Arizona,* made 18 knots for a single hour, on her trial trip. Even at the present time, according to Lloyd's Register, there are not more than thirty ocean-going mail steamships afloat, that are able to steam over 18 knots. It must have been blowing hard enough when the *Lightning's* jib and foretopsail carried away, for these were not old, worn-out sails, put on board to attract the favorable consideration of underwriters, but were of new canvas, made unusually strong, and had not been out of the sail loft more than a couple of weeks.

Strange as it may seem, the "wood butchers of Liverpool," as Donald McKay used to call them, were allowed to fill in the concave lines of the *Lightning's* bow with slabs of oak sheathing, and while she continued to be a fast ship, she doubtless would have proved still faster had her original design not been tampered with.[1]

The second of these ships, the *Champion of the Seas,* measured: length 269 feet, breadth 45 feet, depth 29 feet, dead-rise at half floor 18 inches;

[1] These slabs were subsequently removed, one side being washed away.

length of mainyard 95 feet. The concavity of her water-line forward was 2½ inches, from which it will be seen that she was a differently designed ship from the *Lightning*. She was considered by many to be even a handsomer vessel. Her stern was ornamented with the arms of Australia, while at her bow she carried a full-length figurehead of a handsome sailorman rigged out in all his best go-ashore togs. She was commanded by Captain Alexander Newlands, who came from Liverpool to superintend her construction and equipment, the whole inside arrangements of the ship, including the complicated plan for light and ventilation and the details of the cabin, being made according to his designs. After fitting out at Grand Junction Wharf, East Boston, she was towed to New York by the *R. B. Forbes,* where she loaded for Liverpool, and made the passage to that port during the month of June, 1854, in 16 days.

The *James Baines* measured: length 266 feet, breadth 46 feet 8 inches, depth 31 feet, with 18 inches dead-rise at half floor. Her mainyard was 100 feet in length, and a single suit of sails contained 13,000 running yards of canvas 18 inches wide. Originally she carried a main skysail only, but later she was fitted with three skysails, main moonsail, and skysail studdingsails, and so far as I know, she was the only clipper ship so rigged. There was only a very slight difference between the lines of the *Champion of the Seas* and those of the *James Baines,* the latter ship having a somewhat more raking stem, which brought her lines out forward a little longer and sharper above the water-line. Her bow was ornamented with a finely executed bust of her namesake, which was carved in England and was said to be an excellent likeness. Across her stern she carried a carved medallion of the globe, supported by the arms of Great Britain and the United States. She was commanded by Captain McDonnell, late of the *Marco Polo,* who sailed from Liverpool for Boston soon after his return from Melbourne.

The *James Baines* sailed from Boston, September 12, 1854, and made the run from Boston Light to the Rock Light, Liverpool, in the record time of 12 days 6 hours. An English correspondent of one of the Boston papers remarked: "You wish to know what professional men say about the ship *James Baines.* Her unrivalled passage, of course, brought her prominently before the public, and she has already been visited by many of the most eminent mechanics in the country. She is so strongly built, so finely finished, and is of so beautiful a model, that even envy cannot prompt a fault against her. On all hands she has been praised as the most perfect sailing ship that ever entered the river Mersey."

The last of this quartette, the *Donald McKay,* measured: length 269 feet, breadth 47 feet, depth 29 feet, with 18 inches dead-rise at half floor, and her mainyard was 100 feet long. While her water-lines were fuller than those of the *James Baines,* she was still an extremely sharp vessel, and with the single exception of the *Great Republic* was the largest merchant ship afloat. She sailed from Boston, February 21, 1855, under the command of

Captain Warner, late of the *Sovereign of the Seas,* and made the run to Cape Clear in 12 days, and thence to Liverpool in 5 days. On February 27th, she ran 421 miles in twenty-four hours, and on that date her log records: "First part, strong gales from northwest; middle blowing a hurricane from west-northwest, ship scudding under topsails and foresail at the rate of 18 knots; latter part, still blowing from west-northwest with heavy hail squalls; very high sea running."

The *Lightning* sailed from Liverpool on her first voyage to Melbourne, May 14, 1854. She encountered light winds and calms to the equator, which she crossed in 25 days from the Mersey; such was the nature of the winds that the topgallantsails were not taken in during the passage, and her best day's runs were only 332, 348, 300, 311, and 329 miles on various dates. She arrived out in 77 days, but the passage home to Liverpool was made in the record time of 63 days. In ten consecutive days of twenty-four hours each, she sailed no less than 3722 miles, her best day's run being 412 miles. On this voyage she brought home gold and dust to the value of £1,000,000 sterling.

The *James Baines* sailed from Liverpool for Melbourne December 9, 1854, and made the passage out in the record time of 63 days, her best twenty-four hours' run being 420 miles. She made the passage home in 69 days, thus sailing around the globe in the record time of 132 days. On a subsequent voyage in 1856 her log records, "June 16th. At noon sighted a ship in the distance ahead; at 1 P.M. alongside of her; at 2 P.M., out of sight astern.

The *James Baines* was going 17 knots with main skysail set; the *Libertas*, for such was her name, was under double-reefed topsails." "June 17th. Latitude 44° S., longitude 106° E., ship going 21 knots with main skysail set." This appears to be the highest rate of speed ever made by a sailing vessel of which any reliable record has been preserved.

The *Champion of the Seas* made the passage out in 71 days and home in 84 days, and the *Donald McKay* made the voyage in about the same time, but the *Lightning* and *James Baines* proved the most famous of these ships. So well pleased was Mr. Baines that he wrote to Mr. McKay, saying, "In these ships you have given us all and more than we expected." These were the last extreme clipper ships built by Donald McKay.

During the Sepoy Mutiny in 1857 a large number of British and American merchant ships were chartered by the British Government to carry troops to India, and among others the *James Baines, Champion of the Seas,* and *Lightning*. The *James Baines* sailed from Portsmouth for Calcutta on August 8th, with the Ninety-seventh Regiment on board, and the *Illustrated London News,* in a notice of her departure, remarked: "Previous to her starting she was honored by a visit of Her Majesty, who highly eulogized the vessel and is said to have declared that she was not aware that so splendid a merchant ship belonged to her dominions."

The *Champion of the Seas* sailed from Portsmouth on the same day, also bound for Calcutta with troops, and the race between these clippers was close and exciting. Nine days out they fell in

The "James Baines"

with the steamship *Oneida* homeward bound, and the *Illustrated London News,* again mentioning the *James Baines,* said: "When met by the *Oneida,* on the 17th of August, on her way to Calcutta with troops, she presented a most magnificent appearance, having in addition to her ordinary canvas, studdingsails, skysails, and moonsail, set and drawing, in all thirty-four sails, a perfect cloud of canvas: the troops all well, and cheering lustily as the vessels passed each other. The sister ship, the *Champion of the Seas,* was not far astern, both vessels making great headway."

These two ships arrived off the mouth of the Hooghly together, each 101 days from Portsmouth, and the finish of this race was talked about by the Calcutta pilots for a good many years: how these splendid clippers raced in from sea almost side by side, with a fresh three-skysail, scupper breeze, the regimental bands on board of both ships playing national airs, while the soldiers were cheering and wild with the joy and excitement of seeing land once more.

The *Lightning* sailed at a more favorable season, and made the passage from Portsmouth to the Hooghly in 87 days, beating the entire fleet of sailing transports, including those fitted with auxiliary screw propellers.

Of the large number of ships bought or chartered in the United States for the Australian trade by British ship-owners at this period, those mentioned, with the *Red Rover, Comet, Tornado, Sierra Nevada,* and *Invincible,* each with a record of less than 75 days from Liverpool or London to Melbourne, the *Belle of the Sea,* 64 days from London to Melbourne, and *North Wind,* 67 days from London to Sydney, N. S. W., were the most celebrated.

There were also many American ships that made the voyage from New York to Melbourne, and among the fast passages may be mentioned those of: the *Mandarin,* in 71 days; *Flying Scud* and *Nightingale,* 75 days; *Whirlwind,* 80 days; *Flying Dutchman* and *Panama,* 81 days; *Snow Squall,* 79 days, and *Ringleader,* 78 days. Most if not all these ships loaded in R. W. Cameron's line, and it is worth noting that, of all the great shipping firms that flourished in New York half a century ago, this is the only one which now survives.

It was only natural that ship-owners of Great Britain should feel keenly the invasion of their trade by the American clippers, and in 1855, James Baines & Co. placed an order with Alexander Hall & Co., of Aberdeen, then the leading clipper shipbuilders in Great Britain, for a large clipper ship for the Australian trade, to "outdo the Americans." This vessel was the *Schomberg,* 2600 tons; length 262 feet, breadth 45 feet, depth 29 feet. She was very sharp forward and had a long, clean run, with considerable dead-rise at her midship section. She was built of wood and heavily sparred, with single topsail yards and three skysails.

When this ship came around from Aberdeen to load at Liverpool for Melbourne, she was greatly admired and it was generally believed that she would prove faster than her American rivals, especially as Captain Forbes, late of the *Marco Polo* and *Lightning,* had been appointed to command her. She sailed from Liverpool on October 6, 1855. Captain Forbes was a proud man that day, for the pierheads of the port were thronged with a patriotic, cheering crowd to see the *Schomberg* off, and as she towed down the Mersey, the signals reading, "Sixty days to Melbourne," fluttered gayly from her mizen truck.

She had moderate winds to the equator, which she crossed 28 days from the Mersey, and then drifted into calms and light airs which continued for ten days and from which she did not possess the nimble speed to extricate herself. Her best day's work, while running her easting down, was 368 miles. When 81 days out she was wrecked and became a total loss on an uncharted reef about 150 miles to the westward of Melbourne, the passengers, crew, and mails being saved. This was by no means a record passage, and it is to be regretted that her career was so short, as it would be interesting to know what she might have done under more favorable conditions. She certainly possessed the qualities of a fast ship, and was ably commanded.

There were also many fine ships of English build sailing out of London in the Australian trade; the *Norfolk* and *Lincolnshire,* built and owned by Money, Wigram & Sons; the *Kent, Trafalgar,* and *Renown,* built and owned by R. & H. Green; and many others. These ships were built of teak, oak, and elm; were copper-fastened and sheathed with red copper. They resembled smart frigates more than merchantmen, and were about the perfection of that type—splendid ships to be at sea in, though not so fast as the sharper American clippers. None of these vessels was over 1500 tons, and it was thought by shipping men in London and Liverpool that much of the speed of the American ships was due to their greater tonnage. There may have been some truth in this, but it should be remembered that with these large wooden vessels an increase in size made the difficulties in building greater, as well as in getting their wooden masts to stand with hemp rigging, to say nothing of handling their enormous single topsails in heavy weather.

Meanwhile attempts were being made by various companies to introduce steam in place of the clipper ships that had carried the passengers, mails, and specie after the discovery of gold in Australia, but these efforts were beset with many difficulties and heavy financial losses.

The *Australian*, an iron screw steamer of 2000 tons, was the first steamship to carry the mails from England to Melbourne. She sailed from Plymouth, June 5, 1852, and called at St. Vincent, St. Helena, Table Bay, and St. George's Sound for coal, which had been sent out by ship from England to meet her. She arrived at Melbourne in 89 days from Plymouth, and returned by the Cape of Good Hope in 76 days. She arrived at London, January 11, 1853, having been 7 months and 6 days upon the voyage, a creditable but not a very brilliant performance. The *Australian* was soon followed by the *Great Britain, Adelaide, Queen of the South, Sydney, Cleopatra, Antelope,* and other iron screw steamers; but these vessels nearly ruined

The "Schomberg"

their owners and did not greatly interfere with the clippers.

In 1854 the *Argo,* a full-rigged iron ship of 1850 tons register, with plenty of canvas and fitted with an auxiliary engine and screw, made the passage from London to Melbourne in 64 days and home round Cape Horn in 63 days; and though she sailed during the greater portion of the voyage, using her engines only in calms and light winds, she was the first merchant vessel using steam-power to circumnavigate the globe. This voyage is peculiarly adapted to auxiliary steam vessels, as, by following the sailing-ship track, very few strong head winds are met, and of course the screw is of great assistance in light winds and calms.

The *Argo* was followed (1855–1856) by the *Royal Charter, Istamboul,* and *Khersonese* and other iron auxiliary "steam clippers," as they were called. These vessels carried as much canvas as the clipper ships, and were more expensive to handle and not much faster; the rivalry was therefore keen. The clippers still secured their full share of the cabin and steerage passengers, the mails and gold, and were by no means vanquished; indeed, the auxiliaries proved no more successful than the steamships, and brought much the same result to their owners.

It was not till after the close of the Crimean War in 1856, when the Peninsular & Oriental Steam Navigation Company extended their line to the Australian colonies, that the clipper ships began seriously to feel the competition of steam. From that time iron sailing vessels for this trade were built with a view to carrying large cargoes and steerage passengers, so that by 1860 the day of the Australian clippers had passed away, although the later China tea-clippers sometimes made this voyage. Almost countless splendid iron and steel sailing ships have since been built in Great Britain, and many fine passages have been made to and from Australia, yet the records of the *James Baines, North Wind, Lightning, Mandarin,* and *Lord of the Isles* remain unbroken.

CHAPTER XIX

LAST YEARS OF THE AMERICAN CLIPPER SHIP ERA—SUMMARY OF CALIFORNIA PASSAGES

DURING the Crimean War a large number of merchant ships, many of which were American, were chartered by the British and French Governments to carry troops, but when peace was declared in 1856 and this demand for tonnage ceased, it was found that there were more ships afloat than could find profitable employment, or indeed employment of any kind.

Only eight ships were added to the California fleet in 1856—the *Alarm, Euterpe, Flying Mist, Florence, Intrepid, Mary L. Sutton, Norseman,* and the second *Witch of the Wave.* These were all handsome medium clippers, and possessed what is so sadly lacking in sailing ships of the present day—style, distinction. The *Florence* was built by Samuel Hall, Jr., who had succeeded his father as a ship-builder and continued in the same yard at East Boston. She was owned by Captain R. B. Forbes and others of Boston. Captain Dumaresq commanded her and also owned an interest in her until his death in 1860. As Captain Forbes used to say, "He was the prince of sea captains."

The *Sweepstakes* made the fastest passage to San

Francisco in 1856—94 days from New York—followed by the *Antelope,* 97 days; *Phantom,* 101 days; and *David Brown,* 103 days; the *Ringleader* made the passage from Boston in 100 days. The abstract log of the *Sweepstakes* is as follows:

From Sandy Hook to the equator....	18	days.
From the equator to 50° S..........	23	"
From 50° in the Atlantic to 50° in the Pacific..........................	15	"
From 50° S. to the equator..........	17	"
From the equator to San Francisco....	21	"
Total..........................	94	"

The year 1857 was one of financial depression throughout the United States, which was severely felt by the shipping interests of the country and continued until the Civil War. The rates of freight from New York to San Francisco, which during the years immediately following the discovery of gold in California were $60 a ton, gradually declined, and in 1857 had fallen to $10 per ton. Ships that had formerly loaded cargoes for San Francisco night and day and were hurried to sea as quickly as possible, now lay at their loading berths for weeks, leisurely taking on board such cargo as their agents could engage. During this period vessels lay idle at the wharves of Atlantic ports for weeks and even months, in charge of ship-keepers, with sails unbent, waiting for employment.

The former activity in the ship-building yards had also subsided. During the four years prior to the Civil War, Donald McKay built only one ship,

The "Sweepstakes"

the *Alhambra* (1857), and William H. Webb built only one ship for the California trade, the *Black Hawk,* beside the *Resolute,* and the barque *Trieste* (1857), and the barque *Harvest Queen* (1858). The same depression was felt in all the yards along the Atlantic coast. British ship-builders had made such rapid progress in the construction and speed of their vessels that it was now difficult for American ships to obtain charters from China to England. From 1857 to 1861, they were to be found lying idle for months at a time in Manila Bay, Hong-kong harbor, Foo-chow, Shanghai, and Calcutta, seeking employment.

The depression in the oversea carrying trade was felt quite as much by the ship-owners of Great Britain as by those of the United States, and while of short duration, was as serious there as in the United States. It was at this period, however, that Great Britain began to feel the benefit of Free Trade in her ship-building industry, and entered upon her conquest of the world's oversea carrying trade. In this her ship-builders were greatly assisted by the introduction of iron as a material for construction. In 1855 the Committee of Lloyd's Register had framed rules for the classification of iron ships, as their number had so increased, and the demand of ship-owners for their official recognition had become so general, that they could no longer be ignored. The screw propeller was also beginning to supersede side-wheels as a means of propulsion, and some of the ablest men in Great Britain were engaged upon the development and improvement of the marine engine and boiler.

The steam tonnage of the British Empire—mostly engaged in the oversea carrying trade—had increased from 204,654 tons in 1851 to 417,717 tons in 1856, whereas the steam tonnage of the United States engaged in the oversea carrying trade had increased from 62,390 tons in 1851 to 115,045 tons in 1855, but had decreased to 89,715 tons in 1856. It should be noted that while a large proportion of the steam tonnage of Great Britain consisted of iron vessels, many of them being screw steamers, the steam vessels of the United States were very nearly, if not all, still constructed of wood and propelled by side-wheels.

The first symptoms of the decadence of the American merchant marine were the falling-off in the sales of American tonnage to foreign countries —the reduction being from 65,000 tons in 1855 to 42,000 tons in 1856, declining to 26,000 tons in 1858 and to 17,000 tons in 1860, a falling-off of 75% in five years—then in the total tonnage of vessels built in the United States, which fell from 583,450 tons in 1855 to 469,393 tons in 1856, and to 378,804 tons in 1857.

These facts refute the historic falsehood that the *Alabama* and her consorts were the first and immediate cause of decadence in the American merchant marine. As a matter of fact, neither the depression preceding the Civil War, nor the depredations of Confederate privateers, nor the Civil War itself, have had any material bearing upon the decline of American shipping during the last fifty years. The gigantic task of driving the American flag from the ocean has been accomplished by far more insidious and potent means than these. It has been the inevitable consequence of irrational and unjust laws, and until these are repealed, as those of Great Britain were in 1849, we may hope in vain that the ensign of the United States will be restored to its place upon the sea.

Amid the discouraging conditions of these years preceding the Civil War, American sea-captains never lost faith in their ships nor in themselves. They seemed to think, the lower the rate of freight, the more reason that it should be earned quickly, and when once clear of the disheartening influences of a seaport and well off soundings, they sent their ships along with the same energy and skill for which they had become famous in more prosperous days.

It was in the year 1857 that the *Great Republic* made her remarkable passage of 92 days from New York to San Francisco, and established a new record of 16 days from Sandy Hook to the equator. She was still commanded by Captain Limeburner, who had as his first officer, Montgomery Parker, an accomplished seaman and navigator, afterward commander of the ships *Judge Shaw* and *Lord Lyndhurst*. The crew of 50 men before the mast were the usual assortment, 15 or 20 good seamen, the rest adventurers and mongrels of various brands, of whom little could be expected. Captain Limeburner and his officers always went armed, and it was perhaps fortunate, with such a crew, that the topgallantsails were never clewed up during the passage, and that Cape Horn was rounded with skysails set.

The abstract log of the *Great Republic* is as follows:

From Sandy Hook to the equator......	16	days.
From the equator to 50° S...........	25	"
From 50° S. in the Atlantic to 50° S. in the Pacific....................	9	"
From 50° S. to the equator...........	23	"
From the equator to San Francisco....	19	"
Total............................	92	"

Lieutenant Maury, in a letter on the subject to the Secretary of the Navy, remarks: "This vessel did not have the luck to get a wind that could keep her up to her mettle for twenty-four hours consecutively. Here and there she got into favorable streaks of wind, but she appears to have run out of them faster than they could follow. She made the run to San Francisco in 92 days.

"The shortest passage that in the present state of ship-building will probably ever be made from New York to San Francisco, is 85 days; and the very clever first officer of this ship, writing from California, expresses the opinion that 'should she continue to run between New York and San Francisco, from the experience of this voyage, she will one day make the trip within your possible 85 days.'

"The friends of this noble specimen of naval architecture, however, can scarcely hope for a fair trial and proper display of her prowess until she shall be sent on a voyage to Australia. The brave west winds of the Southern hemisphere, which she will then encounter, will enable her to show herself; elsewhere, she can scarcely find a sea wide enough, with belts of wind broad enough for the full display of her qualities and capabilities."

There can be little doubt that with her original spars and sail plan, the *Great Republic* would have made this passage in 85 days or less, and it is to be regretted that, even with her reduced rig, she never made a voyage between England and Australia, the service for which she was built and especially adapted. Her best twenty-four hours' run, made upon a subsequent voyage while under the command of Captain Josiah Paul, was 413 miles.

In 1857 the *Flying Dragon* made the passage to San Francisco in 97 days; the *Westward Ho* and the *Andrew Jackson* in 100 days, both from New York; and the *Flying Fish* in 106 days from Boston. In 1858 the *Twilight* made the passage from New York in 100 days; the *Andrew Jackson* in 103 days; and in 1859 the *Sierra Nevada* in 97 days and the *Andrew Jackson* in 102 days. In 1860 the *Andrew Jackson* made the trip in 89 days.

As before noted, the *Andrew Jackson* was built in 1855. Her builders were Irons & Grinnell, of Mystic, Connecticut; she was owned by J. H. Brower & Co., of New York, and was commanded by Captain John E. Williams, of Mystic. She was 1679 tons register and measured: length 222 feet, breadth 40 feet, depth 22 feet, and while not an extreme clipper, she was a very handsome, well-designed ship. She was heavily sparred and carried double topsails, skysails, and royal studdingsails. Her figurehead was a full-length statue of the famous warrior and statesman in whose honor she was named.

Upon Captain Williams's arrival at San Francisco, in 89 days from New York, he was presented with a Commodore's pennant, and on his return to New York the owners presented him with a valuable chronometer watch bearing the following inscription: "Presented by J. H. Brower & Co. to Captain J. E. Williams of the clipper ship *Andrew Jackson* for the shortest passage to San Francisco. Time 89 days 4 hours, 1860."

With this superb record by the *Andrew Jackson* —four consecutive passages averaging 98½ days each—the American clipper ship era may well bring its brilliant career to a close.

It would be invidious, even if it were possible, to name the fastest of the splendid fleet of California clippers which sailed during the years 1850–1860, as their voyages were made in different years and at different seasons of the year; still, a comparison of their records is of interest.

Eighteen ships made single passages of less than 100 days from New York or Boston to San Francisco during this period. The *Flying Cloud* and *Andrew Jackson* share the honor of 89 days each, and are closely followed by the *Sword Fish,* 90 days; *Flying Fish* and *Great Republic,* 92 days; *John Gilpin,* 93 days; *Sweepstakes,* 94 days; *Surprise* and *Romance of the Seas,* 96 days; *Sea Witch, Contest, Antelope, Sierra Nevada, Flying Dragon,* and *Witchcraft,* 97 days; *Flying Fish* and *David Brown,* 98 days, and *Herald of the Morning* and *Hurricane,* 99 days each.

Four of these ships, the *Flying Cloud, Flying Fish, Great Republic,* and *Romance of the Seas,* were built by Donald McKay, and two of the four, the *Flying Cloud* and *Flying Fish,* each came within the limit twice. Two others, the *John Gilpin* and *Surprise,* were built by Samuel Hall, and two, the *Contest* and *Sweepstakes,* by Jacob A. Westervelt, with one ship each by other builders. Beside Captain Creesy of the *Flying Cloud* and Captain Nickels of the *Flying Fish,* Captain Dumaresq also made the passage twice in less than 100 days, in command of the *Surprise* and *Romance of the* Seas.

For an average of the two fastest passages by one ship, the record of the *Flying Cloud*—two in 89 days each—stands at the head. The others are: the *Andrew Jackson,* 89 and 100—94½ days; *Flying Fish,* 92 and 98—95 days; *Sword-Fish,* 90 and 105—97½ days; *David Brown,* 98 and 103—101½ days; *Westward Ho,* 100 and 103—101½ days; *Sea Witch,* 97 and 108—102½ days; *Contest,* 108 and 97—102½ days; *Herald of the Morning,* 99 and 106 --102½; *Phantom,* 101 and 104—102½ days; John *Gilpin,* 93 and 115—104 days; *Romance of the Seas,* 96 and 113—104½ days; *Ringleader,* 100 and 109 —104½ days; *Sweepstakes,* 94 and 116—105 days; *Flying Dutchman,* 104 and 106—105 days; *Flying Dragon,* 97 and 114—105½ days; *Surprise,* 96 and 116—106 days; *Young America,* 105 and 109—107 days; *Neptune's Car,* 100 and 112—106; *Eagle,* 103 and 111—107 days; *Comet,* 103 and 112—107½ days; *Golden Gate,* 102 and 113—107½ days; *Golden City,* 105 and 113—109 days; *Flyaway,* 106 and 112—109 days; *Sea Serpent,* 107 and 112—109½ days; *Shooting Star,* 105 and 115—110 days.

The fastest three passages in 1850–1860 were made by the *Flying Cloud,* 89, 89, 105—94 1/3 days; *Andrew Jackson,* 89, 100, 102—97 days; *Flying Fish,* 92, 98, 105—98 1/3 days; *Westward Ho,* 103, 106, 100—103 days; *Sword-Fish,* 90, 105, 116—103 2/3 days; *Sea Witch,* 97, 108, 110—105 days; *Young America,* 105, 107, 110—107 1/3 days; *Surprise,* 96, 116, 117—109 2/3 days; *Sea Serpent,* 107, 112, 115—111 1/3 days.

The best four passages were made by the *Flying Cloud,* 89, 89, 105, 108—97 ¾ days; *Andrew Jackson,* 89, 100, 102, 103—98 ½ days; *Flying Fish,* 92, 98, 105, 106—100 ¼ days.

By dividing this great race-course into sections, a further comparison of the relative speed of the clipper ships may be obtained. Thus the following separate runs were made during the years in question:

From Sandy Hook to the equator: *Great Republic,* 16 days; *Flying Cloud, Northern Light, Sea Serpent, Storm* (barque), *White Swallow,* 17 days; *Adelaide, Jacob Bell, Surprise, Sweepstakes,* 18 days; *Atlanta, Flying Fish, Golden Gate, Hornet, Samuel Russell, Tingqua,* 19 days; *Archer, Antelope, Climax, Courier, Comet, David Brown, Hazard, Sirocco, Tornado, White Squall,* 20 days. In February, 1858, the *Stag Hound,* commanded by Captain Hussey, made the run from Boston Light to the equator in the phenomenal time of 13 days, eclipsing all records.

From Cape St. Roque to 50° S.: *Samuel Russell,*

16 days; *Hornet, Ocean Pearl,* 17 days; *Bald Eagle, Comet, Electric, Hurricane, Ocean Express, Raven,* 18 days; *Electric Spark, Galatea, Governor Morton, John Gilpin, Sovereign of the Seas, Sword-Fish, Witch of the Wave,* 19 days; *Aurora, Flying Fish, Golden Gate, John Wade, Mandarin, North America, Panama, Ringleader, Seaman, Sea Witch, Skylark, Trade Wind,* 20 days.

From 50° S. in the Atlantic to 50° S. in the Pacific: *Young America,* 6 days; *Flying Fish, Flying Cloud, Robin Hood,* 7 days; *Flying Dutchman* (twice), *Herald of the Morning, Stag Hound, Sword-Fish,* 8 days; *Mary L. Sutton, Sovereign of the Seas, Great Republic,* 9 days; *Atlanta, Golden City, Hornet, Snap Dragon* (barque), *Sweepstakes, Typhoon, Whistler,* 10 days.

From 50° S. in the Pacific to the equator: *Live Yankee, Mary L. Sutton,* 16 days; *Flying Cloud, Sweepstakes,* 17 days; *Celestial, Eagle, Hurricane, John Bertram, Surprise, Young America,* 18 days; *Belle of the West, Courser, Don Quixote, Flying Dutchman* (twice), *Flying Fish, Mermaid, Neptune's Car, Ocean Telegraph, Sirocco, Starlight, Sword-Fish, Wild Pigeon, Winged Arrow,* 19 days; *Alarm, Archer, Electric, Flying Dragon, Golden Eagle, John Gilpin, Malay, Stag Hound, Starr King, Syren, Shooting Star, Telegraph, Unknown,* 20 days.

From the equator to San Francisco: *White Squall,* 14 days; *Flying Cloud, John Gilpin, Phantom,* 15 days; *Antelope, Comet, Contest, Flying Dutchman, Game-Cock, Trade Wind,* 16 days; *Aurora, Flying Fish* (twice), *Sovereign of the Seas, Surprise, Young America,* 17 days; *Cleopatra, Chal-*

lenge, Golden City, John Bertram, Samuel Appleton, Seaman, Sea Witch, Staffordshire, Typhoon, Westward Ho, Winged Arrow, 18 days; *Bald Eagle, Boston Light, Defender, Eagle, Electric, Golden Eagle, Great Republic, Hornet, N. B. Palmer, Wild Pigeon,* 19 days; *Celestial, Cyclone, Eureka, Governor Morton, Herald of the Morning, Intrepid, Living Age, Ocean Telegraph, Raven, Samuel Russell, Sparkling Wave, Sword-Fish,* 20 days.

These records indicate the remarkable sailing qualities of the clipper ships, for, if the quickest single runs are added together—the *Stag Hound's* 13 days from Boston Light to the equator with an allowance of 2 days for the run from the equator to Cape St. Roque; the *Samuel Russell's* 16 days from Cape St. Roque to 50° S.; the *Young America's* 6 days from 50° S. in the Atlantic to 50° S. in the Pacific; the *Live Yankee's* and *Mary L. Sutton's* 16 days from 50° S. to the equator; and the *White Squall's* 14 days from the equator to San Francisco —we find that these six ships sailed long distances at the rate of a passage of 67 days from Boston Light to San Francisco, or 22 days less than the record of the *Flying Cloud* and *Andrew Jackson*— 89 days. Yet no one of the six ships which made these splendid runs made the passage from an Atlantic port to San Francisco in less than 100 days.

The records of the other ships are even more remarkable, for allowing 20 days as the outside limit of the four longer runs, with 10 days from 50° S. in the Atlantic to 50° S. in the Pacific and 2 days from the equator to Cape St. Roque, we find that no less than 157 runs were made over distances of thousands of miles, most of them considerably within an average rate of 92 days from Sandy Hook to San Francisco, or well within 3 days of the fastest record time. These records prove, if proof were needed, that the reputation of American clipper ships for speed does not rest upon the fast passages of a few ships, but is based upon the established records of many swift vessels.

Judged by any standard of beauty, the American clipper ships were handsome, noble-looking vessels. During the past fifty years I have seen many fleets of men-of-war and merchant ships, besides naval reviews, and at various times the squadrons of yachts that gather each summer in Cowes Roads and Newport Harbor, but I have never seen a collection of vessels which could compare in stately beauty with the fleet of American clipper ships which lay in the harbor of Hong-kong during the autumn of 1858.

The American clippers were all built of wood and their hulls were painted black from the metal up, though the *Invincible* carried a crimson stripe, and the *Challenge, N. B. Palmer, Sweepstakes,* and perhaps two or three others, a stripe of gold. Their yards and bowsprits were usually painted black, the lower masts white to the tops, with the tops and doublings above scraped bright and varnished, but the *Challenge, Young America,* and *Mandarin* carried black lower masts, and a few other ships kept their lower masts bright.

Many of their figureheads were of considerable artistic excellence, being designed by skilful artists, some of whom have already been mentioned. The *Romance of the Seas* carried the full-length figure of an ancient navigator, whose original might have stood on the high poop of Magellan's flag-ship, with head bent forward and right hand raised to shade his eager eyes, as he gazed upon an unknown land in an uncharted sea. The *Sea Serpent* carried a long slender serpent, whose life-like, slimy-looking body, picked out in shades of green and gold, suggested his recent escape from the waters of one of the summer resorts along the Atlantic coast. The *Nightingale* carried a beautiful bust of Jenny Lind, for whom she was named. The *Panama* carried at her bow a nude, full-length figure of a beautiful woman with arms extended, pure white and of great artistic merit, perhaps the most beautiful figurehead ever carried by a ship. The *Flying Fish* carried a fish on the wing, of life-like color and giving a vivid sense of speed; the *Witchcraft,* a grim Salem witch riding upon her aerial broomstick; the *Game-Cock,* a fighting bird with outstretched neck and head, apparently eager for combat; the *Northern Light,* the full-length figure of an angelic creature in flowing white drapery, one graceful arm extended above her head, and bearing in her slender hand a torch with golden flame.

One of the most striking figureheads was the tall square-built sailor, with dark curly hair and bronzed clean-shaven face, who stood at the bow of the *Champion of the Seas.* A black belt with a massive brass buckle supported his white trousers, which were as tight about the hips as the skin of an eel, and had wide, bell-shaped bottoms that almost hid his black polished pumps. He wore a loose-fitting blue-and-white-checked shirt, with wide, rolling collar, and black neck handkerchief of ample size, tied in the most rakish of square knots with long flowing ends. But perhaps the most impressive of this mariner's togs were his dark-blue jacket, and the shiny tarpaulin hat which he waved aloft in the grip of his brawny, tattooed right hand. The only exception that one could possibly take to this stalwart sailorman was that his living prototype was likely to be met with so very seldom in real life. There were many other figureheads that might be mentioned, but these are best remembered.

In those days New York was one of the most beautiful and picturesque seaports of the world; the water-front was lined with majestic clippers, stately Indiamen, and noble packet ships, their American ensigns and well-known house flags of many brilliant colors floating in the breeze.[1] The

[1] The following are some of these house flags: The crimson field and black ball, of Charles H. Marshall; the red, white, and blue swallowtail, of Grinnell, Minturn & Co.; the yellow, red, and yellow horizontal bars with white "L" in centre, of A. A. Low & Brother; the thirteen blue and twelve white squares, of N. L. & G. Griswold; the crimson field and yellow beehive, of Sutton & Co.; the crimson field, white border, and white "D" in centre, of George Daniels; the red, white, and red vertical stripes with red "B" in centre, of Vernon H. Brown; the blue and white half-diamonds, of Russell & Co.; the crimson field and white diamond, of Augustine Heard & Co.; the white above blue and red ball in the centre, of Sampson & Tappan; the white above yellow and red star in centre, of Glidden & Williams; the narrow blue and white horizontal stripes with red ball in the centre, of Napier, John-

view and skyline of the port from the harbor were very beautiful; Battery Park with its fine lawns and trees in the foreground, the graceful spire of Trinity Church forming a prominent landmark, while clustered on every side were the modest yet dignified and substantial residences, gardens, and warehouses of the merchants, with a quiet, refined atmosphere of prosperity and contentment, long since departed.

---

son & Co.; the white field and blue cross, of George B. Upton; the crimson swallowtail and blue cross, of Charles R. Green; the white swallowtail, red cross with white diamond in the centre, of R. W. Cameron; the crimson swallowtail, blue cross, and white ball in the centre, of Wells & Emanuel; the blue above white, white ball in blue and red ball in white, of D. & A. Kingsland; the white field and red cross in the centre of D. G. & W. B. Bacon; the white swallowtail and black S. & B., of Snow & Burgess; the white field and black horse, of William F. Weld & Co. The flag of Howland & Aspinwall had a blue square in the upper corner of the luff and lower corner of the fly; the rest of the flag was white with narrow blue lines in the lower corner of the luff and upper corner of the fly, which formed squares, and also formed a white cross extending the full hoist and length of the flag. David Ogden's flag was a white field and red cross; Crocker & Warren's, blue above yellow with a yellow "C" in the blue and blue "W" in the yellow. Then there was the red swallowtail with white cross and black star in the centre, of Samuel Thompson & Nephew; the blue field, white diamond, and black star, of Williams & Guion; the crimson field and black "X" of John Griswold. These were the private signals of most of the leading New York and Boston ship-owners, which, half a century ago, enlivened the water front of New York, though there were some others which have now faded from memory.

The New York pilot-boats were remarkably fast and able schooners of from 80 to 90 tons, which cruised to the eastward as far as the Grand Banks, with a hand in the crow's nest on the lookout for the packets and steamships bound for New York. Among these stanch little vessels were the *Washington, Ezra Nye, George W. Blunt, William H. Aspinwall, Mary Taylor, Moses H. Grinnell, Charles H. Marshall, Mary Fish, George Steers,* and *Jacob Bell.* The New York pilots themselves were a very superior class of men, who always wore beaver hats when boarding a vessel, and owned their boats, and it was regarded as a compliment and an honor for a citizen of New York to have one of their vessels named for him.

Of the men who commanded the American clipper ships, it may be said that they carried the ensign of the United States to every quarter of the globe, with honor to their country and themselves. They were not, however, all cast in the same mould. Each had his strongly marked individual traits of character, and his human weaknesses. Nothing could be more remote from the truth than to imagine these men as blustering bullies at sea or rollicking shellbacks on shore; neither were they Chesterfields or carpet knights, afloat or ashore, nor at all the type of skipper that one is apt to meet in works of fiction. Many of them might easily have been mistaken for prosperous merchants or professional men, until a more intimate acquaintance disclosed the aura of salted winds and surging seas, and a worldwide knowledge of men and cities. These were the qualities which made so many of these master mariners delightful companions and welcome guests at the firesides of refined and luxurious homes, whose doors could not be opened by golden keys. It may well be doubted whether braver, truer-hearted gentlemen or finer seamen than many of the American clipper ship captains of half a century ago have ever sailed the seas.

Many of the clipper ship captains were accompanied on their voyages by their wives, whose influence at sea was humanizing, while their companionship was a comfort and solace to their husbands. In foreign ports, especially in China and India, they were made much of. The merchants vied with each other to render their visits enjoyable, and nothing in the way of lavish entertainment or costly gift was regarded as too good for them. Mrs. Babcock, of the *Sword-Fish* and *Young America;* Mrs. Low, of the *N. B. Palmer;* Mrs. Very, of the *Hurricane;* Mrs. Creecy, of the *Flying Cloud,* and Mrs. Andrews, of the *Red Gauntlet,* were veritable sea belles, while Mrs. Patten of the *Neptune's Car* proved herself a true heroine.

The *Neptune's Car* sailed from New York for San Francisco in June, 1856, and before she reached Cape Horn, Captain Patten was compelled to put his chief officer under arrest on account of incompetence and neglect of duty. That winter off Cape Horn was unusually cold and stormy, and the exposure and fatigue which Captain Patten was obliged to endure brought on an attack of brain fever which soon resulted in his becoming entirely blind. The second mate was a good seaman but knew nothing about navigation. Mrs. Patten at that time was not more than twenty-four years old, but she had acquired a thorough knowledge of navigation upon a previous voyage with her husband round the globe, and she at once assumed command of the ship. For 52 days she navigated this heavily masted clipper of over 1600 tons, taking her safely into the harbor of San Francisco, besides acting as nurse and physician to her husband and keeping him alive by constant care and watchfulness. The chief mate asked to return to duty, but Mrs. Patten declined his aid, as she had no faith in his ability or loyalty, and preferred to trust the faithful though illiterate second mate.

Captain Patten never recovered his health and died at Boston on July 26, 1857, in his thirty-sixth year. His funeral took place at Christ Church in that city, with the colors of the shipping in the harbor at half mast, and the bells of the church tolling in his honor. Captain Joshua A. Patten was born in Rockland, Maine, and had followed the sea from boyhood. He was a prominent Mason, and for several years had been a member of Christ Church. Mrs. Mary Patten was a beautiful woman of the finest New England type, with a refined, gentle voice and manner. While not active in the then newly-organized women's rights movement, she was unwillingly made to appear as the star example of woman's ability to compete successfully in the pursuits and avocations of man.

CHAPTER XX

THE GREATNESS AND THE DECLINE OF THE AMERICAN MERCHANT MARINE

THE year 1851 is memorable in our maritime annals, because at that time the United States was at the zenith of her power upon the ocean, and had completely outstripped her rival Great Britain in the efficiency and extent of her oversea carrying trade. It is true that the total tonnage of merchant shipping owned in the United States in this year, including steam, was only 3,718,640 tons, against 4,332,085 owned by the British Empire with all its dependencies; but these figures, like many statistics of this nature, are somewhat misleading. The primary reason for the existence of a merchant ship is, of course, her ability to pay her way and earn money for her owners. When a ship ceases to be able to do this, the sooner she is converted into a hulk or broken up, the better. So the true measure of a nation's merchant marine is its earning capacity, not merely the number or tonnage of its ships; and judged by this standard, the merchant marine of the United States was at this time far in advance of the merchant shipping of the whole British Empire.

In the first place, the merchant ships of the British Empire were of such massive construction that they could not carry at the very most more than ninety per cent. of the cargo carried by ships of similar tonnage owned in the United States; then in the matter of speed, an American merchantman would make five voyages while a British ship was making four of equal length; and as to freights, the American ships had the splendid rates to San Francisco all to themselves, while from China to England the rates of freight were quite double in their favor, as compared with British ships.

If any one with a liking for statistics will apply these facts to the foregoing figures, the seeming advantage of tonnage possessed by the British Empire will disappear and it will be found that the merchant marine of the United States at that time held a commanding position in the maritime carrying trade of the world. Furthermore, the shipbuilders of this country still excelled in every branch of merchant marine architecture.

On the North Atlantic in 1851, the American Collins Line steamships *Arctic, Atlantic, Baltic,* and *Pacific* were competing successfully with the British Cunarders *Niagara, Canada, Asia,* and *Africa:* the *Baltic* holding the speed record for both the eastern and the western passages between New York and Liverpool; while the New York, Philadelphia, and Boston packet ships still held their own. No sailing ships of other nationalities could compete with them, and though hard pressed by steamships of the various lines, they still retained their popularity with passengers and shipping merchants. American ships from home ports were profitably engaged in the India, China, African, and South American trades; the New Bedford and Nantucket whaling ships were to be found upon every sea; the Mississippi, Hudson River, and Long Island Sound steamboats were the most perfect types of this period for inland navigation; and the Massachusetts fishing schooners, the North River sloops, and the New York pilot-boats were far famed for speed and beauty; while the American clippers were now known and admired throughout the maritime world.

It was in this year also that the Royal Yacht Squadron presented a cup to be sailed for at Cowes by yachts belonging to the yacht clubs of all nations, which, as every one knows, was won by the *America,* representing the New York Yacht Club.

> "To teach the Mistress of the Sea
> What beam and mast and sail should be,
> To teach her how to walk the wave
> With graceful step, is such a lore
> As never had been taught before;
> Dumb are the wise, aghast the brave."[1]

Surely De Tocqueville was right when he said: "Nations, as well as men, almost always betray the most prominent features of their future destiny in their earliest years. When I contemplate the ardor with which the Anglo-Americans prosecute commercial enterprise, the advantages which befriend them, and the success of their undertakings, I cannot refrain from believing that they will one

[1] Walter Savage Landor.

day become the first maritime power of the globe. They are born to rule the seas, as the Romans were to conquer the world."[1]

This day had then come. The victory of the *America* off the Isle of Wight may be likened to the gilded weathercock at the top of some lofty spire, being highly decorative and at the same time showing the direction of the wind. At that time the commercial greatness of the United States rested upon the splendid qualities shown by her sailing ships and their captains upon the ocean. And after all the only really rational sovereignty of the seas that exists, or has ever existed, is maintained by the merchant marine, whose ships and seamen contribute not only to the welfare and happiness of mankind, but also to the wealth of the nations under whose flags they sail.

In those early days, as the flaming posters in the downtown streets of New York used to announce, it was "Sail versus Steam" and the packet ships justified their claim more than once by beating a steamship from port to port. When, as not infrequently happened, a packet ship running before a strong westerly gale in mid-ocean overhauled a wallowing side-wheel steamer bound the same way, the joyous shouts and derisive yells of the steerage passengers on board the packet, as she ranged alongside and swept past the "tea-kettle," were good for the ears of sailormen to hear. In those days no sailors liked steamships, not even those who went to sea in them. If a

[1] *Democracy in America* (1835); Second American edition, p. 408.

packet captain sighted a steamer ahead going the same way, he usually steered for her and passed to windward as close as possible, in order that the dramatic effect of the exploit might not be lost upon the passengers of either vessel.

The Atlantic steamship lines with which the packet ships had to compete, the Cunard, Collins, Havre, Bremen, and Vanderbilt lines, ran only wooden side-wheel steamers; but when the Inman Line was founded in 1850, and began to run iron screw steamers between Liverpool and Philadelphia, the Atlantic packet ships began to lose their trade. Indeed, from 1840, when the Cunard Line was established, until the Inman Line began to run their fast iron screw steamships to New York in 1857, the rivalry between sail and steam was keen and spirited. During these years the Atlantic mail steamships carried almost as much canvas as sailing vessels, and they continued to do so for many years. Most of the Cunarders were barque-rigged, and the famous *Russia* of that line carried topmast and topgallant studdingsails. The Allan liners were also barque-rigged, and the Inman steamships were full ship-rigged, while the White Star liners were ship-rigged with a jiggermast. It was not until 1889, when the White Star Line brought out the *Majestic* and the *Teutonic* with twin screws, pole masts, and no canvas, that the Atlantic Ocean began to be navigated by vessels propelled entirely by steam; so that the complete transition from sail to steam required very nearly half a century.

It cannot be said that steam competition had any direct effect upon the California clippers, as it is only of late years that there has been direct communication by sea between the Atlantic and Pacific coasts, and the Pacific Mail Company, after once getting its steamers round into the Pacific, had always carried passengers, the mails, and specie with transshipment at Panama. The demand for the California clippers ceased when rapid transportation of cargoes round Cape Horn became no longer necessary.

Besides the competition between sail and steam, there was also going on for many years, as has already been suggested, the attempt to substitute iron for wood in the construction of vessels, and screw propellers for paddle-wheels as a means of propulsion by steam. In both branches of this transition, which were parallel but not necessarily connected, Great Britain took the lead, and she has rightfully reaped the benefit.

How gradually the change came about will be seen from the following facts and figures: The first iron sailing ship was the *Vulcan,* built on the Clyde in 1818, and in the following year the first sailing vessel with an auxiliary engine crossed the Atlantic. This was the *Savannah,* a wooden ship of 350 tons, with portable paddles and an engine and boiler on deck. She was built at New York. The first vessel to cross the Atlantic using steam-power during the entire voyage was the *Royal William,* which was taken from Quebec to London in 1833; and in 1838 the first steamers of British build, the *Great Western* and the *Sirius,* made the westward passage. The first steamer constructed of iron was the *Aaron Manby,* a small paddle-wheel vessel about 50 feet long, built at Horsley, England, in 1821; and the first screw steamer of any importance was the *Archimedes,* an iron vessel of 237 tons, built in England in 1839. The *Great Britain,* built at Bristol, England, in 1843, was the first screw, as well as the first iron steamer to cross the Atlantic, but it was not until 1850, when the Inman liner *City of Glasgow* began to run regularly between Liverpool and Philadelphia, that iron screw steamers took a recognized place upon the ocean.

It is to be noticed how closely these last dates correspond with those of the clipper ship era, which opened with the advent of the *Rainbow* in 1843, and was brought to its greatest brilliancy through the discovery of gold in California and Australia in 1848 and 1851. At this time each nation was devoting its best talents to developing the material that lay nearest at hand; and while the American wooden-built type was earlier brought to perfection, its possibilities were more limited by natural causes. Greater economy, durability, and regularity of speed on the part of the iron screw steamer were the qualities that finally drove from the seas the far more picturesque and beautiful wooden sailing ship.

The supremacy held by the merchant marine of the United States in 1851 was maintained until about 1856, and during this period American ships continued to be built, bought, and chartered by British ship-owners; but after the great financial depression which affected both countries from 1857 to 1859, British ship-owners no longer needed American-built ships, for in Great Britain iron had by this time superseded wood in the construction of large vessels. Thus the advantage to the United States of having an abundant supply of timber was taken away, while the advantage of Free Trade, with low cost of living, was on the side of England. Moreover, the spirit of enterprise, which had been growing in Great Britain during the years of free competition in the carrying trade since 1849, was having its effect.

Following the repeal of the Navigation Laws, the Merchant Shipping Act of 1854, a wise and far-seeing measure, completed the foundation upon which the merchant marine of Great Britain has been developed. This act of Parliament contains 548 clauses, dealing with all questions which relate to British merchant ships and seamen, including tonnage. The ship-builders of Great Britain had been much hampered by the old tonnage laws and were glad to see them abolished.[1] The new tonnage rules, which are still in force, were based upon the actual cubic capacity of the hull, the unit of 100 cubic feet being one ton register, so that a vessel measuring 100,000 cubic feet internal capacity registers 1000 tons, and is able to carry 2000 tons at 50 cubic feet per ton. This new system of measurement encouraged the application of scientific knowledge to the design of vessels, and, as we shall see, helped somewhat to prolong the clipper ship era in England, when it was practically dead in the United States.

It is true that during our Civil War American

[1] See Appendix IV.

ships were still sold in England, but this was rather because their owners had no profitable use for them at home than from any lack of British iron vessels. Since that period, the decline of American shipping, for reasons that should be well understood, has been constant.

I refer to the Navigation Laws and Protective Tariff of the United States. The former, first enacted in 1792 and revised and added to since that time only in unimportant details, have long outlived the usefulness they may once have possessed, and completely fail to meet the requirements of the changes in ocean navigation that have taken place during the period of more than a century that has since elapsed. As is well known, they prohibit an American citizen from owning a foreign-built merchant ship. Meanwhile the Protective Tariff so increases the cost of living and with it the cost of the labor and materials that go into the construction of a modern ship, that the American ship-builder cannot produce a steel or iron vessel at anything like a cost that will enable her to compete successfully with a ship of the same class constructed in a European shipyard. Were it not for this hindrance, the immense natural advantages of such broad, deep waters as those of the Delaware and Chesapeake, where the finest coal and iron ore are within easy transportation, and the abundant food supplies of the neighboring garden States and of the West which are easily accessible, would make them ideal spots for the construction of ships. So it will be seen that the Navigation Laws and Protective Tariff are the millstones between which the American ship-owner and ship-builder at present find themselves ground with an ever-receding prospect of escape from this cunningly devised dilemma. Meanwhile, the ensign of the United States no longer contributes in any marked degree to the gayety of foreign seaports; whereas, Great Britain, with inferior coal and iron ore, compelled to import the food and clothing material for her shipwrights from distant lands, and with certainly no keener intelligence nor greater energy among her ship-owners and builders, but guided by the enlightened policy of Free Trade, sends her endless procession of merchant ships, both sail and steam, to every seaport upon the globe.

CHAPTER XXI

THE LATER BRITISH TEA CLIPPERS

IN what may be called the ante-Suez Canal days, China was a pretty comfortable place to be in. The East India Company, with its pomp and grandeur, had passed away, but the older residents treasured the picturesque traditions of former times, and the comfort and luxury of the old days still survived.

All white foreigners in China were known as Europeans, and at the little treaty ports along the coast their communities were closely united by ties of social necessity, the barriers of national prejudice, if they existed, being soon obliterated in the effort of each member to contribute to the well-being of all. Hong-kong was the European capital. With its cathedral, Government House, regiment of soldiers, court of justice, race-course, social clubs, and annual Derby and Regatta week, it was a most entertaining pocket edition of England, set down at the base of a lofty island mountain-peak, between the bluest of seas and the brightest of skies. Almost the only things that reminded one of the Orient were the tiers of junks that lay moored at the western end of the town, and the industrious well-mannered Chinese who mingled so unobtrusively with their visitors from the west.

All of these things worked together for good. There were no cables or telegraphs to vex the souls of the righteous. The P. & O. steamer, via the Red Sea and the Indian Ocean, usually arrived every month, though frequently four or five days overdue, and once in a while she would not appear at all, having fetched up on one of the numerous uncharted reefs or shoals that then infested these seas. When she did arrive, there was a ripple of excitement over receiving letters and newspapars from home, and when she had departed, the little colony settled once more into agreeable repose. The towns and cities of America and Europe seemed far away—bright, shadowy visions that dwelt in our hearts as "home."

In 1862 the Messageries Imperiales of France extended their steamship line to China, and in 1867 the first steamship of the Pacific Mail Company from San Francisco arrived at Hong-kong. Vast numbers of globe-trotters then began to appear, most of them far too energetic; they insisted, among other things, on tying their own shoestrings, and in general proved very inferior lotus-eaters. When the Suez Canal was opened and telegraph cables began to be laid, then the remnant of charm that had made the old life in China so pleasant vanished forever.

In 1859 quite a new type of China tea clipper appeared in Great Britain. The first of these beautiful vessels was the *Falcon,* built by Robert Steele & Co., at Greenock, and owned by Shaw,

Maxton & Co. She was a wooden vessel of 937 tons register; length 191 feet 4 inches, breadth 32 feet 2 inches, depth 20 feet 2 inches, and was commanded by Captain Maxton, who had been in command of the *Lord of the Isles*. The *Falcon* was the first of the really handsome tea clippers sailing out of London. Like her, the *Fiery Cross*, built by Chalour & Co., of Liverpool, in 1860; the *Min*, by Robert Steele & Co., of Greenock, and the *Kelso*, by William Pile, of Sunderland, in 1861; the *Belted Will*, by Feel & Co., of Workington, and the *Serica*, by Robert Steele & Co., in 1863, were all wooden ships sheathed with red copper. The *Fiery Cross*, the largest of these, was only 888 tons. They were all beautiful vessels of an entirely original type and with nothing about them to remind one of the American clippers; for they had considerably less sheer, much less freeboard, and lower bulwarks, and their comparatively small breadth gave them a slim, graceful appearance.

These ships and the tea clippers which followed them had very clear decks for working ship. The deck-houses were small, and with the rails, bulwarks, waterways, bitts, hatch-coamings, companions, and skylights were of India teak varnished; the decks, also of India teak, were holystoned; and this, with the polished brasswork and the spare spars lashed amidships, made them very smart and shipshape.

The tea-trade in the early sixties was comparatively small, and did not require many vessels, but speed in the delivery of new teas was of the utmost importance, and it was this demand that brought these clippers into existence. They were designed with great skill for this special purpose, and as they invariably sailed from China with new teas during the southwest monsoon, it was necessary that they should be smart in moderate weather going to windward, as well as in getting through the northeast trades in the Atlantic. It was under these conditions that they did their best work. They did not carry as heavy spars nor as much canvas as the American clippers of the same length, and probably could not have done so to advantage, as their breadth was considerably less, and with their easy lines they did not require much canvas to drive them. They were remarkably fast in light and moderate winds, and made fine averages rather than exceptional daily records of speed, none of them reaching the extreme speed of many of the sharper and more powerful American clipper ships. Only twenty-five or thirty of these vessels were built from first to last, and not more than four or five in any one year. A list of the most celebrated of them will be found in Appendix III.

The captains were men of great ability, who handled their ships with skill and judgment; some of them accumulated considerable fortunes, being part owners of the vessels which they commanded. These ships were manned by fine British seamen, many of whom had served in the Royal Navy. When these fellows got safely to sea and properly sobered up, there were no smarter sailors afloat, whether aloft or with marlinspike, palm and needle, or watch tackle.

In 1863 the first tea clippers of composite construction were brought out—the *Taeping,* built by Robert Steele & Co.; the *Eliza Shaw,* by Alexander Stephen, and the *Yang-tze* and *Black Prince,* by Alexander Hall. This system of ship-building—iron frames and wood planking—was invented by John Jordan, son of a member of the firm of L. H. Macintyre & Co., ship-builders of Liverpool, who built the schooner *Excelsior* upon this principle in 1850, and the barque *Marion Macintyre,* in 1851, these being the first composite vessels constructed.

This system combined the strength of iron frames with the advantage that the wooden planking could be coppered to prevent fouling, which was a serious matter in this trade. Great care had to be taken in building these vessels to prevent galvanic action so far as possible. Gutta-percha was placed between the frames and planking as a non-conductor; the planking was then fastened with yellow-metal screw bolts with counter-sunk heads, the holes being afterwards filled with a composition prepared for the purpose. Mr. Jordan obtained a patent for his invention, but it did not attract much attention until adopted in the construction of the *Taeping, Eliza Shaw, Yang-tze,* and *Black Prince.* From that time all the tea clippers were of composite build, though it was not until 1867 that the Committee of Lloyd's Register issued rules for their construction.

It was in 1863 also that the *Seaforth,* an iron ship of 1200 tons, built for the Calcutta trade by Jones, Quiggin & Co., of Liverpool, was fitted with steel lower masts, topmasts, topsails yards, and bowsprit, and with standing rigging of steel wire

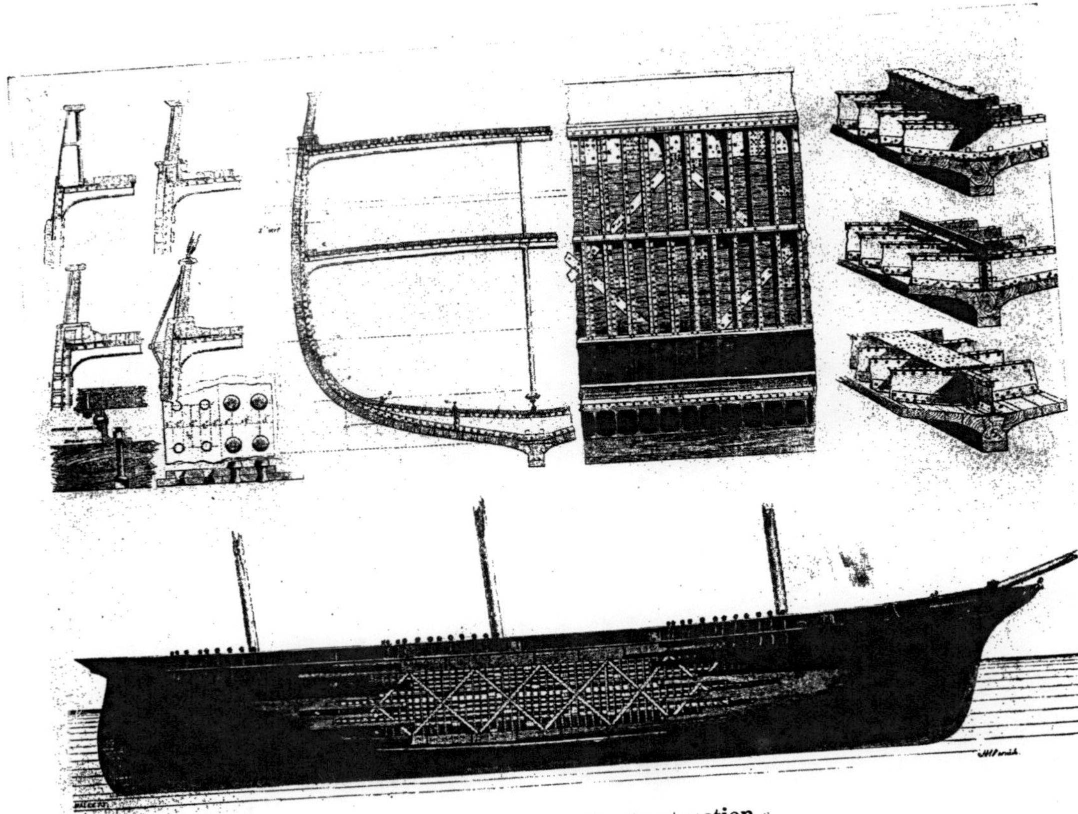

The Composite Construction

rope. It was estimated that by replacing wood and hemp with steel, she saved 21 tons weight aloft, besides getting less wind resistance and a very considerable increase in strength. The *Seaforth* was the first vessel to have steel spars and rigging, but they soon came into use on board the tea clippers.

The wild, speculative years of ship-owning which followed the discovery of gold in California and Australia, when a clipper ship was expected to pay for herself every voyage or two, had now passed away. Ship-owners retained a lively recollection of the crash in 1857 and the depression which followed, so the tea clippers were built with an eye to economy as well as speed. The rates of freight, which in the early fifties had been £6 and even as high as £8 per ton, were in 1863 £4 10s. to £5 per ton—still fine paying rates on the investment of capital, after allowing for running expenses and depreciation. Ship-owning in Great Britain had now become established upon a less profitable, though more rational and substantial basis.

The tea clippers carried from 200 to 300 tons of clean shingle ballast, laid beautifully smooth and even, upon which the chests of tea were stowed, and a considerable quantity of dunnage wood, for which allowances were made in reckoning the actual cargo capacity. The *Taeping,* which under the new rules based on the cubic capacity of the hull registered 767 tons, carried 1234 tons of tea at 50 cubit feet per ton, with a crew of 30 men all told. Vessels were now designed on scientific principles, and it may be doubted whether the qualities then desirable in a merchant sailing ship

—speed, strength, carrying capacity, and economy—have ever been so successfully united as in these famous China tea clippers.

Some exciting contests took place between the various clippers of the new type, the *Falcon, Fiery Cross, Serica,* and *Taeping* proving the most successful. In the year 1865 the *Fiery Cross* and *Serica* sailed from Foo-chow side by side, on May 28th, both bound for London. After a close race during which they sighted each other several times, both ships made their signals off St. Catharine's, Isle of Wight, at almost the same moment, 106 days from Foo-chow, and continued up Channel before a light westerly breeze. Off Beechy Head they fell in with the tugs sent out to meet them, the *Serica* at that time having a lead of about two miles. The *Fiery Cross,* however, secured the most powerful tug and reached her dock one tide before the *Serica,* thus winning the premium of 10 shillings per ton. The *Taeping* sailed from Foo-chow some days later and made the passage to the Downs in 101 days. As may be supposed, this system of awarding premiums led to a good deal of unpleasantness.

In 1865, Robert Steele & Co. brought out the sister ships *Ariel* and *Sir Launcelot;* Alexander Hall, the *Ada,* and Connell & Co., of Glasgow, the *Taitsing,* all of composite construction; and in the following year the most famous race between these vessels—the one which the tea brokers of Mincing Lane still discuss with enthusiasm—was sailed. It was arranged that nine clippers should sail from Foo-chow as nearly the same date as possible, and during the last week in May the picturesque Pagoda Anchorage presented a scene of unusual activity. The *Ada, Black Prince, Chinaman, Fiery Cross, Flying Spur, Serica, Ariel, Taeping,* and *Taitsing* were all hurrying to finish loading and get to sea. Cargo junks and lorchers [1] were being warped alongside at all hours of the day and night; double gangs of good-natured, chattering coolies were on board each ship ready to handle and stow the matted chests of tea as they came alongside; comfortable sampans worked by merry barefooted Chinese women sailed or rowed in haste between the ships and the shore; slender six-oared gigs with crews of stalwart Chinamen in white duck uniforms darted about the harbor; while dignified master mariners, dressed in white linen or straw-colored pongee silk, with pipe-clayed shoes and broad pith hats, impatiently handled the yoke lines.

On shore the tyepans and their clerks hurried about in sedan chairs carried on the shoulders of perspiring coolies, with quick, firm step to the rhythm of their mild but energetic "woo ho—woo-ho—woo ho." The broad, cool veranda of the club-house was almost deserted; in the great hongs of Adamson, Bell; Gilman & Co.; Jardine, Matheson; Gibb, Livingston; and Sassoon, the gentry of Foochow toiled by candle-light over manifests and bills of lading and exchange, sustained far into the night by slowly swinging punkahs, iced tea, and the fragrant Manila cheroot.

[1] A lorcher is a fast Chinese vessel, used a good deal by fishermen, and in former times by the Chinese pirates and smugglers.

The *Fiery Cross* was the first ship to get her final chest of tea on board, at midnight, and she towed to sea early on the morning of May 29th; the *Ariel* left the Pagoda Anchorage at 10:30 and the *Serica* and *Taeping* at 10:50 A.M. on the 30th; the *Taitsing* followed at midnight on the 31st. Here we must bid good-bye to the *Ada, Black Prince, Chinaman,* and *Flying Spur,* for these vessels, unfortunately, did not finish loading in time to take part in the race. The five competing ships, however, represented the flower of the fleet, and for this reason had been the favorites with shippers. The *Fiery Cross, Taeping,* and *Serica* were fast and well-tried vessels, while the *Ariel* and *Taitsing* were just beginning their successful career. The captains, Keay, of the *Ariel;* Robinson, of the *Fiery Cross;* Innes, of the *Serica;* McKinnon, of the *Taeping,* and Nutsfield, of the *Taitsing,* were all seamen of skill and experience, well known in the China trade.

The *Fiery Cross* found a light northeast breeze outside, and passed through the Formosa Channel with royal studdingsails set, followed by the other four ships. They all carried this breeze for four hundred miles, when the *Fiery Cross* drifted into a calm which let the other ships run up, but she was the first to get the southwest monsoon, and soon drew away again. On June 8th the *Fiery Cross* and *Ariel* met on opposite tacks, both ships having a strong southwest breeze, and the *Fiery Cross* passed three miles to windward. She kept her lead through the Straits of Sunda, passing Anjer Point at noon on June 19th, and was followed by the *Ariel* on the morning of June 20th and the *Taeping* during that afternoon; the *Serica* passed Anjer Point on the 22d and the *Taitsing* on the 25th. From Anjer Point to the meridian of Mauritius they all carried fresh trade winds, and it was on this stretch across the Indian Ocean that each ship made her best twenty-four hours' run—the *Ariel,* 317; *Taeping,* 319; *Serica,* 291; *Fiery Cross,* 328; and *Taitsing,* 318 miles.

The *Fiery Cross* rounded the Cape of Good Hope on July 14th, 46 days from Foo-chow, followed by the *Ariel* also 46 days; *Taeping,* 47 days; *Serica,* 50 days, and *Taitsing,* 54 days. The *Fiery Cross* was on the equator, August 3d, 20 days from the Cape of Good Hope, with the *Ariel* still only one day astern, while the *Taeping* and *Taitsing* had each gained 1 and the *Serica* 2 days on this stretch. On August 9th, in latitude 12° 29′ N., the *Fiery Cross* and *Taeping* exchanged signals, and they continued in company, with calms and variable winds until the 17th, when the *Taeping* picked up a breeze which carried her out of sight while the *Fiery Cross* lay becalmed for another twenty-four hours. Meanwhile, the *Ariel,* which was about thirty miles further to the westward, found better winds and now led the fleet, while the *Taitsing* brought up a good breeze and passed the *Taeping, Serica,* and *Fiery Cross* and was closing on the *Ariel.* At the Azores the *Ariel* still held the lead, though closely followed by the *Taitsing, Fiery Cross, Serica,* and *Taeping* in the order named. From the Azores to the entrance of the English Channel, the *Taeping* and *Serica* passed the *Taitsing* and *Fiery Cross* and closed on the *Ariel,* the *Taeping* leading the *Serica* by about six hours.

At daybreak on the morning of September 5th, two of the clippers sighted each other running in for the Lizard; they were about five miles apart, beam and beam, steering on slightly converging courses. There was a strong southerly wind with smooth sea, and both ships were being driven at their utmost speed—a good fifteen knots—their lee scuppers smothered in foam, with the wind well abaft the starboard beam; both were under the same canvas, main skysail, topmast, topgallant, royal, and square lower studdingsails. Neither captain required the example of the other to send his ship along at her best speed—they had been doing that for ninety-eight days and nights. When their signals could be made out these ships proved to be the *Ariel* and the *Taeping.* After passing the Lizard the wind moderated, and they raced up channel almost side by side, now one and then the other gaining a slight advantage, but never far apart, and as they passed the various headlands along the coast they presented a spirited marine picture. They were off the pilot station at Dungeness at three o'clock the next morning and burned their blue lights for pilots, who boarded both ships at the same time. With a moderate wind they were now making not more than five or six knots through the water, but the tide was sweeping them along fast. Off the South Foreland the wind slackened again with the rising sun. Here the *Ariel* held a slight lead and she passed Deal at 8 o'clock, followed by the *Taeping* eight minutes later, but as the latter vessel had sailed from the Pagoda An-

The "Ariel" and "Taeping" Running up Channel, September 5, 1866

chorage twenty minutes after the *Ariel*, ninety-nine days before, she had won the race by twelve minutes. Both ships had sailed 16,000 miles.

The *Serica* passed Deal four hours later; all three ships went up the Thames on the same tide, and after the usual tugboat race, the *Taeping* arrived in the London Docks at 9:45, the *Ariel* in the East India Docks at 10:15, and the *Serica* in the West India Docks at 11:30 P.M. on September 6th. The *Fiery Cross* passed Deal on the 7th and the *Taitsing* on the 9th, each 101 days from the Pagoda Anchorage.

The following is an abstract of their logs:

	Ariel	*Taeping*	*Serica*	*Fiery Cross*	*Taitsing*
From the Pagoda Anchorage to Anjer	21 days	21 days	23 days	21 days	26 days.
From Anjer to the Cape of Good Hope	25 "	26 "	27 "	25 "	28 "
From the Cape of Good Hope to the equator	20 "	19 "	18 "	20 "	19 "
From the equator to Deal	33 "	33 "	31 "	35 "	28 "
Total	99 "	99 "	99 "	101 "	101 "

The best twenty-four hours' runs were as follows:

			Average
Ariel	June 25......	317 miles......	13.2 knots.
Taeping	" 25......	319 "	13.3 "
Serica	" 29......	291 "	12.1 "
Fiery Cross.....	" 24......	328 "	13.7 "
Taitsing	July 2......	318 "	13.25 "

This contest of 1866 was one of the grandest ocean races ever sailed, partly on account of the number of evenly matched vessels engaged in it, but chiefly by reason of the splendid manner in which it was contested and the close, exciting finish. The tea cargoes of the five ships were: *Taeping,* 1,108,709 lbs.; *Ariel,* 1,230,900 lbs.; *Serica,* 954,236 lbs.; *Fiery Cross,* 854,236 lbs.; *Taitsing,* 1,093,130 lbs.

The usual altercation arose over the award of premium, which this year was 10 shillings per ton; Shaw, Maxton & Co., owners of the *Ariel,* protested that their ship had arrived first at Deal and was therefore entitled to the prize money, but the contention of Rodger & Co., owners of the *Taeping,* that their ship had made the fastest passage and had also reached her dock first, prevailed, and the matter was finally adjusted by dividing the premium. The captains all dined together at the Ship and Turtle Tavern in Leadenhall Street, and harmony was restored, but there were no premiums after this race. The system of awards had always led to controversy, and such an effort to combine sport and business could not be made to flourish. There had also been heavy betting on these races, large sums of money changing hands, and this continued; but it was better understood whether wagers were being laid on the clippers or tugboats, for under the old system, there had been nothing except expense to prevent a ship towing from the Azores.

In the next two years the fleet was increased by a number of fine vessels, built to meet the competition of steam, which was now beginning to be felt in the China trade. We have seen how fierce and prolonged a contest there had been between sail and steam on the Atlantic, where the brave old packet ships had finally been driven into other trades, and how the California and Australian clippers had gradually been superseded by other means of transportation. The difficulty and peculiar conditions of the China voyage made this a harder field to conquer.

Since 1845 the P. & O. steamers had carried passengers between England and China via the Red Sea, but they were expensive vessels to operate, and there were difficulty and delay in transportation across the Isthmus of Suez; consequently, their rates of freight were high and they were unable to compete with the tea clippers. On the other hand, auxiliary vessels did not have sufficient power to drive them against the southwest monsoon when new teas were shipped from China, as their heavy masts, yards, and rigging held them back in head winds. A number of auxiliaries were tried in the China trade, among them the *Scotland, Erl King, Robert Lowe,* and *Far East,* but they were not successful. As late as 1866 there were no steamers that could make the voyage between England and China with sufficient cargo to meet expenses, and very few persons at that time believed that the direct trade between Europe and China could ever be carried on by steamers, or that the Suez Canal, even if completed, would prove of any commercial value.

In this year, however, Alfred Holt, of Liverpool, brought out three iron screw steamships with compound engines—the *Ajax, Achilles,* and *Agamemnon,* —2270 tons gross and 1550 tons net register—and put them in the China trade. These vessels could steam from London to Mauritius, a distance of 8500 miles, without coaling, a remarkable performance in those days, and they made the passage from Foo-chow to London in 58 days, at an average speed of 235 miles per day. These were the first steamships to perform long ocean voyages successfully, and they marked a new era in steam navigation, although they were expensive vessels to operate compared with steamers of the present day, and it was at first doubted whether they could be made to pay.

The owners, builders, and captains of the tea clippers were not men to yield without a contest; they met this new and aggressive invasion of steam by building in rapid succession such noted fliers as the *Titania, Spindrift, Forward Ho, Lahloo, Leander, Thermopylæ, Windhover, Cutty Sark, Caliph, Wylo, Kaisow,* and *Lothair.* These, with the older tea clippers, held their own against the steamers until the opening of the Suez Canal in November, 1869, greatly lessened the length of the voyage and the difficulty and expense of obtaining coal.

In 1868 the *Ariel, Taeping,* and *Sir Launcelot*

sailed from Foo-chow on May 28th, the *Spindrift* on the 29th, the *Lahloo* on the 30th, the *Serica* on June 1st, and the *Leander* on June 3d. The *Ariel* and *Spindrift* made the passage to Deal in 97 days, the *Sir Launcelot* in 98 days, the *Lahloo* in 100 days; *Taeping,* 102 days; *Leander,* 109 days, and *Serica,* 113 days.

The famous tea clipper *Thermopylæ* was launched in this year. She was of composite construction, built by Walter Hood, of Aberdeen, for George Thompson & Co., who also owned the *Star of Peace, Ethiopian, Aristides, Patriarch, Salamis,* and other fine ships well known in the Australian trade. The *Thermopylæ* was 947 tons register; length 210 feet, breadth 36 feet, depth 21 feet; she carried double topsails, but no skysail, and like all the Thompson ships, her hull was painted sea green from the copper up with white yards and lower masts. She carried a handsome figurehead of the brave Leonidas, and was a very beautiful ship. She was designed by Bernard Weymouth, an accomplished naval architect who was for many years the secretary to Lloyd's Register of Shipping. He had before this designed the tea clipper *Leander,* and later designed the *Melbourne,* a fast ship in the Australian trade, built and owned by Richard Green, of London, of which further mention will be made later.

On her first voyage the *Thermopylæ* sailed from London to Melbourne under command of Captain Kemball, who had formerly commanded the *Fairlight* and the *Yang-tze.* She left Gravesend, November 7, 1868, and arrived at Melbourne, January 9, 1869, thus making the passage in the remarkable record time of 63 days, the same time as the record passage of the *James Baines,* from Liverpool to Melbourne fourteen years before. She had a fast run of 21 days to the equator; on the three days before and after crossing the line she made 202, 140, 228, 271, 288, and 293 miles—an unusual rate of speed for that part of the ocean. Her best days' runs were made on January 3d and 4th—330 and 326 miles; her log records on both days "northerly, strong," so that it may be assumed that she had as much fair wind as she needed. Her log records nine days during the passage when her runs were over 300 miles, and five days of less than 100 miles. The entries on December 9th and 10th are: "Northwesterly, fresh gale, 240 miles," and "southwesterly, blowing a gale, 224 miles." These were fair winds. An analysis of this log leads to the conclusion that the *Thermopylæ* was a very fast ship in average weather at sea, but in heavy weather could not be driven at a high rate of speed for a vessel of her length, probably on account of her small breadth and low foreboard.[1]

She next made the run from Newcastle, New South Wales, to Shanghai in 28 days, which is the record between those ports. On this passage large days' runs are not to be expected, but on one day she made 300 miles, and she showed the same fast averages in moderate weather as before.

There was great excitement in the hongs at the coast ports of China in this year (1869) when it

[1] The *Thermopylæ* repeated this remarkable passage of sixty-three days from London to Melbourne during the following year.

became known that the *Thermopylæ* was chartered to load new teas at Foo-chow for London; for no racing yachts ever had firmer friends and backers than the tea clippers; moreover, the rivalry between Aberdeen and the Clyde was acute. Of late years the Clyde clippers had carried all before them, and it was now felt that Aberdeen was about to regain her former glory; but this did not prove to be the case. The *Ariel* sailed from the Pagoda Anchorage on June 30th; the *Leander,* July 1st; *Thermopylæ,* July 3d; *Spindrift,* July 4th; *Taeping,* July 9th, and the *Sir Launcelot,* July 17th. They arrived off Deal as follows: *Sir Launcelot,* 89 days; *Thermopylæ,* 91 days; *Taeping,* 102 days; *Leander,* 103 days; *Ariel,* 104 days, and *Spindrift,* 106 days.

The winner, the *Sir Launcelot,* was commanded by Captain Robinson, formerly of the *Fiery Cross,* a seaman of great energy and experience. On this passage she sailed 354 miles in twenty-four hours while running through the trades in the Indian Ocean, which is believed to be the greatest speed ever made by any of the tea clippers of that period. This vessel was 886 tons register; length 197 feet 6 inches, breadth 33 feet 7 inches, depth 21 feet, drawing 18 feet 9 inches aft and 18 feet 7 inches forward, and carried 45,500 square feet of canvas, with a crew of 30 hands all told. She delivered 1430 tons of tea at fifty cubic feet per ton, and in addition to 200 tons of shingle ballast, she carried 100 tons of kentledge, cast to fit the floors along the keelson between the fore and mizzen masts. Her owner, James McCunn, of Greenock, claimed that she was the fastest of the tea clippers, which her record passage of 89 days from Foo-chow to London and her twenty-four hours' run of 354 miles would seem to justify, though there were probably very slight differences in speed between any of these vessels under similar conditions of wind and weather.

The race of 1870 from Foo-chow to London was won by the *Lahloo* in 97 days, the other vessels being: the *Windhover,* 100 days; *Sir Launcelot,* 102 days *Leander,* 103 days; *Thermopylæ,* 106 days. In 1871 the *Titania* won in 93 days; the *Lahloo,* 111 days, from Foo-chow to London; and from Shanghai to London the *Thermopylæ* was 106 days; *Cutty Sark,* 110 days, and *Forward Ho,* 118 days. This was about the last of the tea clipper racing, for the combined competition of steam and the Suez Canal proved too powerful for sail. No more tea clippers were built after 1869; by degrees these beautiful vessels were driven into other trades; and so the Clipper Ship Era drifted into history.

Great Britain had regained her empire upon the sea, and few British ship-owners could be found who any longer doubted the wisdom of Free Trade. Through the irony of fate, Duncan Dunbar, who had been one of the most vehement opponents of the repeal of the Navigation Laws, became under the new conditions, the largest ship-owner and one of the wealthiest in the United Kingdom, leaving at his death an estate of £1,500,000.

In comparing the speed of the British tea clippers with that of American clipper ships, a good deal depends on what is meant by speed. In ordinary weather at sea, when great power to carry sail is

The "Lahloo"

not required, the British tea clippers were extremely fast vessels, chiefly on account of their narrow beam, which gave their hulls a comparatively small wetted surface, and their smooth copper bottoms which reduced skin resistance. Under these conditions they were, perhaps, as fast as the American clippers of the same class, though from very different causes; —such ships, for instance, as the *Sea Witch, Samuel Russell, Game Cock, Phantom, White Squall, Nightingale, Shooting Star, Northern Light, Surprise, Witch of the Wave, Sword-Fish,* and others. But if speed is to be considered as the maximum performance of a ship under the most favorable conditions, though these conditions may not often occur, then the British tea clippers were certainly no match for the larger American ships such as the *Flying Cloud, Typhoon, Neptune's Car, Challenge, Comet, Hurricane, Flying Fish, Stag-Hound, Young America, Trade-Wind,* and others of this class, to say nothing of the *James Baines, Red Jacket, Champion of the Seas, Lightning, Sovereign of the Seas,* and *Great Republic.* The greater breadth of the American ships in proportion to their length, meant, in sailing vessels of this type, not only power to carry canvas, but also power in the form of buoyancy; and this, with their longer and sharper ends, enabled the American clippers to be driven at much greater speed than the British clippers in strong gales and before heavy seas. It should, however, be remembered that none of the British tea clippers exceeded 1000 tons register, and it may again be said that they probably combined the good qualities of a merchant ship in a higher degree than any other vessels that have ever been built.

The *Melbourne,* already mentioned, was perhaps the fastest ship ever built in Great Britain. In 1875, commanded by Captain Marsden, she made the passage from London to Melbourne in the not very remarkable time of 74 days, but when running her easting down in strong westerly gales she sailed 5100 miles in 17 days, an average of 300 miles a day, and her best twenty-four hours' run was 374 miles, an average of over 15½ knots. She was an iron vessel of 1865 tons register; length 269 feet, breadth 40 feet, depth 23 feet 7 inches, and while not an extreme clipper, was a finely designed ship.

It should be remembered that both the American and the British clippers were dependent upon the form of their lines for stability; this problem in their design was therefore a far more intricate and difficult one to deal with than that of producing stability by hanging a huge mass of lead below the body of a hull, as is the custom with our modern racing yachts.

Yachting is the grandest of sports when yachtsmen handle their yachts themselves, and there are a good number of yachtsman who are excellent seamen and navigators. It is pleasant to recall that in the race for the Emperor's Cup in 1905, four of the competing yachts were sailed and navigated by their owners; and although there is far too much wasteful extravagance and enervating luxury in yachting, still, the increasing number of yachtsmen who show a keen interest and are amateur experts in the design, construction, rigging, and sailing of their yachts, is an encouraging sign for the future of the sport.

Nevertheless, it must be frankly admitted that yacht racing, even across the Atlantic, in comparison with the old clipper ship racing, resembles snipe shooting as compared with hunting big game in the wilds of Africa, while the gold and silver yacht racing cups appear as mere baubles beside the momentous stake of commercial supremacy for which the clippers stretched their wings.

CHAPTER XXII

THE FATE OF THE CLIPPER SHIPS

WE have already seen how, about the year 1855, the extreme clippers were succeeded in the United States by a class of vessels known as medium clippers. These vessels were not so sharp and did not carry as heavy spars or so much canvas as the old clippers, but they could carry more cargo and could be handled with fewer men. This made them more profitable when the demand for speed and the rates of freight had declined, and the extreme clippers were unable to command any higher rate than the medium clippers. After the Civil War ship-building for the oversea carrying trade steadily declined, though it was not until 1893 that the last American wooden sailing ship, the *Aryan,* was launched. During these thirty-eight years a good many ships were built, and by degrees a new type of vessel, designed to carry large cargoes at moderate speed, was developed, which enterprising agents advertised as clippers; but those who had known the real clippers were not deceived. Many of the old names survived; thus there were a second *Memnon,* another *Rainbow, Sea Witch, Oriental, Eclipse, Comet, Northern Light, Ringleader,*

Invincible, Witch of the Wave, Blue Jacket, Charmer, Sovereign of the Seas, Lightning, and *Andrew Jackson* which should not be mistaken for the famous clippers after which they were named.

One may well ask what became of all the splendid clipper ships? The fate of some of them has already been told in these pages, others have disappeared from one cause or another, as time went on, until now scarcely one is left. During the Civil War many of them were sold and sailed under foreign flags, their names were changed and their identity all but lost.

Of the more famous early clippers, the *Houqua* foundered in a typhoon in the China seas in 1865 while under command of Captain McKenzie. The *Sea Witch* made her last voyage to San Francisco in 1852 and then returned to the China trade for which she had been built. On her voyage to China in 1855 Captain Fraser was murdered at sea by his chief mate, and the vessel put into Rio Janeiro, where Captain Lang took command. On the homeward voyage from Amoy to Havana with a cargo of coolies, the *Sea Witch* was wrecked and became a total loss on the eastern coast of Cuba, March 26, 1856. The *Samuel Russell* was wrecked in the Gaspar Straits in 1870, under command of Captain Frederick Lucas.

The *Stag-Hound* was burnt off the coast of Brazil in 1863, her United States ensign, which the captain brought off and returned to the owners in Boston, being the sole relic. The *Surprise,* under command of Captain F. Johnson, struck a sunken rock while beating into Yokohama Bay and became a total wreck, February 4, 1876; the *Game-Cock* was condemned at the Cape of Good Hope in 1880.

The *Staffordshire* was lost off Cape Sable, while bound from Liverpool for Boston in December, 1854. She struck on a ledge during a thick fog and foundered in deep water. Two days before her wreck Captain Richardson had fallen on deck and fractured his spine, and while he lay helpless in his berth, Joseph Alden, his chief mate, reported that the ship was sinking. Captain Richardson gave directions to the mate for saving the women and children passengers, but declined assistance for himself. His last words were: "God's will be done," and as the vessel settled deeper and deeper in the water and the waves closed in upon her deck, the brave spirit of her captain returned to God who gave it, to join the innumerable host of heroes and martyrs of the sea.

The *Flying Cloud* was sold to James Baines in 1863 and was destroyed by fire at St. John, N. B., in 1874. The *Flying Fish* was wrecked in November, 1858, while coming out of Foo-chow, bound for New York with a cargo of tea, and was abandoned to the underwriters, who sold her to a Spanish merchant of Manila. She was subsequently floated and rebuilt at Wampoa, her name being changed to *El Bueno Suceso*. She sailed for some years between Manila and Cadiz, and finally foundered in the China Sea. The *Typhoon* was sold to the United States Government during the Civil War, and was finally broken up. The *Northern Light* was abandoned at sea, December 25, 1861, after being in collision while bound from Havre for New York.

The *Comet* was sold under the British flag and renamed the *Fiery Star*. She sailed between England and Australia for several years and was finally burned at sea in 1865, while on a voyage from Moreton Bay, Queensland, for London. She had been on fire for twenty-one days when the crew were rescued by the ship *Dauntless*. The *Trade Wind,* while bound from Mobile for Liverpool, in 1854, was in collision with the ship *Olympus,* from Liverpool for New York. Both vessels foundered, forty-four of the sixty-four passengers and crew of the *Trade-Wind* and fifty-two of the fifty-eight on board the *Olympus* being rescued by the Belgian barque *Stadt Antwerpen,* Captain Wyteerhoven, and landed at New York.

The *Nightingale* was sold to a firm in Salem and sent to Rio Janeiro, where she was bought and sailed in the African slave trade under the Brazilian flag. About the year 1860 she was captured by a United States war-vessel and sent home as a prize. She was subsequently fitted out by the Government as an armed cruiser during the Civil War, and at the close of the war was sold and sailed in the California and China trade. Later she sailed for many years under the flag of Norway. The *Shooting Star* was sold to a merchant of Siam in 1862 and was wrecked on the coast of Formosa in 1867. Captain Low remained in command of the *N. B. Palmer* until she was sold abroad in 1872. The *Tornado, Whirlwind,* and *Neptune's Car* were sold in England and disappeared from the Shipping Lists many years ago.

The *Golden Light* under command of Captain C.

F. Winsor, sailed from Boston on her first voyage bound for San Francisco, February 12, 1853, and ten days out was struck by lightning which set fire to cargo in the forehold. After every exertion had been made to save the vessel, Captain Winsor gave orders to abandon the ship, and at 6 P.M., February 23d, her people took to the boats. At that time the ship was in flames. Her foremast had burnt off and fallen; soon after her main- and mizzen-masts went over the side. She had eleven passengers, including three ladies who were in the long boat with the captain. There were five boats in all, four of which, after being adrift eight days, were picked up by the British ship *Shand* from Calcutta bound for Boston; the other boat, in charge of the mate, reached Barbadoes in safety, so that all hands were saved.

The *Sovereign of the Seas* was sold to a Hamburg firm and was wrecked on the Pyramid Shoal in the Straits of Malacca, August 6, 1859, becoming a total loss. The *Contest* and *Winged Racer* were destroyed by the *Alabama* off the coast of Java in 1863, and the *Jacob Bell* by the *Florida* during the same year. The *Harvey Birch* was destroyed by the *Nashville* in 1861. The *Flying Dutchman* went ashore on the Brigantine Shoal, off the coast of New Jersey, during a thick snowstorm in February, 1858, and became a total loss. The *Highflyer*, under command of Captain Gordon B. Waterman, sailed from San Francisco, October 24, 1856, bound for Hong-kong and was never heard from. The *John Gilpin* struck an iceberg off Cape Horn and foundered, January 29, 1858, while bound from

Honolulu for New Bedford under command of Captain John F. Ropes, all hands, including fifteen passengers, being saved by the British ship *Herefordshire.*

The *Phantom* was lost on Prates Shoal, about two hundred miles east-southeast of Hong-kong, in 1862, while under command of Captain Henry Sargent. All hands were saved in the boats, which reached Hong-kong safely, and a large amount of treasure that she had on board was also saved. Captain Sargent received great credit for his brave and judicious action at the time of the wreck; for in those days the China Sea was filled with junks whose crews required only the sight of a vessel in distress to turn them into most barbarous pirates. Captain Sargent soon after took command of the clipper barque *Emily C. Starr* and sailed from Shanghai for Yokohama. She was never heard from, and it was supposed that she foundered in a typhoon. Captain Sargent belonged to an old Boston family whose home was on Beacon Street. He had sailed with Captain Nickels in the *Flying Fish* and had also commanded the ship *Rockland.* He was one of the youngest and most accomplished of all the American clipper ship captains.

The *Bald Eagle* and *Romance of the Seas* both sailed from Hong-kong in 1860 and were never heard from. The *Reporter* foundered off Cape Horn in 1863, and in the same year the *Undaunted* was condemned at Rio Janeiro.

The *Sweepstakes* was condemned in Batavia in 1864. The *Great Republic* was sold to the Merchants' Trading Company, of Liverpool, in 1869 and her name was changed to the *Denmark*. She finally foundered in a hurricane off Bermuda in 1872. The *Morning Star* was sold to a Liverpool firm, who renamed her the *Rockingham;* she foundered while on a voyage from Samarang for Falmouth in 1879. The *Ocean Telegraph* was sold to an English firm and renamed the *Light Brigade* and was finally condemned at Gibraltar and converted into a coal hulk.

The *Marco Polo, Red Jacket,* and *Donald McKay* ended their days in the Quebec lumber trade, and the *Lightning* disappeared from the Shipping List in 1866. The *Champion of the Seas* foundered while homeward bound round Cape Horn in 1877. The *James Baines* was burnt at Liverpool in 1858, and her wreck was converted into the old landing stage for Atlantic steamship passengers, few of whom probably realized that they were walking over the remains of one of the grandest ships that ever sailed the sea.

Of the British-built clippers, the first *Lord of the Isles* built in 1854 was burnt in 1862. The second of the name, built in 1864 by Robert Steele & Co., of Greenock, was sold in France and became known as the *Paul Albert.* The *Spindrift* and *Serica* were both wrecked in 1869. The *Forward Ho* was lost in 1881. The *Sir Launcelot* was sold to a merchant of Bombay and sailed for many years between that port and Mauritius, and was finally wrecked in 1895. The *Cutty Sark* was sold to a merchant in Lisbon in 1895. The *Chinaman* was sunk by a steamer on the coast of China in 1880. The *Windhover* was wrecked on the coast of Australia in

1884. The *Falcon* was sold in Australia, her name being changed to the *Sophia Branilla.* She was wrecked on the coast of Java in 1871. The *Thermopylæ* is now a schoolship at the mouth of the Tagus. The *Yang-tze* was lost in 1872. The first *Guinevere,* built by Robert Steele & Co., in 1862, was lost in 1866, while the second *Guinevere,* built by Randolph Elder & Co., in 1868, was sold in Norway. The *Ariel* sailed for Melbourne and was never heard from. The *Taitsing* was wrecked on the coast of Zanzibar in 1883.

The *Titania* is the only one of all the old clipper ships that can now be traced as in active service. She is owned by Madame Maresca, of Castellamare, and sails under the flag of Italy, usually between European and South American ports. A few years ago she arrived at New York, and I was much interested in going on board of her, as I had known the ship and her captain many years before in China. She appeared so little changed that it was difficult to realize that nearly forty years had passed away since I last stood upon her deck one bright June morning at the Pagoda Anchorage, bidding Captain Burgoyne good-bye as he was getting under way bound for London with new teas. Her spars had been somewhat reduced and her rig changed to a barque, but the beautiful India teak used in the construction of her hull, decks, and bulwarks, with the polished brasswork of her rails, skylights, bells, and capstans, blinking cheerfully in the autumn sunshine, seemed to have paid little heed to the flight and ravages of time.

And so I have endeavored to record the leading events of an era in maritime history long ago departed; and however much the remarkable development of steam navigation may have contributed to the welfare of mankind, I think that the memory of the clipper ships and the men who built and commanded them, will always find a welcome in the hearts of those who know and love the sea.

Appendix I

CALIFORNIA CLIPPER SHIPS BUILT IN THE UNITED STATES FROM 1850 TO 1857 INCLUSIVE

1850

SHIP	TONS	CAPTAIN	BUILDER	OWNER & PORT
Celestial	860	Gardner	William H. Webb, New York	Bucklin & Crane, New York.
Eclipse	1223	Hamilton	J. Williams & Son, Williamsburg, N. Y.	T. Wardle & Co., New York.
Game-Cock	1392	Hollis	Samuel Hall, East Boston	Daniel C. Bacon, East Boston.
Governor Morton	1318	Burgess	James M. Hood, Somerset	Handy & Everett, New York.
John Bertram	1080	Landholm	R. E. Jackson, East Boston	Glidden & Williams, Boston.
Mandarin	776	Stoddard	Smith & Dimon, New York	Goodhue & Co., New York.
Race Horse	512	King	Samuel Hall, East Boston	Goddard & Co., Boston

SHIP	TONS	CAPTAIN	BUILDER	OWNER & PORT
Seaman	546	Myrick	Bell & Co., Baltimore	Funch & Meincke, Baltimore.
Sea Serpent	1337	Howland	George Raynes, Portsmouth, N. H.	Grinnell, Minturn & Co., New York.
Stag-Hound	1535	Richardson	Donald McKay, East Boston	George B. Upton and Sampson & Tappan, Boston.
Surprise	1361	Dumaresq	Samuel Hall, East Boston	A. A. Low & Brother, New York.
White Squall	1118	Lockwood	Jacob Bell, New York	W. Platt & Son, Philadelphia.
Witchcraft	1310	Rogers	Paul Curtis, Chelsea, Mass.	S. Rogers & W. D. Pickman, Salem.
			1851	
Alert	764	Bursley	Damariscotta, Me.	Crocker & Warren, New York.
Challenge	2006	Waterman	William H. Webb, New York	N. L. & G. Griswold, New York.
Comet	1836	Gardner	William H. Webb, New York	Bucklin & Crane, New York.
Courser	1026	Berry	Paul Curtis, East Boston	Richardson & Co., Boston.
Eagle	1340	Farran	Perrin, Patterson & Stack, Williamsburg, N. Y.	Harbeck & Co., New York.

SHIP	TONS	CAPTAIN	BUILDER	OWNER & PORT
Eureka	1050	Canfield	Jacob A. Westervelt & Son, New York	
Flying Cloud	1793	Creesy	Donald McKay, East Boston	Grinnell, Minturn & Co., New York.
Flying Fish	1505	Nickels	Donald McKay, East Boston	Sampson & Tappan, Boston.
Gazelle	1244	Henderson	William H. Webb New York	Chamberlain & Heyser, New York.
Golden Gate	1347	Barstow	New York	Taylor & Merrill, New York.
Hornet	1426	Lawrence	Jacob A. Westervelt & Son, New York	Chamberlain & Co., New York.
Hurricane	1607	Very	Smith & Co., Hoboken, N. J.	C. W. & H. Thomas, New York.
Invincible	1767	Johnson	William H. Webb, New York	J. W. Phillips, New York.
Ino	895	Plummer	Perrin, Patterson & Stack, Williamsburg, N. Y.	Sifkin & Ironside, New York.
John Wade	639	Willis	Medford, Mass.	Augustine Heard & Co., Boston.
Monsoon	773	Winsor	Trufant & Drummond, Bath, Me.	G. Hussey, New Bedford.
Northern Light	1021	Hatch	Briggs Brothers, South Boston	James Huckins & Sons, Boston.

SHIP	TONS	CAPTAIN	BUILDER	OWNER & PORT
N. B. Palmer	1490	Low	Jacob A. Westervelt, New York	A. A. Low & Brother, New York.
Queen of the East	1275	Bartlett	Metcalf & Co., Damariscotta, Me.	Crocker & Warren, New York.
Raven	715	Henry	Hood & Co., Somerset	Crocker & Warren, New York.
Shooting Star	903	Baker	J. O. Curtis, Medford, Mass.	S. G. Reed & Co., Boston.
Snow Squall	742	Bursley	Portland, Me.	Charles R. Green & Co., New York.
Southern Cross	950	Stevens	Briggs Brothers, Boston	Baker & Morrell, Boston.
Staffordshire	1817	Richardson	Donald McKay, East Boston	Enoch Train & Co., Boston.
Sword-Fish	1036	Babcock	William H. Webb, New York	Barclay & Livingston, New York.
Syren	1064	Silsbee	Isaac Taylor, Medford, Mass.	G. Z. Silsbee & Co., Boston.
Tornado	1801	Mumford	J. Williams, Williamsburg, N. Y.	W. T. Frost & Co., New York.
Trade-Wind	2030	Osgood	Jacob Bell, New York	W. Platt & Son, Philadelphia.
Typhoon	1610	Salter	Fernald & Pettigrew, Portsmouth, N. H.	D. & A. Kingsland, New York.

SHIP	TONS	CAPTAIN	BUILDER	OWNER & PORT
Wild Pigeon	996	Putnam	George Raynes, Portsmouth, N. H.	Olyphant & Co., New York.
Witch of the Wave	1500	Millett	George Raynes, Portsmouth, N. H.	Glidden & Williams, Boston.
			1852	
Antelope	1187	Cole	J. Williams & Son, Williamsburg, N. Y.	Harbeck & Co., New York.
Ariel	1340	Delano	Patten & Co., Bath, Me.	Patten & Co., Bath, Me.
Bald Eagle	1790	Dumaresq	Donald McKay, East Boston	George B. Upton, Boston.
Celestial Empire	1399	Pierce	J. Stetson, East Boston	C. H. Parsons & Co., New York.
Cleopatra	1562	Thayer	Paul Curtis, East Boston	
Climax	1051	Howes		Howes & Crowell, Boston.
Contest	1150	Brewster	Jacob A. Westervelt, New York	A. A. Low & Brother, New York.
Dauntless	791	Miller		
Fleetwood	666	Dale	George Raynes, Portsmouth, N. H.	Captain and others, Boston.

SHIP	TONS	CAPTAIN	BUILDER	OWNER & PORT
Flying Childers	1125	Cunningham	Samuel Hall, East Boston	Cunningham & Sons, Boston.
Flying Dutchman	1257	Hubbard	William H. Webb, New York	
Golden City	810	Canfield	Jacob A. Westervelt, New York	H. A. Pierce & Co., Boston.
Golden Eagle	1120	Fabens	Hayden & Co., Medford, Mass.	William Lincoln & Co., Boston.
Golden Light	1141	Winsor	Briggs Brothers, South Boston	James Huckins & Sons. Boston.
Golden State	1363	Barstow	Jacob A. Westervelt, New York	A. A. Low & Brother, New York.
Golden West	1443	Kerwin	Paul Curtis, Boston	Glidden & Williams, Boston.
Highflyer	1092	Waterman	Currier & Townsend, Newburyport	David Ogden, New York.
Jacob Bell	1382	Kilham	Jacob Bell, New York	A. A. Low & Brother, New York.
John Gilpin	1089	Doane	Samuel Hall, East Boston	Pierce & Hunnewell, Boston.
Messenger	1350	Corning	Jacob Bell, New York	Slade & Co., New York.
Meteor	1063	Pike	Briggs Brothers, South Boston	Curtis & Peabody, Boston.

SHIP	TONS	CAPTAIN	BUILDER	OWNER & PORT
Phantom	1177	Paterson	J. O. Curtis, Medford, Mass.	Henry P. Sturgis, Boston.
Polynesia	1068	Watson	Samuel Hall, Boston	Hunnewell, Pierce & Co., Boston.
Queen of the Seas	1400	Knight	Paul Curtis, East Boston	Glidden & Williams, Boston.
Radiant	1300	Hallet	Paul Curtis, East Boston	Baker & Morrell, Boston.
Red Rover	1021	Putnam	Fernald & Pettigrew, Portsmouth, N. H.	R. C. Taylor, New York.
Simoon	1436	Smith	Jabez Williams, New York	B. A. Mumford & Co., New York.
Sovereign of the Seas	2421	McKay	Donald McKay, East Boston	Grinnell, Minturn & Co., New York.
Storm (barque)	545	Roberts	Sag Harbor	Chamberlain & Heyser, New York.
Westward Ho	1600	Hussey	Donald McKay, East Boston	Sampson & Tappan, Boston.
Whirlwind	962	Burgess	J. O. Curtis, Medford, Mass.	W. & F. H. Whitmore, Boston.
Winged Racer	1760	Esterbrook	R. E. Jackson, East Boston	R. L. Taylor, New York.
Wizard	1600	Woodside	Samuel Hall, Boston	Slade & Co., New York.

1853

SHIP	TONS	CAPTAIN	BUILDER	OWNER & PORT
Amphitrite	1687		Samuel Hall, East Boston	
Archer	1098	Bursley	Hood & Co., Somerset	Crocker & Warren, New York.
Belle of the West	936	Howes	Dennis	Glidden & Williams, Boston.
Black Warrior	1878	Murphy	Austin & Co., Damariscotta, Me.	W. Wilson & Sons, Baltimore.
Bonita	1127	Windsor	Boston	Hallett & Co., Boston.
Boston Light	1164	Crowell	Briggs Brothers, Boston	James Huckins & Sons, Boston.
Challenger	1334	Hill	R. E. Jackson, East Boston	Whitmore & Son, Boston.
Cyclone	1109	Osgood	Briggs Brothers, Boston	Curtis & Peabody, Boston.
Dashing Wave	1239	Young	Fernald & Pettigrew, Portsmouth, N. H.	S. Tilton, Boston.
David Brown	1715	Brewster	Roosevelt & Joyce, New York	A. A. Low & Brother, New York.
David Crockett	1679	Spicer	Greenman & Co., Mystic, Conn.	Handy & Everett, New York.

SHIP	TONS	CAPTAIN	BUILDER	OWNER & PORT
Don Quixote	1470	Nott	Medford, Mass.	John E. Lodge, Boston.
Eagle Wing	1174	Linnell	J. O. Curtis, Medford, Mass.	Chase & Tappan, Boston.
Edwin Forrest	1200		D. D. Kelly, East Boston	
Empress of the Seas	2200	Putnam	Donald McKay, East Boston	W. Wilson & Son, Baltimore.
Fearless	1183	Manson	A. & G. T. Sampson, East Boston	W. F. Weld & Co., Boston.
Flora Temple	1915	Myers	J. Abraham, Baltimore	Abraham & Oshcroft, Baltimore.
Flying Dragon	1140	Baker	Trufant & Drummond, Bath, Me.	S. G. Reed & Co., Boston.
Gauntlet	1860	Borland	T. J. Southard, Richmond, Me.	Stephenson & Thurston, New York.
Great Republic	3357	Limeburner	Donald McKay, East Boston	A. A. Low & Brother, New York.
Guiding Star	899	Hale	J. Currier, Newburyport, Mass.	C. Hill & Co., Newburyport, Mass.
John Land	1061	Howes	Briggs Brothers, South Boston	Baker & Morrell, Boston.
Kate Hooper	1507	Johnson	Hunt & Wagner, Baltimore	J. Hooper, Baltimore.

SHIP	TONS	CAPTAIN	BUILDER	OWNER & PORT
Kathay	1460	Stoddard	Jacob A. Westervelt, New York	
Kingfisher	1300	Crosby	Medford, Mass.	William Lincoln & Co., Boston.
Lightfoot	1996		Jackson & Ewell, East Boston	
Live Yankee	1637	Thorndike	Rockland, Me.	Foster & Nickerson, New York.
Matchless	1033	Potter	Chelsea, Mass.	N. S. Goddard, Boston.
Morning Light	1713	Knight	Toby & Littlefield, Portsmouth, N. H.	Glidden & Williams, Boston.
Mystery	1200		Samuel Hall, East Boston	
Neptune's Car	1616	Patten	Portsmouth, Va.	Foster & Nickerson, New York.
North Wind	1041	Gore	Jacob Bell, New York	Grinnell, Minturn & Co., New York.
Oriental	1654	Fletcher	Samuel Hall, East Boston	D. G. & W. B. Bacon. Boston.
Pamparo	1376	Coggins	Charles Mallory, Mystic, Conn.	J. Bishop & Co., New York.
Panama	1349	Cave	Thomas Collyer, New York	N. L. & G. Griswold, New York.

SHIP	TONS	CAPTAIN	BUILDER	OWNER & PORT
Queen of Clippers	2360	Zerega	Jackson & Ewell, East Boston	Zerega & Co., New York.
Red Gauntlet	1038	Andrews	J. W. Cox, Robbinston, Me.	F. Boyd & Co., Boston.
Reporter	1474	Howes	Paul Curtis, East Boston	E. Snow, Boston.
Ringleader	1156	Matthews	Medford, Mass.	Howes & Crowell, Boston.
Romance of the Seas	1782	Dumaresq	Donald McKay, East Boston	George B. Upton, Boston.
Skylark	1209	Henry	Hood & Co., Somerset	Crocker & Warren, New York.
Snapdragon (barque)	619	Brown	William H. Webb, New York	
Spirit of the Times	1206	Klein	Cooper & Slicer, Baltimore	Aymer & Co., New York.
Spitfire	1550	Arey	Frankfort, Me.	Manning & Stanwood, Boston.
Storm King	1408	Callahan	Isaac Taylor, Chelsea, Mass.	John E. Lodge, Boston.
Sweepstakes	1735	Lane	Jacob A. Westervelt, New York	Grinnell, Minturn & Co., New York.
Undaunted	1371	Freeman	Snow & Hall, Bath, Me.	W. H. Foster & Co., Boston.

SHIP	TONS	CAPTAIN	BUILDER	OWNER & PORT
Viking	1449	Windsor	Trufant & Drummond, Bath, Me.	G. Hussey, New Bedford.
Whistler	820	Brown	George W. Jackman, Newburyport, Mass.	Bush & Wildes, Boston.
Wild Wave	1547	Knowles	G. H. Ferrin, Richmond, Me.	Benjamin Bangs, Boston.
Young America	1961	Babcock	William H. Webb, New York	George Daniels, New York.
			1854	
Adelaide	1831	Wakeman	Jacob Bell, New York	Williams & Guion, New York.
Canvas Back	735	Clarke	Baltimore	S. Lurman, Baltimore.
Black Prince	1050	Brown	George W. Jackman, Newburyport, Mass.	Bush & Wildes, Boston.
Electric	1271	Gates	Mystic, Conn.	C. Adams, New York.
Fleetwing	912	Howes	Hayden & Cudworth, Medford, Mass.	Crowell, Brooks, Boston.
Grace Darling	1240	Doane	Briggs Brothers, South Boston	C. B. Fessenden, Boston.

SHIP	TONS	CAPTAIN	BUILDER	OWNER & PORT
Harvey Birch	1488	Nelson	Irons & Grinnell, Mystic, Conn.	J. H. Brower & Co., New York.
Midnight	1000	Hatch	Fernald & Pettigrew, Portsmouth, N. H.	Henry Hastings, Boston.
Nabob	1254	Baxter	J. Taylor, Chelsea, Mass.	William Appleton, Boston.
Nonpareil	1431		Dunham & Co., Frankfort, Me.	T. Richardson & Co., New York.
Nor'wester	1267	Gregory	S. Lapham, Medford, Mass.	Coolidge & Co., Boston.
Ocean Telegraph	1492	Willis	J. O. Curtis, Medford, Mass.	S. G. Reed & Co., Boston.
Rattler	794	Forrest	Forster & Borze, Baltimore	D. Stewart, Baltimore.
Robin Hood	1185	Sears	Hayden & Cudworth, Medford, Mass.	Howe & Crowell, Boston.
Sancho Panza	850	Friend	Medford, Mass.	John E. Lodge, Boston.
Saracen	1266	Barry	Briggs Brothers, South Boston	Curtis & Peabody, Boston.
Sierra Nevada	1942	Penhallow	Toby & Littlefield, Portsmouth, N. H.	Glidden & Williams, Boston.
Starlight	1150	Matthews	Briggs Brothers, South Boston,	Baker & Morrell, Boston.

SHIP	TONS	CAPTAIN	BUILDER	OWNER & PORT
Starr King	1170	Turner	George W. Jackman, Newburyport, Mass.	Bates & Thaxter, Boston.
Swallow	1435	Tucker	Robert E. Jackson, East Boston.	W. T. Dugan, New York.
			1855	
Andrew Jackson	1676	Williams	Irons & Grinnell, Mystic, Conn.	J. H. Brower & Co., New York.
Beacon Light	1320	Barwell	Chelsea, Mass.	J. A. Stetson, Boston.
Carrier Dove	1694	Conner	J. Abraham, Baltimore.	Montell & Co., Baltimore.
Charmer	1060	Lucas	George W. Jackman, Newburyport, Mass.	Burt & Wildes, Boston.
Courier	1025	Smith	Newburyport, Mass.	Foster & Elliott, New York.
Daring	1097	Simonson	George W. Jackman, Newburyport, Mass.	Bush & Comstock, Boston.
Electric Spark	1215	Howes	Thacher & Magoun, Medford, Mass.	Magoun & Co., Boston.
Golden Fleece	1538	Manson	Paul Curtis, East Boston.	Weld & Baker, Boston.

SHIP	TONS	CAPTAIN	BUILDER	OWNER & PORT
Herald of the Morning	1300	Baker	Thacher & Magoun, Medford, Mass.	Magoun & Co., Boston.
Mary Whitridge	978	Cheesebrough	Hunt & Wagner, Baltimore.	T. Whitridge, Baltimore.
Noonday	1177	Gerry	Fernald & Pettigrew, Portsmouth, N. H.	Henry Hastings, Boston.
Ocean Express	1699	Cunningham	J. O. Curtis, Medford, Mass.	Reed & Wade, Boston.
War Hawk	1067	Simmons	George W. Jackman, Newburyport, Mass.	Captain and others, Boston.

1856

SHIP	TONS	CAPTAIN	BUILDER	OWNER & PORT
Alarm	1184	Matthews	Briggs Brothers, South Boston.	Baker & Morrell, Boston.
Euterpe	1984	Avery	H. Merriman, Rockland, Me.	Foster & Nickerson, New York.
Florence	1310	Dumaresq	Samuel Hall, Jr., East Boston,	R. B. & John M. Forbes, Boston.
Flying Mist	1150	Fennell	J. O. Curtis, Medford, Mass.	T. Chase & Co., Boston.
Intrepid	1173	Gardner	William H. Webb, New York.	Bucklin & Crane, New York.

SHIP	TONS	CAPTAIN	BUILDER	OWNER & PORT
Mary L. Sutton	1450	Rowland	Charles Mallory, Mystic, Conn.	Charles Mallory, Mystic, Conn.
Norseman	820	Haskell	R. E. Jackson, East Boston.	Cunningham Brothers, Boston.
Witch of the Wave	1200	Todd	Portsmouth, N. H.	Titcomb & Co., Newburyport, Mass.
			1857	
Black Hawk	1108	Bowers	William H. Webb, New York.	Bucklin & Crane, New York.
Black Hawk	970	Shoof	J. Currier, Newburyport, Mass.	M. Devenport & Co., Newburyport, Mass.
Hotspur	862	Porter	Roosevelt & Joyce, New York.	Wisner, McCready & Co., New York.
Twilight	1482	Gates	Charles Mallory, Mystic, Conn.	G. Gates & Co., Mystic, Conn.

Appendix II

RECORD PASSAGES OF THE CALIFORNIA CLIPPER SHIPS MADE IN 110 DAYS OR LESS FROM 1850 TO 1860, INCLUSIVE

1850

SHIP	PORT OF DEPARTURE	ARRIVAL AT SAN FRANCISCO	DAYS
Celestial	New York	November 1	104
Race Horse	Boston	November 24	109
Samuel Russell	New York	May 1	109
Sea Witch	New York	July 24	97

1851

SHIP	PORT OF DEPARTURE	ARRIVAL AT SAN FRANCISCO	DAYS
Challenge	New York	October 29	108
Flying Cloud	New York	August 31	89
N. B. Palmer	New York	August 21	106
Raven	Boston	November 19	105
Sea Witch	New York	November 20	110
Seaman	New York	March 11	107
Stag-Hound	New York	May 26	107
Surprise	New York	March 19	96
Typhoon	New York	November 18	106
Witchcraft	New York	August 11	103

1852

SHIP	PORT OF DEPARTURE	ARRIVAL AT SAN FRANCISCO	DAYS
Celestial	New York	February 17	106
Comet	New York	January 13	103

SHIP	PORT OF DEPARTURE	ARRIVAL AT SAN FRANCISCO	DAYS
Courser	Boston	April 28	108
Eclipse	New York	April 22	104
Northern Light	Boston	March 8	109
Sea Witch	New York	December 8	108
Staffordshire	Boston	August 13	101
Sword-Fish	New York	February 10	90
Flying Fish	Boston	February 17	98
John Bertram	Boston	March 26	105
Shooting Star	Boston	August 17	105
White Squall	New York	July 29	110
Wild Pigeon	New York	January 28	104
Sovereign of the Seas	New York	November 15	103
	1853		
Bald Eagle	New York	April 11	107
Contest	New York	February 24	108
Contest	New York	October 24	97
Flying Cloud	New York	August 12	105
Flying Dutchman	New York	January 27	104
Flying Dutchman	New York	October 7	106
Flying Fish	New York	February 1	92
Golden Age (barque)	Boston	May 31	103
Golden Gate	New York	March 20	102
Hornet	New York	August 12	105
Invincible	New York	September 9	110
John Gilpin	New York	February 2	93
Meteor	Boston	March 10	110
Oriental	New York	May 7	100
Phantom	Boston	April 21	104
Rebekah (barque)	Baltimore	May 10	106
Sea Serpent	New York	June 1	107
Sword-Fish	New York	May 30	105
Storm (barque)	New York	April 10	109
Tornado	New York	May 2	109
Trade-Wind	New York	February 24	102
Westward Ho	Boston	February 1	103
Witchcraft	New York	July 8	110

SHIP	PORT OF DEPARTURE	ARRIVAL AT SAN FRANCISCO	DAYS
Winged Racer	New York	March 30	105
Young America	New York	August 29	110
	1854		
Archer	New York	April 29	106
Challenger	Boston	June 9	110
Courier	Boston	April 28	108
David Brown	New York	March 23	98
Eagle	New York	February 16	103
Eagle Wing	Boston	April 5	106
Flying Cloud	New York	April 20	89
Golden City	New York	February 8	105
Herald of the Morning	Boston	May 7	106
Hurricane	New York	September 4	99
Matchless	Boston	February 8	109
Pamparo	New York	January 25	105
Polynesia	New York	April 10	104
Ringleader	Boston	February 8	109
Romance of the Seas	Boston	March 23	96
Samuel Russell	New York	January 20	106
San Francisco	New York	February 8	105
Stag-Hound	New York	August 14	110
Westward Ho	New York	February 28	106
Witchcraft	New York	August 15	97
Young America	New York	October 20	110
	1855		
Boston Light	Boston	April 11	102
Cleopatra	New York	March 4	107
Don Quixote	Boston	March 29	108
Electric	New York	March 4	109
Flying Cloud	New York	June 6	108
Flying Fish	Boston	January 10	109
Flying Fish	Boston	December 27	105
Golden Eagle	New York	August 25	106

SHIP	PORT OF DEPARTURE	ARRIVAL AT SAN FRANCISCO	DAYS
Governor Morton	New York	April 2	104
Greenfield (barque)	New York	May 6	110
Herald of the Morning	New York	May 16	99
Meteor	Boston	August 30	108
Neptune's Car	New York	April 25	100
Red Rover	New York	June 13	107
Telegraph	Boston	April 9	109
Westward Ho	Boston	April 24	100

1856

Antelope	New York	March 15	97
David Brown	New York	April 28	103
Don Quixote	Boston	May 31	108
Electric Spark	Boston	April 9	106
Flyaway	New York	April 8	106
Mary L. Sutton	New York	July 20	110
North Wind	Boston	July 21	110
Phantom	New York	April 29	101
Red Rover	New York	April 7	110
Reporter	New York	March 27	107
Ringleader	Boston	February 3	106
Sweepstakes	New York	May 25	94
Tornado	New York	March 27	110
Wild Hunter	Boston	April 29	108
Young America	New York	October 14	107

1857

Andrew Jackson	New York	February 28	100
Flying Dragon	New York	April 10	97
Flying Dutchman	New York	September 10	102
Flying Fish	Boston	October 2	100
John Land	New York	July 30	104
Reporter	New York	April 17	110
Westward Ho	New York	March 26	100

1858

SHIP	PORT OF DEPARTURE	ARRIVAL AT SAN FRANCISCO	DAYS
Andrew Jackson	New York	April 27	103
Dashing Wave	New York	August 18	107
Don Quixote	New York	March 4	108
Esther May	Boston	May 19	103
John Land	New York	July 24	108
Twilight	New York	April 16	100

1859

SHIP	PORT OF DEPARTURE	ARRIVAL AT SAN FRANCISCO	DAYS
Andrew Jackson	New York	April 5	102
Robin Hood	New York	March 25	107
Sierra Nevada	New York	December 17	97
Young America	New York	July 24	105

1860

SHIP	PORT OF DEPARTURE	ARRIVAL AT SAN FRANCISCO	DAYS
Andrew Jackson	New York	March 23	89
Archer	New York	March 18	106
Lookout	New York	February 20	108
Mary L. Sutton	New York	May 12	103
Ocean Telegraph	New York	March 13	109
White Swallow	New York	August 7	110

During the forty-five years that have elapsed since the close of the Civil War a large number of sailing ships have been built for the California trade, and it is a notable fact that only two of these vessels made the passage from an Atlantic port to San Francisco in less than one hundred days. The *Seminole,* built by Maxon & Fish at Mystic, Connecticut, in 1865, arrived at San Francisco from New York, March 10, 1866, in 96 days, and the *Glory of the Seas,* already mentioned as the last ship built by Donald McKay, made the same voyage, arriving at San Francisco, January 18, 1874, in 94 days.

The two most successful ships in after years were the *David Crocket* and *Young America.* Both were built in

1853, and both continued in the San Francisco trade until 1883, during which time the *David Crockett* made her best twelve passages from New York to San Francisco in an average of 109 $\frac{7}{12}$ days each, her best being 102 days in 1872. The *Young America*, during this period also made twelve passages in an average of 110 $\frac{7}{12}$ days each, her best being 102 days in 1880.

As these ships were by many years the oldest survivors of the California clippers, there was a good deal of rivalry between them, and their records show that they were very evenly matched. It should, however, be remembered that about the year 1860 their spars and canvas were considerably reduced and that they were fitted with double topsail yards, all of which hampered their speed in moderate weather. Indeed, they resembled two faded beauties who in their youth had been rival belles.

Appendix III

CHINA TEA CLIPPERS, 1859–1869

SHIP	TONS	CONSTRUCTION	BUILDER	YEAR
Falcon	937	Wood	Robert Steele & Co., Greenock	1859
Isle of the South	821	"	Laing & Co., Sunderland	1859
Fiery Cross	888	"	Chalour & Co., Liverpool	1860
Min	629	"	Robert Steele & Co., Greenock	1861
Kelso	556	"	Pile & Co., Sunderland	1861
Belted Will	812	"	Feel & Co., Workington	1863
Serica	708	"	Robert Steele & Co., Greenock	1863
Taeping	767	Composite	Robert Steele & Co., Greenock	1863
Eliza Shaw	696	"	Alexander Stephen, Glasgow	1863
Yang-tze	688	"	Alexander Hall, Aberdeen	1863
Black Prince	750	"	Alexander Hall, Aberdeen	1863
Ariel	853	"	Robert Steele & Co., Greenock	1865
Ada	686	"	Alexander Hall, Aberdeen	1865
Sir Launcelot	886	"	Robert Steele & Co., Greenock	1865
Taitsing	815	"	Connell & Co., Glasgow	1865
Titania	879	"	Robert Steele & Co., Greenock	1866
Spindrift	899	"	Connell & Co., Glasgow	1867
Forward Ho	943	"	Alexander Stephen, Glasgow	1867

SHIP	TONS	CONSTRUCTION	BUILDER	YEAR
Leander	883	Composite	Lawrie & Co., Glasgow	1867
Lahloo	779	"	Robert Steele & Co., Greenock	1867
Thermopylæ	947	"	Walter Hood, Aberdeen	1868
Windhover	847	"	Connell & Co., Glasgow	1868
Cutty Sark	921	"	Scott & Co., Greenock	1868
Caliph	914	"	Alexander Hall, Aberdeen	1869
Wylo	799	"	Robert Steele & Co., Greenock	1869
Kaisow	795	"	Robert Steele & Co., Greenock	1869
Lothair	794	"	Walker & Son, London	1869

Appendix IV

RULES FOR TONNAGE MEASUREMENTS

THE English system of measuring the tonnage of vessels in the eighteenth century is given in Falconer's *Marine Dictionary*, 1780, as follows:

" To determine the burden, or, in other words, the tonage, of a ship, it is usual to multiply the length of keel into the extreme breadth of the ship within board, taken along the midship beam, and multiplying the product by the depth in the hold from the plank joining to the keelson upwards to the main-deck, and divide the last product by 94; then will the quotient be the burden required, in tons."

This rule continued in force till 1819, when it was changed by the Lords Commissioners of the Admiralty as follows:

" Multiply the length of the keel by the breadth of beam, and that product by half the breadth of beam, and divide the last product by 94, and the quotient will be the tonnage " (*Marine Dictionary,* William Burney, LL.D., 1830). Dr. Burney remarks: " It appears from the general construction of merchant ships, that more attention is paid to evade the tax on tonnage than to their sailing well with the wind in different directions; and if the real tonnage of ships were taken, an alteration would soon be made in the construction for the better."

This form of the rule continued until 1842, when by Act of Parliament the following method was adopted:

" Divide the length of the upper deck between the after part of the stem and the fore part of the stern-post into six equal parts. Depths: at the foremost, the middle, and the aftermost of these points of division, measure in feet and decimal parts of a foot the depths from the under side of the upper deck to the ceiling at the limber strake. In the case of a break in the upper deck, the depths are to be measured from a line stretched in a continuation of the deck. Breadths: Divide each of those three depths into five equal parts, and measure the inside breadths at the following points—viz., at one fifth and at four fifths from the upper deck of the foremost and aftermost depths, and at two fifths and four fifths from the upper deck of the midship depth. Length: At half the midship depth, measure the length of the vessel from the after part of the stem to the fore part of the stern-post; then, to twice the midship depth add the foremost and the aftermost depths; add together the upper and lower breadths at the foremost division, three times the upper breadth, and the lower breadth, at the midship division and the upper and twice the lower breadth at the after division, for the sum of the breadths; then multiply the sum of the depths by the sum of the breadths, and this product by the length, and divide the final product by three thousand five hundred, which will give the number of tons for register" (Young's *Marine Dictionary*, 1846).

In 1854 this rule was changed by the Merchant Shipping Act, which provided that the actual cubic contents of a vessel's hull should be measured, a registered ton being reckoned as 100 cubic feet. This is known as the Moorsom system, and is still in use and likely to continue. It was adopted by the United States in 1865; Denmark, 1867; Austria, 1871; Germany, France, and Italy, 1873; Spain, 1874; and Sweden, 1875.

The old practice of calculating tonnage in the United States was adapted from the English, and the mode of measurement was as follows:

The length was measured on deck from the fore part of the stem to the after part of the stern-post; the breadth from outside to outside planking at the broadest part of the vessel; the depth of the hold from the plank on deck to the ceiling of the hold. This last measurement was not used, the depth of a vessel for tonnage purposes being assumed to be one half of her breadth. In order to find the tonnage, three fifths of the breadth were deducted from the length and the remainder multiplied by the breadth, and this product multiplied by one half the breadth, or the assumed depth, the last product was then divided by 95, giving the formula:

$$\frac{(L - {}^3/_5 B) \times B \times \frac{1}{2} B}{95}$$

Thus in a vessel measuring 100 ft. x 20 ft. x 18 ft.:

Length of vessel......................	100
Subtract $^3/_5$ breadth..................	12
Length for measurement..............	88
Multiply by the breadth...............	20
	1760
Multiply by half breadth..............	10
	17,600
Divide 17,600 by 95............and the result is............	$185+{}^{12}/_{19}$
Total tonnage..............	$185+{}^{12}/_{19}$

This mode of measurement continued from colonial times until the Moorsom system was adopted in 1865.

The dimensions of ten representative American and British clippers were as follows:

		Length	Breadth
	Nightingale (1851)......	178 "	..36 "
American	*Oriental* (1849)..........	183 ft.	..36 ft.
	Celestial (1850)..........	158 "	..34 " 6 in.
	Stag-Hound (1850).......	209 "	..39 "
	Flying Dutchman (1852).	187 "	..38 " 6 in.
British	*Falcon* (1859)...........	191 " 4 in.	.32 " 2 in.
	Taitsing (1865)..........	192 "	..31 " 5 in.
	Titania (1866)..........	200 "	..35 "
	Spindrift (1867)........	219 " 4 in.	.35 " 6 in.
	Thermopylæ (1868).....	210 "	..36 "

Although these British ships show less breadth than the American, yet they have more breadth in proportion to length than the earlier British clippers, such as the *Stornoway* (1850), *Lord of the Isles* (1855), etc.

INDEX

Vessels not otherwise designated are American

D

E

H

I

J

K

L

N

S